Untying the knot

A short history of divorce

RODERICK PHILLIPS

Carleton University, Ottawa

The right of the
University of Cambridge
to print and publish
all kinds of books
was granted by law
in 1534.
The University has printed
and published continuously
since 1584.

CAMBRIDGE UNIVERSITY PRESS

Cambridge

New York   Port Chester   Melbourne   Sydney

Published by the Press Syndicate of the University of Cambridge
The Pitt Building, Trumpington Street, Cambridge CB2 1RP
40 West 20th Street, York, NY 1001–4211, USA
10 Stamford Road, Oakleigh, Melbourne 3166, Australia

© Cambridge University Press 1991

First published 1991

Printed in Finland by Werner Söderström Oy

Library of Congress Cataloging-in-Publication Data
Phillips, Roderick.
Untying the knot : a short history of divorce / Roderick Phillips.
p. cm.
Includes bibliographical references and index.
ISBN 0-521-42370-8 (paperback)
1. Divorce – History. I. Title.
HQ811.P49 1991
306.89′ – dc20 90–25269

British Library Cataloguing-in-Publication Data
Phillips, Roderick
Untying the knot : a short history of divorce.
1. Divorce, history
I. Title
306.8909

ISBN 0 521 42370 8 paperback

*To my mother
and to the memory
of my sister,
Carol*

Contents

Preface

One of the paradoxes of modern Western society is the simultaneous popularity of marriage and divorce. Even though marriage rates have fallen in some countries in recent years, marriage is, generally speaking, as popular today as it has ever been at any period in the past. In the nineteenth century and earlier, quite large proportions of men and women could not hope to marry, and never did; today in most Western countries almost everyone marries at some time in her or his life. What John Gillis writes in the introduction of his history of marriage in Britain, *For Better, For Worse,* holds true for the rest of Western society: "We live in a conjugal age, when the couple has become the standard for all intimate relationships.... Commerce panders to the conjugal ideal and municipalities zone in its favor. Children play at it; teenagers practice it."

Children might not play at divorce explicitly – although they do so implicitly when their marriage games go sour and one party goes home because the other will not play nicely. Nor do teenagers practice divorce very often, although their marriages are particularly likely to end in divorce when they reach their twenties. Even so, divorce has become the common partner of marriage at the center of the Western marriage system, for divorce, too, has never been as widespread in the Western world as it has become in recent times. Even though divorce rates in some countries have stabilized in the early and mid-1980s, they did so at unprecedentedly high levels, and in other countries divorce rates continue to set records year after year. Precise statistical measurements of divorce, expressed as rates per thousand population or per thousand married women, demonstrate how divorce has increased during the twentieth century, especially since the early 1970s. More widely understood expressions of the increase have entered popular awareness as we are regularly told, depending on where we live, that one in every two, three, or four marriages ends in divorce.

The high divorce rates that have become characteristic of modern Western society have provoked various reactions. Some observers have interpreted them as indicating the decline, a prefiguring of the disappearance, of marriage and the family. Others construe them as part of an emerging marriage pattern in which many, perhaps most, men and women will marry twice or more often during their lifetimes. Divorce is perceived by some as a threat to social stability, while others insist that the Western family system can accommodate a high incidence of divorce. Many different reasons have been given for the increase in divorce over the long and short term. Prominent among them are a shift or decline in morality, the decreased influence of religion, the effects of the women's movement, married women's employment outside the home, and rising expectations of marriage.

This book is first and foremost a history of divorce, but it necessarily addresses some of the issues raised by divorce in modern times. The question most often asked about divorce – "Why is it so common today?" – is implicitly historical, for any answer to it must address the implied question of why divorce was so uncommon in the past. Similarly we must look to the past for a full appreciation of other aspects of divorce in the modern world. Divorce laws, popular attitudes toward divorce and toward divorced men and women, and prevailing secular and ecclesiastical policies toward divorce cannot properly be understood without some idea of their evolution over the long or medium term.

Recent scholarship has contributed a great deal to our knowledge of many aspects of the history of the Western family; books have poured forth, especially since the 1960s, on such important questions as historical trends in household size and structure, kinship patterns, sexual relationships, ages at marriage, premarital pregnancy rates, and the duration of marriage. Divorce and marriage breakdown, however, have generally been treated as tangential issues, poor cousins within the field of the history of the family. The major surveys of the development of the Western family make only passing reference to divorce, marriage breakdown, and separation. Lawrence Stone's ambitious survey of the English family (*The Family, Sex and Marriage in England, 1500–1800*) deals with divorce more systematically, but even there divorce and its associated issues are treated as of minor significance. John Gillis's magisterial study of British marriages deals overwhelmingly with the making, rather than the unmaking, of conjugal matches. Lawrence Stone's *Road to Divorce: England 1530–1987* appeared just as this book was going to press.

The relative neglect of divorce and marriage breakdown by historians of the family is understandable, for it reflects two realities. The first is that except for one or two specific periods, such as the revolutionary years in France, divorces were extremely rare in Western society until the late nineteenth century. Second, signs of marriage breakdown, apart from the infrequent divorces and separations, are generally sparse and inconclusive. There is evidence of desertions, bigamy, wife sales, and the like, and there is also a great deal of evidence of marital stress and violence that might or might not indicate marriage breakdown. Broadly speaking, however, the quality of the data is not encouraging for firm conclusions, and this, together with its treatment in histories of the family, tends to reinforce the image that marriage breakdowns and divorces were infrequent in the past.

Even so, the past twenty years have witnessed the growth of a solid body of research on the history of divorce. We now know a great deal more about the development of divorce laws and policies in many countries, historical attitudes toward marriage breakdown and divorce, the application and use of the divorce laws, and the characteristics of couples that divorced. Many of the studies have placed divorce within definite social, political, and cultural contexts.

This is not the place to catalog the many articles, monographs, unpublished papers, and chapters in more general works that make up modern scholarship on the subject. They are listed in the bibliography and footnotes of *Putting Asunder*, of which the present book is a shorter version. Only some of the more accessible works are cited here, in the "Suggestions for further reading" that follow each chapter. However, I wish to record again my debt to scholars whose research has illuminated such diverse topics as divorce in seventeenth-century Norway, divorce in eighteenth-century Connecticut, the role of divorce in Milton's *Paradise Lost*, Thomas Jefferson's studies of divorce, and the relationship of divorce to married women's property legislation in nineteenth-century England.

In *Untying the Knot* I have attempted to provide a short, readable history of divorce in the Western world from the broadest perspective. The "Western world" here comprises North America, Western Europe, Scandinavia, Great Britain, and Australasia, although at times other areas, like the Soviet Union, are also discussed. Spread across half the globe, and disparate in many social, economic, and cultural respects, this Western world drew on common traditions of family law and policy. European, British, and Scandinavian legislation was influenced by Roman Catholic doctrine and canon law up to and beyond the Reformation, and marriage and divorce policies in America and Australasia were based, in turn, on European models. Such traditions give this broad Western world enough unity to enable us to consider it a coherent unit for the purpose of historical analysis. At the same time there are enough variations and divergences to make this a comparative study. Although general phenomena like the Protestant Reformation led to more or less dramatic matrimonial reform throughout

Europe, in individual countries events as specific and diverse as the English Civil War, the American Revolution, the French Revolution, and the advent of national socialism affected the way divorce laws, policies, and rates developed.

For the most part this book proceeds chronologically from the Middle Ages to the present, although there are specific chapters on major questions such as the meaning and extent of marriage breakdown in the past. In this version, it should be noted, the nineteenth and twentieth centuries occupy a somewhat greater proportion of the book than they did in the original book. I have been sufficiently encouraged by the reviews of *Putting Asunder* that had appeared by the time this abridgment was prepared, not to make any significant changes in argument or interpretation. What is missing from this book is the footnotes and bibliography, and any reader interested in following up any of the points made more briefly here is referred to the original version for a fuller discussion with references.

As for the perspectives adopted by this study, several points might be noted. First, although the development of divorce laws is a central theme, I have tried to avoid a narrowly legal narrative and have attempted to place legal change within the broadest social, economic, political, and cultural contexts. It will become clear that changes in divorce law have often coincided with political change, so closely associated are doctrines of marriage and divorce with political ideology. A second major theme is the social history of divorce: Who divorced, why did they divorce, and why were divorce rates at any given time not higher or lower? A third theme is the distinction between marriage breakdown and divorce. A major question addressed in these pages is whether the rise of divorce in the past century indicates an increased tendency of marriages to break down or whether it means no more than that an increasing proportion of marriage breakdowns has been translated into divorce.

In short, this book seeks a comprehensive view of divorce in the Western world during the past thousand years. It is not exhaustive, however. To have listed all major legal changes would have been very tedious. It would have been equally tedious to have quoted the thoughts on divorce expressed by all the great and famous. Not only did Christ, Erasmus, Luther, Milton, Voltaire, Frederick the Great, Jefferson, Napoleon, Disraeli, Lenin, Mussolini, and Keynes all have something to say about divorce, but so did thousands of other men and women. Only a handful could be represented here. The subject of this book is a massive one, and the following pages represent only a distillation of current knowledge and an interpretation of it. The subject is an important one, however, for we cannot begin to understand current issues surrounding marriage breakdown and divorce in modern Western society until we appreciate their historical origins. I hope that this book contributes not only to a better understanding of this aspect of the history of the family, but also to a more informed discussion of modern social issues.

Ottawa, July 1990

Acknowledgments

In the course of preparing the book of which *Untying the Knot* is an abridged version, I was privileged to receive a great deal of assistance of various sorts, and I am delighted to be able to express my thanks again.

The personnel of the research libraries and archives I used were unfailingly helpful. Principal among them were the British Library (London), Bodleian Library (Oxford), Cambridge University Library (Cambridge), Bibliothèque Nationale (Paris), Uppsala University Library (Uppsala), and the Riksarkiv (Oslo). Access to these and other resources was facilitated by support at various times from the University of Auckland, which granted me a leave of absence, the Queen's University Advisory Research Committee, which provided research funds, the Swedish Institute, which awarded me a fellowship at Uppsala University, and Brock University, which gave me support from funds provided by the Social Sciences and Humanities Research Council of Canada.

Colleagues and friends in different parts of the world were more than hospitable when I arrived in search of divorces. Paul O'Flinn always made me welcome in Wolvercote whenever I was working in the Bodleian. Peter Laslett has always been a gracious host in Cambridge. Jan Trost looked after me in the months I spent in Uppsala, and Sølvi Sogner and Gudmund Sandvik of Oslo University generously assisted me during my all-too-brief stay in Norway. I also wish to thank Piers Mackesy and the Fellows of Pembroke College for having granted me membership to the Senior Common Room during one of my periods of research in Oxford. This is also an opportunity to salute three former colleagues at the University of Auckland: Michael Graves, Peter O'Connor, and John Stagg.

I am especially indebted to former colleagues and teachers who read parts of the manuscript: Michael Graves and Barry Reay of the University of Auckland and Christopher Greene and John Gilchrist of Trent University. They, together with the remarkably efficient readers engaged by Cambridge University Press, saved me from a number of embarrassing errors. I have also benefited over the years from the comments, criticisms, and suggestions that have followed conference and seminar papers I have given on aspects of my research. Among those to whom I owe gratitude in this respect are my friends who convene every two years for the George Rudé Seminars on French history, the members of the Cambridge Group for the History of Population and Social Structure, and the Social History seminar at the University of Essex.

As far as *Untying the Knot* is concerned, I wish to record several additional debts. The first is to my editor at Cambridge University Press, Frank Smith. He not only encouraged me to write the original book, but suggested (with some trepidation) that I then do this abridgment. He has been consistently patient, encouraging, and gracious, and no author could wish for a better editor in any respect. A second debt is to Carleton University for material help that enabled me to finish the abridgment far more quickly than I had expected.

Finally, Alyssa Novick, to whom the original version was dedicated, has continued to be my best friend and critic. For some reason, perhaps because she too loves history, she persists in sharing the ups and downs of research and writing. Her interest and support make everything easier. She and my daughter, Zoë Quinn-Phillips, let me disappear night after night as I worked on this book, and I wish to express to them here not only my thanks, but my love.

Catholics and Protestants

It is paradoxical that we must begin a history of divorce in Western society with a discussion of Roman Catholic teaching about marriage and divorce, for it was (and remains) Catholic doctrine that a validly contracted marriage cannot be dissolved and that divorce is therefore prohibited. This doctrine underlay the ideology and law of marriage in Europe for centuries before the Protestant Reformation (and for centuries after it in some countries), so that the history of divorce since the sixteenth century has been, for the most part, a progressive rejection of the Catholic position. By the end of the twentieth century we have reached a point where civil divorce laws, popular attitudes toward divorce, and mass practices in respect to divorce owe virtually nothing to the Roman Catholic doctrines that were dominant only five centuries earlier.

If we think of the history of divorce as being, on one important level at least, the abandonment of Catholic teaching on marriage, we must begin with a clear understanding of that teaching and its development. This first chapter discusses these issues, together with the most significant single challenge to Catholic matrimonial doctrines, namely the Protestant teachings on marriage and divorce that were articulated in the sixteenth century, during the Reformation.

The Catholic church's position on divorce, as it was when the Protestants rejected it, can be stated with deceptive simplicity: Divorce was forbidden because a validly contracted Christian marriage could be dissolved only by the death of the wife or husband. It was a corollary of this that a married person could not enter into another marriage while his or her spouse was still alive. Yet we can immediately note potential exceptions to what seems an absolute bar to divorce. The first, known as the Pauline Privilege (found in the New Testament in Paul's Letters to the Corinthians [1 Cor. 7:15]), appeared to allow remarriage by a Christian who had been deserted by his or her non-Christian spouse. The second potential exception to divorce concerned a marriage that had not been sexually consummated and where the husband or wife wanted to enter a religious order. In both cases the marriage might be dissolved in "favor of the faith." Despite such qualifications (and the circumstances must have been rarely encountered), it is adequate to describe Catholic doctrine, as it had developed by the thirteenth century, as simply forbidding divorce.

This doctrine, eventually set down in canon law by the Council of Trent in the 1560s, was achieved only after centuries of debate within the church. But before we discuss the development of the doctrine, we must note various meanings of the word *divorce* itself, for its variety of meanings and contexts has led to confusion about the history of the concept.

In this book *divorce* will be used in the restrictive sense of a total dissolution of a validly contracted or celebrated marriage. In the Catholic church's Latin documents it was often referred to as a *divortium a vinculo matrimonii* (divorce from the marriage bond), and it is this sort of divorce that enabled (or would have if the church had allowed it) men and women to remarry. Confusion has arisen, however, because the words *divorce* and *divortium* were also used in two other senses with respect to marriage: annulment and separation. Annulments (or nullifications) of marriage are discussed in some detail later, and here it is enough to note that the difference between a divorce and an annulment is that a divorce dissolves a marriage that exists, whereas an annulment is a declaration that a marriage had never existed between a specific man and woman. The crucial difference between a divorce and a separation, on the other hand, is that a divorce dissolves a marriage and permits the former spouses to remarry (although specific laws might limit that right), whereas a separation does not destroy the marriage bond, although it permits wife and husband to live apart and to lead separate lives.

In its developed form, Catholic doctrine made provision for annulment and separation but not for divorce. It has often been argued, however, that the church circumvented its own doctrine of marital indissolubility by allowing annulments to be used as if they were divorces, so that many annulments in name were divorces in intent. In other words it has been suggested that spouses who wanted to free themselves from their marriages exploited the provisions for annulment, and that the judges of the church courts connived in the practice.

The provisions for annulment rested upon the impediments to marriage that the church laid down. Some of these impediments, called *diriment* or *nullifying* impediments, were a bar to marriage unless the couple obtained a dispensation from them. The best-known such impediments were those of consanguinity and affinity, the relationship of two people by blood or marriage, respectively, such that close relatives could not marry one another. The specific degrees of relationship within which marriage was prohibited were drawn directly from the

Bible, but the list was extended by the church. By the twelfth century marriage was forbidden to the seventh degree, which meant that a man could not marry a woman who was his sixth cousin or more closely related. Jean-Louis Flandrin describes the practical implications of this rule in this way: If in each generation each couple married off one boy and one girl, then a marriageable youth would soon be in a position of being unable to marry all the marriageable girls he could possibly know, together with many he did not know.

Perhaps because of the inconveniences caused by these rules in a society where geographical mobility was limited, and where most marriages united men and women from the same parish, the Fourth Lateran Council (1215) reduced from seven to four the range of degrees within which marriage was banned. This reform permitted the marriage of men and women who were more distantly related than third cousins.

Strict consanguinity and affinity were only two kinds of diriment impediment to marriage. Another was illegitimate affinity (*affinitas illegitima*), which was the relationship formed by sexual intercourse. Under the rules set down in 1215, a man was prevented from marrying the sister, first, second, or third cousin of, or any woman more closely related to, a woman with whom he had had sexual relations. A further bar to marriage was spiritual affinity, which was the relationship between the members of a family and any of the active participants at one of its baptisms or confirmations. An example is the case in the English town of York in the fourteenth century where a man, a widower, was forbidden to marry the woman who had stood as godmother to one of his children by his first marriage.

Catholic doctrine raised yet other impediments to a valid marriage. A prior matrimonial engagement (precontract) to one person prevented an individual from marrying another, as did, of course, an existing marriage. There were impediments of age in that a boy had to be twelve and a girl fourteen before marrying. Impotence – the inability to complete sexual intercourse – was an impediment preventing a valid marriage. And because consent was an essential element of marriage in Catholic doctrine, lack of consent was also a diriment impediment. Yet additional impediments existed where one of the parties had taken religious vows or where one of the parties had attacked the sanctity of the previous marriage of the other (by killing the first spouse or by committing adultery with a promise to marry as soon as the accomplice was free to do so). Finally, marrying clandestinely could be a bar to a marriage being recognized as valid.

Clearly, forming a valid marriage was far from straightforward, and such impediments must have prevented many marriages from taking place. Some couples obtained dispensations in order to marry despite the existence of impediments. The church recognized the difficulties of finding a marriageable partner of acceptable social status in small localities where everyone seemed to be related and would sometimes allow marriages between relatives as close as uncle and niece. Yet it is clear that marriages also took place where there were impediments and without a dispensation having been granted. These were marriages that were technically invalid and were susceptible to being annulled – being declared nonmarriages – if evidence of the impediment were brought to the attention of the ecclesiastical authorities.

The question we must ask is whether medieval men and women abused the rules of marriage by seeking out impediments when they wanted to escape from their marriages, thus using annulments as substitutes for divorce. Some historians have argued that they did. The great medievalist Frederick Maitland, for example, writes that "spouses who had quarrelled began to investigate their pedigrees and were unlucky if they could discover no diriment impediment." Similarly, in his history of divorce and the church A. R. Winnett refers to the "undermining of the indissolubility of marriage by the expediency of annulments." No doubt the impression that annulments were cynically misused has been reinforced by the popular image of Henry VIII, annulling the marriages to wives of whom he apparently had no more use.

However, more recent research on the operations of the medieval church courts has tended to support the view that there was little amiss in their disposition of matrimonial cases. R. H. Helmholz's fine study of marriage litigation in medieval England shows that only a small proportion of cases regarding marriage involved annulment: They comprised twelve out of eighty-eight matrimonial cases in one set of court records and ten out of ninety-eight in another, with an overall representation of between 10 and 20%. Not only were suits for annulment quite rare, but the ecclesiastical judges demanded rigorous proof of an impediment before annulling a marriage, and the evidence of more than one witness was required to establish facts.

Helmholz cites the petition for annulment of the marriage of Richard Broke and his wife Joan because a certain Peter Daneys claimed, first, that he was related to Richard in the second degree of consanguinity, and second, that he had had sexual relations with Joan before her marriage to Richard. If the allegations were true, Richard and Joan would have been related to each other by their respective blood and sexual relations to Peter, the third party, and their mutual though indirect relationship would have been a diriment impediment from which they had not been dispensed before marriage. The evidence brought forward in the case was that of one witness who stated that Richard and Peter "sprang from two sisters" and that it was a matter of public knowledge, though the witness had no firsthand knowledge,

4

that Peter and Joan had had a sexual relationship. In this case the impediment was declared not proved and the marriage was upheld. On balance, Helmholz concludes from his study of annulment petitions that rather than grant annulments easily, the church courts operated on the principle "that it was better to risk allowing consanguineous unions than to risk separating couples God had legitimately joined together."

The church did not seem to operate differently elsewhere. Between 1384 and 1387 the bishop's court in Paris (the most important church court in France) heard almost 500 matrimonial cases, but annulled only 10 marriages. One annulment was based on consanguinity, one on the husband's impotence, and eight on the ground of bigamy (where the second marriage was declared void). As in England, the ecclesiastical courts in France appear to have been reluctant to annul marriages, although they did not hesitate when presented with convincing grounds. One such case was heard by the bishop's court at Troyes in 1530. There a man demanded the annulment of his son's marriage because it was "incestuous"; the son's uncle had had a sexual relationship with the wife before the marriage and had thus created the impediment of illegitimate affinity between husband and wife. The court ordered the husband kept in prison while it deliberated (presumably to prevent further possibly illicit sexual relations) and finally decided that the union should be annulled.

The evidence suggests not that marriage was easy to escape through the apparent loopholes of the rules of annulment, but that marriages were rarely annulled. Perhaps this explains why couples were careful about marriage and anxious to ensure that their future marriages were canonically valid. The church courts were often asked to rule on such questions as whether a precontract existed. In other instances betrothals were nullified at the joint request of the parties, sometimes on the ground that consent was lacking (as when children had been betrothed by their parents), sometimes on the ground that the parties had been young and irresponsible at the time of their betrothal. At other times the misconduct (usually sexual) of one of the parties justified canceling the betrothal. These petitions for release from betrothals, often met with a sympathetic response from the ecclesiastical judges, were altogether different from the suits to have marriages annulled; the latter were less indulgently received.

All this is not to suggest that annulments could not be used as divorces. What are we to think of cases where a wife or husband presented a petition to have her or his marriage annulled because of a recently discovered impediment? On the face of it we should have to conclude that the applicant was so troubled about breaching the church's rules (and by implication God's law) that she or he was

5

prepared to surrender a happy marriage. Whether we think of these cases – rare as they were – as genuine expressions of conscience or as cynical exploitations of the law depends on the motivations we attribute to the petitioners. No doubt some annulment petitions were motivated by religious scruples, whereas others were provoked by an unhappy marriage. In other cases there might have been a happy conjunction of marital unhappiness and the discovery (perhaps a result of a search motivated by the discontent) of an impediment. What is clear, however, is that the image of the Catholic church's courts as corrupt divorce mills is not accurate.

It is quite possible, even so, that the exploitation of annulments was more common in the higher social ranks. Apart from the case of Henry VIII, which is discussed later in this chapter, there is the example of Eleanor of Aquitaine and Louis VII. After many disagreements, Eleanor had their marriage annulled on the ground that she and Louis were within the prohibited degrees. The annulment was agreed to by French bishops in March 1152, and Eleanor married Henry Plantagenet (later Henry II) two months later. Again, though, such cases were rare, and they reflected the tendency for the church to grant social and political elites greater flexibility in marital matters than the common folk were permitted.

But if most annulments cannot be regarded necessarily as attempts by men and women to free themselves from marital misery, separations can. Husbands and wives were obliged by law to live together, and unauthorized separation – whether it was by mutual consent or the refusal of one spouse to live with the other – was a sin punishable in the ecclesiastical courts. In the twelfth century canon law recognized separations (*separationes a mensa et thoro*, or separations from table and bed), which could be granted in circumstances where the principles of true religion were threatened or where the spiritual or physical well-being of one of the spouses was at risk. In practice these guidelines established three main grounds for separation: adultery, cruelty, and heresy or apostasy.

As we have noted, a separation did not dissolve a marriage but simply permitted husband and wife to live independently. The persistence of the marriage bond meant that they were obliged to remain sexually faithful to each other, although each was freed of the obligation of sexual intercourse (the conjugal debt, in Catholic doctrine). But even given these limitations, the church courts were reluctant to agree to separations. Helmholz found that the judges tried hard to reconcile spouses in conflict and allowed separations only when there was evidence of extreme cruelty. Even then the ecclesiastical judges shared the contemporary toleration of extensive violence against a married woman by her husband. One husband was said to have attacked his wife with

6

a knife and forced her to flee and on another occasion to have stabbed her in the arm and broken a bone, but the judges described his actions as reasonable, honest, and done for the purpose of "reducing her from errors." They decided that the assaults did not justify a separation and instead imposed a bond of good behavior on the man and ordered the couple to remain together. In other cases judges bowed to the apparently inevitable. In the 1442 case of John and Margaret Colwell, who declared that they would prefer to die in prison than to live together, the judge conceded that a separation was the safer course of action.

Suits for separation, like those for annulment, seem to have been rare in the church courts of medieval Europe. In the Belgian city of Ghent there were three to six separations a year between 1349 and 1390 out of some 12,000 existing marriages. There were eight a year in Brussels in the fifteenth century. But even though the Belgian courts accepted grounds such as incompatibility for separations, one historian notes that magistrates discouraged separation and preferred couples to reconcile. In general, writes Barbara Hanawalt of marriage litigation in medieval Europe, the clerical magistrates were "more like marriage counselors trying to arrange amicable settlements, than judges."

As few as they were, some of the actions for annulment or separation would almost certainly have been actions for divorce had the Catholic church recognized divorce. Why divorce was not permitted in the doctrine of the medieval church can be understood only in terms of such issues as celibacy, marriage, remarriage and sexuality, and in terms of the evolution of biblical interpretation.

We must first appreciate that in Catholic doctrine celibacy – the state of being not married – was preferable to marriage. This view was institutionalized in the celibate priesthood by the fourth century. Marriage, according to this doctrine, was provided for those who could not remain sexually continent, the key biblical text being that of Paul (1 Corinthians 7:8–9): "I say therefore to the unmarried and widows, it is good for them if they abide even as I [i.e., celibate]. But if they cannot contain [sexually], let them marry: for it is better to marry than to burn." In the eyes of the church, marriage and sexuality were inseparable, such that the prime purpose of marriage was deemed to be procreation. Its second purpose was to prevent fornication by providing a stable sexual relationship for sexually active men and women. The intimate connections between marriage, sexuality, and procreation in Catholic doctrine go a long way to explaining why an unconsummated marriage might be dissolved in some cases and why impotence was a ground for annulment.

One might have thought that because marriage was considered an inferior state, divorce could have been welcomed as a sort of return to celibate status (albeit a tarnished celibacy) as long as it was not

7

followed by remarriage. But not so. Several biblical texts were interpreted by most ecclesiastical authorities as meaning that a validly contracted marriage could not be dissolved. There was an apparent conflict between the New Testament divorce texts of Mark and Luke on the one hand and Matthew on the other, and this led to some uncertainty within the church. According to Mark, Christ asserted that "whosoever shall put away his wife, and marry another, committeth adultery against her. And if a woman shall put away her husband, and be married to another, she committeth adultery" (Mark 10:11–12). Luke's version of this runs: "Whosoever putteth away his wife, and marrieth another, committeth adultery: and whosoever marrieth her that is put away from *her* husband committeth adultery." Matthew, however, seems to make an exception for adultery, reporting Christ as saying that "Whosoever shall put away his wife, saving for the cause of fornication, causeth her to commit adultery" (Matthew 5:32). The same qualification, "except it *be* for fornication," is found in Matthew 19:9.

Other biblical texts stress the indissolubility of marriage. Matthew 19:4–6 has Christ reply to the Pharisees' question "Is it lawful for a man to put away his wife for every cause?" with "Have ye not read, that he which made *them* at the beginning made them male and female. For this cause shall a man leave father and mother, and shall cleave to his wife: and they twain shall be one flesh? What therefore God hath joined together, let no man put asunder." Paul, we have noted, introduced a potential exception (the Pauline Privilege) to the rule of marital indissolubility by sanctioning remarriage by a Christian deserted by an unbelieving spouse: "But if the unbelieving depart, let him depart. A brother or a sister [i.e., a Christian] is not under bondage in such *cases*" (1 Corinthians 7:15).

What came to be interpreted as the Christian doctrine of marital indissolubility was at odds with Jewish and Roman law at the beginning of the Christian Era. Contemporary Jewish law gave the husband extensive authority to repudiate his wife if "it come to pass that she find no favour in his eyes, because he hath found some uncleanness in her" (Deuteronomy 24:1–2). Even so, there were limitations on the husband's powers in this respect, so that he could not divorce his wife if he had maliciously and falsely accused her of premarital fornication or if he had been forced to marry her after having raped her as a virgin. There were, moreover, contemporary trends in Jewish law toward giving women greater rights in initiating divorce.

The Roman law of divorce had itself evolved. In the early republic, mutual or unilateral divorce was possible because marriage required the mutual consent of the parties, but under the emperor Justinian divorce was restricted to cases where there was just cause. Acceptable grounds included the wife's adultery, a husband's falsely accusing his wife of adultery, and the husband's taking a concubine.

Quite clearly, the embryonic Christian position against divorce in any circumstances departed dramatically from prevailing Roman and Jewish doctrines and practices. Although the New Testament references to divorce were ambiguous enough to prevent a rapid consensus within the church that divorce was wholly unacceptable, it is notable that the Christian debate for and against divorce drew on the biblical texts and tended to ignore contemporary Jewish and Roman laws. The main problem Christian theologians had to face was how to reconcile the apparently irreconcilable differences between the texts that prohibited divorce and those that seemed to allow divorce where the wife was guilty of adultery. Some of the early church fathers (such as Hermas, Justin Martyr, Athenagoras, Tertullian, and Clement of Alexandria) suggested that the divorce texts of Matthew allowed a man to dissolve his marriage with an adulterous wife but allowed neither to remarry. Later theologians such as Ambrose, Justinian, and Augustine rallied to the indissolubilist position, and it was endorsed by various church councils, among them those of Arles (314), Mileve (416), and Hereford (673).

Other church councils, however, allowed remarriage after divorce for reason of adultery. The Council of Vannes (465) did so, as did the Council of Verberie (752), although the latter limited the right of remarriage to the husband and only in certain circumstances. The confusion of divorce doctrines was echoed, too, in the penitentials. The seventh-century Penitential of Theodore prescribed seven years' rigorous (or fifteen years' lighter) penance for a man who repudiated his wife and remarried, but only one year's penance if the man remarried after his wife had deserted him. Significantly, in light of the divorce text of Matthew, this penitential permitted a man to repudiate his adulterous wife and remarry and also allowed the wife to remarry as long as she waited five years and did a penance. Finally, the Eastern church allowed divorce for reason of adultery.

Beyond the ambivalence within the early Christian church on the matter of divorce, there were striking variations among contemporary secular legal codes, although the great majority allowed divorce in one form or another. The Roman law of divorce fluctuated and underwent several modifications in the sixth century under Justinian and Justinian II. Germanic legislation from the fifth to the ninth centuries allowed divorce by mutual consent or unilaterally, though the latter generally favored the husband. Frankish law did not permit a wife to initiate a divorce, and Burgundian law provided that a woman who tried to divorce her husband should be smothered in mire. Anglo-Saxon law, similarly, permitted marriages to be dissolved at the request of both or either spouse.

Even though there was no unanimity on divorce within the Catholic church, the weight of authority lay on the indissolubilist side. The perceptible divergence was increasingly between this emerging indissolubilist consensus in the church and the dissolubilist doctrines entrenched in secular laws, but during the eighth century the Catholic position began to achieve dominance. Paradoxically, the key figure in this process was a secular ruler, the emperor Charlemagne, who extended the ecclesiastical doctrine of marital indissolubility to the secular courts throughout his empire. Even then, several church councils in the ninth century demurred. For example, the Roman synod convoked by Pope Eugenius in 826 decreed that divorce was permitted in the case of adultery and that the innocent spouse could remarry.

Despite this, however, the consensus against divorce hardened. One of the first to experience the effects of the policy was Lothar II, king of Lotharingia, who in 858 attempted to rid himself of his wife to marry his concubine. Lothar battled two successive popes for more than ten years before he finally conceded defeat to a papacy that had demonstrated a new determination to enforce marriage.

The victory of the nondissolubilist doctrine within the Roman Catholic church was hard won, and its consolidation by the thirteenth century was associated with other developments within the church. Canon law and the system of ecclesiastical courts were developed, and throughout Europe the church successfully claimed jurisdiction over matrimonial matters. Marriage itself was more clearly defined, and there was agreement on the principle that the consent of the parties was an essential precondition of marriage. Finally, the sacramentality of marriage was accepted as part of church doctrine (although it did not enter canon law until the sixteenth century). Thus the doctrine of marital indissolubility, the doctrine that forbade divorce, was an integral part of a sweeping reformulation of marriage that took more than a millennium of debate and dissent, and that crystallized in the eleventh and twelfth centuries.

It was, of course, one thing for the church to proclaim its matrimonial doctrines. It was quite another thing for it to enforce them in populations that traditionally observed divergent customs and regulations. There is abundant evidence of customary rituals of marriage coexisting with the evolving procedures laid down by the church. In many cultures marriage might be contracted by an exchange of food and drink, as in this 1483 French case (documented by André Burguière) that involved Jean Binet and Henriette, the widow Legouge, whom he had asked to marry him:

Then the father told his daughter to sit at the table beside Jean Binet, then he put some wine in a glass and told Binet to give it to his daughter to drink in the name of marriage. He obeyed without saying a word. That done, Henriette's uncle said to her: "Give it to Jean to drink in the name of marriage, as he gave it to you to drink." Henriette gave the drink to [Binet] ... He drank from her hand, then said "I wish you to receive a kiss from me in the name of marriage," and then he kissed her.

In what was probably a corrupted use of this custom, one Pierre Pellart, before having intercourse with Marguerite, the widow Jacomart, told her: "Marguerite, so that you may not be afraid that I am abusing you, I put my tongue in your mouth, in the name of marriage."

Customary rituals of marriage, especially in cultures at the fringes of Catholic Europe, long survived attempts by the church to impose its own forms of marriage. Among the Basque populations of southern France couples persisted in the practice of marrying only after the woman had become pregnant. The canon law of marriage was received in Iceland in the thirteenth century, but attempts to impose it on a population whose law permitted divorce, dated only from 1429. Although the church successfully replaced the indigenous law of divorce, it was a brief victory, for a century and a half later Iceland warmed to the Reformation and restored divorce. Finally, in the face of Catholic doctrine, the important thirteenth-century legal code of Spain, *Las Siete Partidas*, allowed an innocent spouse to remarry after an annulment for reason of adultery, heresy, or conversion from Christianity. Such annulments could be divorces in all but name.

Despite the emergence of a consensus in favor of the doctrine of marital indissolubility, then, the church faced continuing difficulty in achieving complete obedience to the rules of marriage it sought to impose on Christendom. The major challenge, of course, in broad theological terms as well as in the narrower realm of marriage, was the Protestant Reformation. But even before that there were significant rumblings of dissent within the church. Humanists such as Erasmus and Thomas More called Catholic marriage teachings into question. Erasmus, for instance, cited the church fathers and councils that had approved of divorce for reason of adultery and suggested that the doctrine of indissolubility should at least be reviewed. For his part, More incorporated divorce – for a variety of reasons, including adultery and emotional incompatibility – in the marriage code of his *Utopia*.

Neither Erasmus nor More had any impact on the church's view of marriage, and although the Protestant rejection of Catholic divorce doctrines did have an impact, it was if anything to reinforce the principle of indissolubility. As a result of the challenges to Catholic doctrines generally, the Council of Trent (1560–3) established a new code of canon law. Included in the council's work was a canon law of marriage and divorce that left no question as to where the church stood on these critical issues. Virginity and celibacy were declared superior to marriage, the sacramentality of marriage was asserted dogmatically, and the forms of and impediments to marriage were codified. For our purposes the most important part of the Council of Trent's work was the introduction of the principle of indissolubility into canon law in Canon VII:

If any one saith, that the Church has erred, in that she hath taught, and doth teach, in accordance with the evangelical and apostolical doctrine, that the bond of matrimony cannot be dissolved on account of the adultery of one of the married parties; and that both, or even the innocent one who gave not occasion to the adultery, cannot contract another marriage, during the lifetime of the other; and, that he is guilty of adultery, who, having put away the adulteress, shall take another wife, also she, who, having put away the adulterer, shall take another husband; let him be anathema.

This dogmatic assertion of the principle of indissolubility, and its codification in canon law, was a reaction to the attack on Catholic doctrine by the Protestant Reformers. By the time the Council of Trent dealt with these issues, the Reformers had not only rejected Catholic teaching on marriage and divorce but had also sponsored the legalization of divorce throughout much of Protestant Europe. The Reformation, then, represented a sharp break in the direction of divorce doctrines and policies. The trend toward a homogeneous and enforced principle of marital indissolubility that had begun in the ninth century was, 700 years later, arrested and reversed throughout much of central and northern Europe.

The Reformers, led notably by Martin Luther and John Calvin, rejected not just the Roman Catholic church's doctrine of marital indissolubility but virtually all aspects of its marriage doctrine. They unanimously repudiated the notion that marriage was inferior to celibacy and argued that marriage was a worthy state, ordained by God, and second to no other. Calvin criticized the church's "unrestrained rhapsodic praises of virginity," while Martin Bucer, the Reformer of Strasbourg, condemned the attitude of Augustine and other church authorities as a "preposterous admiration of the celibate life." The quintessential corruption of the Catholic church's marriage system, the Reformers argued, was the system of granting dispensations from the impediments to marriage that the church itself had created. The church's practices had promoted sexual license and had turned its clergy into merchants, proclaimed Luther: "What is it they sell? Vulvas and genitals – merchandise indeed most worthy of such merchants, grown together filthy and obscene through greed and godlessness. For there is no impediment nowadays that may not be legalized through the intercession of mammon." Luther and the other Reformers insisted that the only impediments to marriage that should be recognized were those set out unambiguously in the Bible: consanguinity to the second degree and affinity to the first degree, sexual impotence, and ignorance of what a validly contracted marriage was. Even in these cases Luther was reluctant to suggest that an annulment should be automatically granted. If a man were impotent, he suggested (somewhat impractically), his wife should have intercourse with another man – her husband's brother, perhaps – and, keeping the relationship a secret, attribute to her husband any children that resulted from it.

It was not only impediments and their dispensations that aroused the ire of the Reformers but also the Catholic insistence on a celibate clergy. Vows of celibacy, they argued, were offensive to God's gift of sexuality. Luther, who had himself been a monk and had subsequently married, thought that "only one in several thousands" had the ability to remain a lifelong virgin. He wrote to a German monk in 1525 that God "does not wish man to be alone but desires that he should multiply, and so he makes him a helpmeet to be with him. . . . Therefore whoever will live alone undertakes an impossible task and takes it upon himself to run counter to God's Word." Luther extended the principle to women, writing to three nuns that no woman should be ashamed "of that for which God has created and fashioned her."

The Reformers pointed, too, to the practical effects of enforced celibacy. Heinrich Bullinger waxed eloquent in his denunciation of the Catholic clergy:

For if we judge the tree by the fruits, I pray you, what fruits of single life may we recite? What filthiness, what bawdry, what adulteries, what fornications, what ravishings, what incests and heinous copulations may we rehearse? Who at this day liveth more unchaste or dishonest, than the rabble of priests and monks do?

Finally, the Reformers denounced the sacramentality of marriage. Marriage was indeed ordained by God – Calvin described it as a "good and holy ordinance of God" – but it did not convey grace.

The Catholic church's marriage doctrines and practices were, according to Calvin, a series of "errors, lies, frauds, and misdeeds," and this view was generally representative of the Reformers. The doctrine of marital indissolubility was one item of the series, and it is to the Protestant doctrines of divorce that we must now turn. What is notable is that the Reformers rallied to divorce with more hesitation than to other aspects of their doctrines. As readily as they rejected such principles as the superiority of celibacy and virginity, they often only reluctantly embraced divorce.

The development of Luther's attitudes toward divorce is an example.

13

In 1520 Luther was undecided as to whether or not divorce was permitted by God's law: "As to divorce," he wrote, "it is still a question for debate whether it is allowable. For my part I so greatly detest divorce that I should prefer bigamy to it; but whether it is allowable, I do not venture to decide." The following year Luther seemed to have concluded that divorce was not allowed, at least by mutual consent or for reason of incompatibility; he opposed the principle of annulling vows by arguing that if solemn vows could be renounced at the will of the individual, "you could also make divorce acceptable, if the marriage partners simply cannot get along." But one year later (1522) Luther listed three grounds he considered would justify divorce: impotence (really a ground for annulment), adultery, and refusal "to fulfil the conjugal duty [sexual intercourse] or to live with the other person."

Luther amplified these grounds, beginning with adultery, which he saw as the most straightforward case. Adultery justified divorce in God's law, according to Luther, because marriage was dissolved by death (Romans 7:2) and death was the punishment for adultery (Deuteronomy 22:20–1). He also referred to the references to adultery in the texts of Matthew. As for the injunction that men should not put asunder a couple God had joined together, it simply did not apply in this case, Luther argued: "such a divorce does not mean that it is done by men, because it does not take place without the word of God."

Luther found desertion more problematic, however. It was not explicitly mentioned in the Bible except in the limited form of the Pauline Privilege. In his early works Luther tried to link desertion to adultery by implying that a deserter would almost certainly commit adultery, but eventually he accepted willful desertion as sufficient in its own right. If the deserter spouse refused to obey pleas or instructions to return, he or she could be ordered by the civil or ecclesiastical authorities to be banished, and the deserted spouse could be permitted to remarry.

The other grounds suggested by Luther were somewhat more ambiguous. If a wife persistently refused her husband intercourse, and placed him in danger of committing adultery, he should warn her that "if you will not, another will; the maid will come if the wife will not." If the wife still refused, the husband should rebuke her publicly and make her offense known to all, and if she still refused, the husband should "get rid of her." Unlike sexual incompatibility, general emotional incompatibility did not justify divorce in Luther's eyes. If a couple did not get on together, they should try to stay together nonetheless, but if one or both found the marriage completely intolerable, they might part as long as they did not remarry. This would be tantamount to a separation, of course, not a divorce.

Despite Luther's accepting divorce as permissible in cases of adultery, desertion, and refusal of sexual intercourse, he stressed that it should not be granted easily. The spouse guilty of an offense should seek forgiveness and the innocent spouse should forgive. Divorce should be a last resort, even in the few cases where it might be justified. If a divorce did take place, neither party should remarry quickly – Luther suggested waiting six months or a year – lest they give the impression that the divorce was a happy event. Luther himself, often asked for advice on specific matrimonial problems, found the issues of marriage and divorce depressing and complex. It is recorded that at one point in 1536, "Dr. Martin sighed and said: 'Good God, what a bother these matrimonial cases are to us! It takes great effort and labour to get couples together. Afterwards it requires even more pains to keep them together.' "

As reluctant as Luther was to allow divorce, and as difficult as individual cases could be, divorces began to be granted in Luther's Württemberg, and subsequently in other parts of Germany such as Augsburg and Nuremberg. Luther's influence was also evident in Scandinavia, where the Swedish church legalized divorce in 1572 on principles that drew heavily on Lutheran German laws. The Swedish clergy were enjoined to attempt to reconcile spouses, and spouses could be fined, flogged, or imprisoned if they refused to live in peace and harmony. As a last resort divorce could be granted, but only when one of the spouses committed adultery or deserted the other. Provisions for divorce that broadly followed Luther's principles (the grounds were adultery, desertion, and impotence) were adopted in Denmark and Norway in 1582, and in Iceland three years later.

Elsewhere in sixteenth-century Europe John Calvin had a significant and wide influence on divorce laws: legislation based on his doctrines was introduced in parts of Switzerland, in the Netherlands, and in Scotland. For Calvin, as for Luther, the prime justification of divorce was adultery. In former times, he pointed out, adultery was punished by death, making divorce unnecessary, but "today it is the perverted indulgence of magistrates that makes it necessary for men to divorce their impure wives." Despite the terms of this statement, Calvin placed equal responsibility on both husband and wife to remain sexually faithful, and thus extended the right of divorce to both. Calvin found desertion more complex, and as Luther had done in an early stage, he linked it to adultery. Any man who went against God's injunctions to the extent of deserting his wife, Calvin wrote, could hardly be expected to be "guided by the Lord" so far as remaining chaste was concerned.

Beyond adultery and desertion (which in some of his texts was portrayed as a kind of aggravated adultery), Calvin could see no grounds for divorce. A man or woman married to an impotent spouse, and tempted into extramarital sexual activity, should be guided by God to resist. Incompatibility of temperament was not a ground because unhappiness in marriage was a result of original sin and must be borne like its other effects. Calvin's advice to the miserably married was succinct:

When now a man has a harsh and dreadful wife, whom he cannot manage by any means, let him know, here are the fruits of original sin and also the corruption that is in myself. And the wife on her side must think, there is a good reason that I must receive the payment that comes from my disobedience towards God, because I did not humble myself before him.

Husbands and wives should not simply accept disharmony, Calvin advised, but if they could not be harmonious they should not look to divorce as a solution. Nor should a woman who was subjected to "cruelty or too much rough or inconsiderate treatment" by her husband think of divorcing. Marriage, and "happy concord" within it, were enjoined by God, and unless there was adultery or desertion, the couple should stay together until the first of them died.

Calvin, and his successor as religious leader in Geneva, Theodore Beza, institutionalized these doctrines in matrimonial ordinances of 1545 and 1561. Under these laws either wife or husband could divorce the other for reason of adultery, but only if the petitioner were demonstrably innocent of the offense. In terms of desertion, a distinction was made between unintended and willful absence. When there was evidence that a soldier was held a prisoner somewhere, or that a traveling merchant had been detained against his will, the wife could not divorce. When the absence was deliberate, however, a divorce could be granted, but only after protracted attempts to have the deserter return. If a deserter husband failed to return after several requests, or returned but then persisted in deserting, the wife might divorce him. If the deserter was the wife, however, the husband was obliged to take her back, if she returned when summoned, only if he were satisfied that she had not committed adultery while absent. Such terms betray the uneasy relationship between desertion and adultery in Calvin's divorce doctrines, together with the persistence of the double standard of sexual morality despite affirmations of the equal responsibility of husbands and wives to remain faithful.

The restrictions on divorce in sixteenth-century Geneva contributed to a low divorce rate. So did the criminalization of sexual offenses: Fornication (intercourse between two unmarried people) was punished by imprisonment with a regime of bread and water, adultery involving an unmarried accomplice was punished by banishment, and adultery involving two married persons was punished by death. Between 1559 and 1569 some 302 Genevans were excommunicated for marital quarrels and disputes of various kinds, but divorces numbered no more than one a year on average through the sixteenth and early seventeenth centuries. The reluctance of Geneva's judges to grant divorce was exemplified by their refusal, in 1572, to grant one Jacques Quiblet a divorce even though his wife had been banished from the city as a witch and could return only on pain of death. While her return and execution would have put an end to the marriage and solved her husband's dilemma, she was understandably reluctant to make the sacrifice. Quiblet was left unable to escape the marriage that had ended in all but name.

The interpretation of Calvin's doctrines was somewhat more liberal in Scotland, where they became law in 1563 under the guidance of John Knox. Adultery was the primary ground for divorce, and the guilty party could be sentenced to death or to excommunication until he or she repented, in which latter case remarriage might be permitted. In 1573 malicious desertion for four or more years was added to adultery as a ground, specifically for the benefit of the earl of Argyle, Chancellor of Scotland, who wanted to divorce Jean Stewart, half-sister of Mary, queen of Scots. Adultery and desertion remained the only grounds for divorce in Scotland until 1938, a testament to the endurance of Calvin's divorce doctrines long after Switzerland had abandoned them.

Calvin's and Luther's teachings on divorce were arguably the most important doctrines articulated during the Reformation because they underlay legislation in much of Europe. In some Protestant territories, however, individual Reformers developed their own divorce doctrines and sponsored legislation on their own terms. One was Huldreich Zwingli, the Reformer of Zurich, who interpreted the biblical texts as meaning not that adultery was the prime ground for divorce but that it was the most minor offense that might justify dissolving a marriage. For if adultery could lead to divorce, he argued, so could any "greater reason." Among these he listed "destroying life, endangering life, being mad or crazy, offending by whorishness, leaving one's spouse without permission, remaining abroad a long time, [and] having leprosy." But rather than set down a definitive list of grounds, Zwingli (and after him Heinrich Bullinger, his successor in Zurich) thought that judges ought to take each case on its own merits "and proceed as God and the character of the case shall demand." In 1525 Zwingli established a marriage tribunal (*Ehegericht*), composed of both clergy and secular judges, to apply Zurich's reformed marriage laws. But even though it had a relatively liberal mandate as far as divorce was concerned, divorces were not easily obtained in the city: between 1525 and 1531 (when Zwingli died) the tribunal granted twenty-eight petitions, or 35% of the eighty lodged. It was still a lot more than in Geneva later in the century.

Divorces were also granted in the Swiss territory of Basel, where the reform of marriage law was supervised by Johannes Oecolampadius, a close friend of Zwingli. Under ordinances passed in 1533, divorce was possible for reason of adultery, refusal to cohabit, abuse, impotence, and conviction for a capital offense. As such they were more extensive than those recognized by Luther and Calvin but less extensive than those accepted by Zwingli. Thomas Max Safley's study of the Basel court shows that of 1,356 matrimonial cases between 1550 and 1592 (an average of 34 a year), only 226 (17%) were divorce petitions and 18 (1%) were suits for separation. Half the divorce petitions (114 cases) were based on adultery, 84 on refusal to cohabit, 21 on various kinds of abuse, and 7 on impotence. Slightly more than half the petitioners (127, or 56%) were women. The court agreed to more than half the petitions (125 of the 226), rejected 65 definitively and instructed the spouses in 35 cases to resolve their differences amicably.

Other streams within Continental Protestantism adopted more restrictive approaches to divorce. Sects such as the Hutterites and Mennonites tended to refer more closely to the biblical texts and generally allowed divorces only for reason of adultery or in the context of the Pauline Privilege. The Hutterite Five Articles of 1547, for example, allowed divorce only for adultery, for although it permitted a Hutterite wife to divorce her "unbelieving" husband (and then only if her or their children's faith was endangered by him), it forbade the divorced woman to remarry while her "husband" was still alive. Similarly the 1554 Mennonite Wismar Resolution allowed the believer in a religiously mixed marriage to separate but did not permit remarriage unless the unbeliever broke the marriage by committing adultery or entering a new marriage. Even then, the believing spouse could remarry only "subject to the advice of the elders of the congregation."

Divorce, and marriage issues more generally, came to the fore in different contexts during the Reformation. Some of the smaller sects, for example, argued that polygamy ought to be permitted. One such advocate was John of Leyden, the spiritual leader of the German city of Münster. From 1534 polygamy was not only permitted but encouraged in Münster, ostensibly in order to promote population growth and to emulate the biblical patriarchs, although it is thought more likely that John of Leyden (who was already married) saw in polygamy a way of marrying a woman to whom he was attracted. Such was the enthusiasm of Münster's male population to obey this law that in January 1535 a decree was issued to allow any woman who had been forced into a marriage to have it dissolved. Of the 2,000 women married in the preceding five months, some 200 obtained divorces.

Münster's experience of matrimonial reform was eccentric, to say the least, but it was not notably liberal, for marriages and divorces were strictly controlled. For the most liberal divorce doctrines propounded during the Reformation we must look to Martin Bucer, the Reformer of Strasbourg. Bucer developed a doctrine of divorce that envisaged the dissolution of marriages by mutual consent and in various specific circumstances, and in so doing he placed himself outside mainstream sixteenth-century Protestant thought on divorce. Bucer's doctrines were no more acceptable a century later when they were expounded by John Milton.

Bucer tied his divorce principles more closely than others to his conception of marriage. Rejecting the Roman Catholic teaching that marriage was primarily for procreation (if that were so, he wrote, there was no marriage between Mary and Joseph), Bucer insisted on the primacy of the emotional relationship between wife and husband: "The most proper and highest and main end of marriage is the communication of all duties, both divine and human, with the utmost benevolence." What did this mean? That a couple should live together and love each other, that they should be sexually faithful, and that the husband should be the head and protector of his wife and the wife a help to him. If these qualities were missing and if the couple refused to or could not perform their obligations, "there is no true marriage, nor should they be considered husband and wife." Such a doctrine permitted divorce not only for desertion and adultery, but also by mutual consent and for emotional incompatibility.

In addition, Bucer identified a list of specific grounds that would justify divorce. It included witchcraft, sacrilege, the husband's frequenting lewd women within his wife's sight, and marital violence. Bucer explicitly repudiated the notion of Calvin and others that matrimonial misery ought to be borne like a cross; Bucer insisted that God had never intended that a decent man or woman should be tied for life to an infamous partner. It was not that Bucer took marriage lightly (although the allegation was made by his opponents), for he wanted marriages overseen by "grave and devout men" who would attempt to ensure that wives and husbands lived harmoniously together. In the end, however, Bucer was prepared to accept the reality of what would later be called "marriage breakdown," and to allow men and women to quit marriages that were oppressive, intolerable, or simply unpleasant.

If Martin Bucer represented the permissive end of the spectrum of sixteenth-century divorce doctrines, the Church of England represented the restrictive end, for England was unique among Protestant countries or states in that its Reformed church did not reject the Roman Catholic doctrine of marital indissolubility. This was ironic because the catalyst for the breach between the English church and Rome was the pope's refusal to allow King Henry VIII to annul his marriage to Catherine of Aragon so that he could marry Anne Boleyn. Henry's matrimonial trials, in fact, throw light on contemporary debates among Catholics and Protestants, and were the background to the history of divorce policy and law in England.

Most of the facts of Henry VIII's matrimonial career are well known, though his annulments are usually referred to, misleadingly, as "divorces." The first annulment, of the marriage to Catherine of Aragon, was pursued within the Catholic rules of impediments that were described earlier in this chapter. Catherine had first married Henry's older brother, Arthur, in 1501, but was widowed when Arthur died the next year. Because a link between Spain and England was deemed useful, it was decided that Catherine would marry Henry as soon as he reached the age of fifteen. Because there was an impediment of affinity between Henry and Catherine because of her marriage to his brother, a dispensation was obtained from Pope Julius II, and the couple duly married in 1509.

Eighteen years later, in June 1527, Henry informed Catherine that he believed their marriage to be canonically invalid. It is not clear when Henry began to doubt the validity of the marriage, nor is it clear whether his infatuation with Anne Boleyn predated or antedated his doubts. What is clear is that Henry was obsessed with producing a male heir to stabilize the Tudor dynasty and that he was unlikely to do this with Catherine. Their marriage had produced one daughter, the future Queen Mary, but Catherine had borne five other children, none of whom had survived, and had had several miscarriages. Marrying a younger woman was the most likely means of having a male heir, and the appearance of Anne Boleyn must have seemed to Henry a godsend.

Because the English church was Catholic, Henry could not divorce, and he formed a case for annulment by arguing that Catherine's marriage to his older brother had created an impediment to his marriage to her such that even the pope could not dispense them from it. Among the biblical texts Henry appealed to was one in Leviticus: "If a man shall take his brother's wife, it is an impurity; he hath uncovered his brother's nakedness; they shall be childless" (Leviticus 20:21). Henry and Catherine were not childless, but in view of the sad catalog of infant deaths and miscarriages, the text impressed Henry and convinced him that his marriage was blighted in the eyes of God.

In 1529 Henry petitioned Pope Clement VII for an annulment but was met with a refusal. Not only was Clement reluctant to nullify one of his predecessor's dispensations, but he himself was virtually a prisoner of Emperor Charles V, who was Catherine of Aragon's nephew. It was not in Charles's best interests to have his aunt removed from the throne of England, which was what an annulment would have entailed. Moreover, Henry's petition had been challenged by Catherine's supporters who had come to her aid and had marshaled their own biblical and other authorities in support of her defense of the validity of her marriage.

There were some questions of fact at issue, notably whether the marriage between Arthur and Catherine had been consummated. If it had, the impediment between Henry and Catherine would have been one of affinity formed by sexual intercourse, but if it had not, the impediment would have been a lesser one of "public honesty," which was formed by a betrothal or unconsummated marriage. For her part Catherine insisted that her marriage to Arthur had not been consummated and that she had been a virgin when she married Henry, but the king and his supporters argued otherwise. They drew upon a reported statement by Arthur "the next Morning after his Marriage, that he had been that Night in the Midst of Spain." Only at the end of the proceedings did Henry concede that Catherine had married him a virgin.

Without going into the intricacies of Henry's suit to have his first marriage annulled, we can note that having failed to secure an annulment from the pope, Henry adopted the view that his marriage was null and void according to God's law, and he proceeded to marry Anne Boleyn secretly in January 1533, soon after she was found to be pregnant. Three months later the Southern Convocation of the Church of England ruled that Henry's marriage to Catherine had been impeded by divine law and that the papal dispensation had been to no effect. Before long the breach between Henry and the pope was formalized and Henry became head of the Anglican church.

What is interesting, from the point of view of the history of divorce, is that Henry did not *divorce* Catherine. It would have been possible for Henry to have broken with Rome and established his own church (as he did) and to have legalized divorce just as Reformed churches were doing on the Continent. Not only did Henry not go this far, but the Continental Reformers whom he consulted on the annulment issue excluded divorce from their solutions. Some, like Zwingli, supported the annulment, while others, like Oecolampadius, argued that even if the marriage had been invalid at the beginning, it had been validated by consummation and the years of cohabitation. Many of the scholars consulted, including Luther, Melanchthon, Bucer, and Erasmus, suggested that Henry remarry without annulling the marriage to Catherine, that is to say, that he commit bigamy. Luther wrote that "before I would approve of such a divorce [annulment] I would rather permit the king to marry still another woman and to have, according to the example of the patriarchs and kings, two women or queens at the same time." This was the advice given to, and followed by, the Landgrave Philip of Hesse in 1539, after he advised Luther and others that he could not live with his wife and yet could not remain sexually inactive.

It is true that Henry's marriage was not an ordinary marriage, for on it rested the stability of the young Tudor dynasty. It was therefore important that any male heir be born in a marriage whose validity could not be impugned by a rival. A divorce was less likely than an annulment to have been regarded as valid, and this must have weighed heavily in the calculations of Henry, his supporters, and those he consulted. Yet it is also significant that Protestants who had established divorce in their own territories would not countenance a divorce in the exceptional circumstances presented by Henry VIII. The case demonstrates the reluctance with which even these innovators approached divorce, and their concern that the proper forms of matrimony be followed. Henry's insistence on pursuing the annulment suggests that he himself, despite his popular image, was more fastidious in matrimonial matters than he is normally given credit for being.

The voiding of his marriage to Catherine of Aragon was, however, only the first of three annulments that punctuated Henry VIII's marital career. The marriage to Anne Boleyn was itself annulled in 1536, although the precise grounds alleged are not known. (Anne Boleyn was convicted of adultery and incest and was executed.) Henry's fourth marriage, to Anne of Cleves, was also annulled but again the precise grounds are not known. In his deposition, Henry argued that he had not truly consented to the marriage, that Anne had not been a virgin when it took place, and that her physical appearance was such as to have rendered him impotent and unable to consummate the marriage. For this third time the Church of England acquiesced in the king's doctrinal contortions and seems to have allowed the rules of annulment to be exploited in precisely the way the Reformers had condemned the Roman Catholic church of doing.

Henry VIII's refusal to consider divorce, whether it was based on religious or political considerations, set the tone for the development of divorce in England for the next 300 years. For although a limited form of divorce was established in the eighteenth century, it was not until the mid-nineteenth century that a divorce law was passed in England. The refusal of the Church of England to reject the Catholic doctrine of marital indissolubility, as the other Reformed churches had done, was not without its critics, for many of the early English Reformers advocated the legalization of divorce. William Tyndale, for one, thought that divorce ought to be available for adultery (at least, adultery by the wife) and desertion. Thomas Becon, a chaplain to Archbishop Cranmer, interpreted the Bible more literally and proposed that divorce should be allowed only in cases of the wife's adultery and in strict terms of the Pauline Privilege. John Hooper, bishop of Gloucester, thought adultery by either spouse would justify divorce, as would the desertion of a believer by an unbeliever (the Pauline Privilege).

Perhaps the most interesting English theologian of the time, as far as the history of divorce is concerned, was Thomas Cranmer, archbishop of Canterbury from 1532 to 1553 and a longtime confidant of Henry VIII. In the light of Henry's pursuit of annulments it is surely significant that Cranmer was opposed to divorce under any circumstances. In 1540 he wrote to one of the Reformers, "What can possibly be alleged in your excuse when you allow a man, after a divorce, when both man and woman are living, to contract a fresh marriage?"

Yet within a decade Cranmer had changed his mind and was prepared to admit divorce for reason of adultery. The cause of this change was the case of William Parr, marquis of Northampton, who in 1542 obtained a separation from a church court on the ground of his wife's adultery. Northampton subsequently sought permission to remarry (even though his first marriage had not been dissolved and his wife was still alive), and in 1547 Cranmer was commissioned to investigate the case to see if a remarriage might be permitted. This in itself was a concession by the Church of England, but before Cranmer could report, Northampton remarried, claiming "that by the Word of God he was discharged of his tye to his former Wife; and the making marriages indissoluble was but a part of the Popish Law." This was a serious challenge to the Anglican church in that Northampton's words and deed claimed, first, that adultery was a ground for dissolution of marriage and, second, that the act of adultery alone – not a court judgment – dissolved the marriage. Neither of these contentions was immediately accepted, and Northampton and his second wife were ordered to separate until Cranmer had reported. When the archbishop did report, it was that divorce was certainly justified by adultery and might also be permitted for reason of desertion. Still, the weight of opinion in English church and state was against divorce, and although Northampton's first marriage was annulled by a special Act of Parliament, it was not intended to provide a precedent for others.

The Northampton case did have implications, however. In 1543 Henry VIII had set up a commission of bishops, other theologians, laymen, and lawyers to draft a canon law for the Church of England. The commission's report, *Reformatio Legum Ecclesiasticarum*, presented in the 1550s and thought to have been particularly influenced by Cranmer (who by this time had rendered the judgment on Northampton's case), recommended that Anglican canon law abolish separations and legalize divorce. The proposed grounds were adultery (only the innocent spouse to be allowed to remarry), desertion or prolonged absence without news, "deadly hostility" (attempted murder), or violence by a husband against his wife unless it were justified by his need to punish her. (This qualification is a reference to the husband's legal ability to "moderately correct" his wife; it is discussed in Chapter 7.) The net effect of the *Reformatio Legum Ecclesiasticarum* was to recommend a more liberal divorce policy than any other country or Reformed church had adopted by that time. The report was discussed briefly in Parliament, but proved unacceptable to the Church of England. When the first systematic revision of canon law of the Anglican church was promulgated in 1604, it permitted separations but explicitly ruled out the possibility of divorce.

Among the European states whose churches broke with Rome in the sixteenth century, England was alone in not abandoning the doctrine of marital indissolubility and making some provision for divorce. Protestant Germany and Switzerland, the Netherlands, Denmark, Norway, Sweden, Iceland, and Scotland, all permitted divorce in one form or another, and most accepted what became the classic Protestant grounds, adultery and desertion. Adultery, though, was the matrimonial offense par excellence – we have noted that Luther and Calvin saw desertion to some extent as associated with adultery – and some explanation for the importance of adultery in Protestant divorce doctrines is necessary.

The primary reason for the unanimous agreement (the Church of England excepted) that adultery was a ground for divorce is surely that it was explicitly cited in the Bible as an exception to the rule of indissolubility. But beyond that, adultery responded to the Protestant emphasis on the essentially sexual character of marriage. One part of Roman Catholic marriage doctrines that most of the Reformers did not reject was the purposes of marriage. For the Catholic church, Luther, Calvin, and most others, the primary end of marriage was procreation, the second was as a means of avoiding illicit sexual activity (usually referred to as "the avoidance of fornication"), and the third end was the mutual companionship and help that spouses provided. The English Reformer Peter Martyr listed these purposes of marriage this way: "for the increasing of children, for the taking away of whoredome, and that thereby the life of man might have helpes and commodities." Only a few of the Reformers rejected this notion of the purposes of marriage; Martin Bucer, the matrimonial odd man out, stressed the social and affective aspects of marriage, rather than the sexual.

The emphasis on sexuality within marriage contributed, in the Reformers' divorce doctrines, to the emphasis on adultery as the clearest breach of marriage that warranted divorce. If marriage was designed to produce legitimate children and keep men and women sexually chaste, then adultery negated marriage by creating doubt about paternity and by being by nature unchaste. The low ranking of the emotional relationship within marriage in the Reformers' marriage doctrines similarly goes a long way to explaining their rejection of incompatibility as a ground for divorce. To them a happy, harmonious relationship was desirable but not an essential component of marriage. It is noteworthy that Bucer, who did stress the affective relationship between wife and husband, permitted divorce for reason of incompatibility.

We should also take into account, when explaining the stress on adultery in their divorce doctrines, the Reformers' horror at the extent of illicit sexual activity apparently permitted by the Catholic church and even encouraged by its hypocritical doctrines of celibacy and virginity. The English theologian Thomas Becon fulminated against the "stinking puddle of whoredom" and "the outrageous seas of adultery, whoredom, fornication, and uncleanness, [which] have not only brast in, but have overflowed almost the whole world." The Reformers condemned the Catholic church's indulgence toward illicit sexual activities, exemplified by its abandonment of the death penalty for adultery that had been enjoined in the Bible. This indulgence, claimed Calvin and some others, had made divorce necessary as a substitute for the death of the adulterous spouse. Calvin, in fact, saw that adultery was made a capital offense in Geneva for some time in the sixteenth century, and the same penalty was imposed in Scotland and Munster. Other jurisdictions, such as England, would make adultery a capital crime in the next century.

A variety of considerations led to adultery becoming the one ground for divorce upon which almost all the Reformers agreed. They were almost unanimous, too, that divorce was a matter of fault. Bucer recognized divorce by mutual consent, but the rest sought circumstances where one spouse was clearly the offender, the other clearly innocent. Thus it was that in some Protestant divorce laws a husband or wife could divorce his or her adulterous partner only if he or she were demonstrably innocent of the offense. Moreover, many of the divorce laws forbade the guilty spouse to remarry. Even so, there were circumstances that justified divorce in some laws that were less clearly than others matters of fault. The Swedish church's divorce law, for example, permitted the divorce of a spouse who had been absent for a long time, even when there was no evidence that it was due to a willful desertion.

We should note, too, that the Reformers did not believe that a matrimonial offense, even such a heinous one as adultery, automatically justified divorce. Most codes provided for compulsory attempts at conciliation and some for mandatory periods of cohabitation, even when one spouse had been guilty of adultery. In cases of desertion attempts were to be made to persuade the deserter to return and make good the marriage. Only after these attempts to retrieve the marriage had failed was divorce countenanced, and to this extent the Reformers did take into account the condition of a marital relationship. A matrimonial offense triggered a divorce procedure, it is true, but the will of both spouses to maintain the marriage could override the offense. Only if they did not have the will or ability to continue together was divorce used, and to this extent the Protestant divorce laws implicitly recognized marriage breakdown.

The often protracted procedures reinforce the image of reluctance with which the Reformers accepted divorce. Not only the theologians but also the judges and other officials tried to keep divorces to a minimum. We have noted that the number of divorce petitions was low in sixteenth-century Europe, but that even so, many of them failed. The judges of Zurich granted 28 out of 80 petitions between 1525 and 1531, and 125 of the 226 petitions in Basel from 1550 and 1592 succeeded. In Zwickau, according to Safley, "divorce was practically as hard to obtain from the Protestant regime as it had been from the Catholic."

To explain the hesitancy of the Protestant spiritual leaders and judges we may appeal to a sense of tradition – these were men who were still influenced by the principle of marital indissolubility – and also to their desire to uphold the integrity of marriage and individual marriages. The Reformers conceived of marriage as an important weapon in the constant battle of believers against evil. In marriage, an estate ordained by God, which provided a forum for licit sexual activity and the virtues of mutual assistance, Christians had a strong basis for salvation. One had only to compare the dangers facing the individual shut out of marriage – the temptations of sexuality and the license promoted by the absence of this fundamental structure of authority – to appreciate how important marriage was for the maintenance not only of virtue, but also of social order.

The Protestant doctrines of marriage and divorce, then, broke with important parts of Catholic doctrine but were informed by many of the same values and some of the same fundamental moral orientations. This paradoxical character of Protestant divorce reflected the paradox of divorce itself. Divorce has generally been seen as detrimental to the family: Nothing seems at first sight more evident than that a process that dissolves a marriage is a negative one. Yet there is an argument to be made that permission to divorce in the Protestant Reformation reflected a higher estimation of marriage than in Roman Catholic doctrine, a shift in emphasis away from the forms of marriage to its content, to the quality of marriage for those involved. In the sixteenth century the Protestants were groping toward a broader conception of marriage than Catholic doctrines and laws had permitted. But they were still too close to the breach with Rome to be able to shed entirely the unease inspired by the conclusions about divorce to which the logic of their social theology drove them.

Suggestions for further reading

Bels, Pierre, *Le mariage des Protestants français jusqu'en 1685* (Paris, 1968).

Brundage, James A., *Law, Sex and Christian Society in Medieval Europe* (Chicago, 1987).

Burguière, André, "Les rituels du mariage en France: pratiques ecclésiastiques et pratiques populaires (XVIe–XVIIIe siècles)," *Annales E.S.C.* 33:3 (May–June 1978), 637–49.

Duby, Georges, *Medieval Marriage* (Baltimore, 1978).

Duby, Georges, *The Knight, the Lady and the Priest: The Making of Modern Marriage in Medieval France* (Cambridge, 1983).

Flandrin, Jean-Louis, *Families in Former Times* (Cambridge, 1979).

Hanawalt, Barbara A., *The Ties That Bound: Peasant Families in Medieval England* (New York, 1986).

Helmholz, R. H., *Marriage Litigation in Medieval England* (Cambridge, 1974).

Kelly, Henry Ansgar, *The Matrimonial Trials of Henry VIII* (Stanford, 1976).

Norskov Olsen, V., *The New Testament Logia on Divorce* (Tübingen, 1971).

Nylander, Ivar, *Studier Rörande den Svenska Äktenskapsrättens Historia* (Stockholm, 1961).

Ozment, Steven, *When Fathers Ruled: Family Life in Reformation Europe* (Cambridge, Mass., 1983).

Rheinstein, Max, *Marriage Stability, Divorce and the Law* (Chicago, 1972).

Safley, Thomas Max, *Let No Man Put Asunder. The Control of Marriage in the German Southwest: A Comparative Study, 1550–1600* (Kirksville, 1984).

Winnett, A. R., *Divorce and Remarriage in Anglicanism* (London, 1958).

2

Seventeenth-century England and its American colonies

By the beginning of the seventeenth century the divorce map of Europe had taken shape: Divorce was absent wherever the Roman Catholic church had resisted the Reformation, and, with the exception of England, it had been legalized wherever a Protestant confession was entrenched. The exceptional status of the Anglican church makes England particularly interesting, for although the divorce debate was settled one way or the other in the rest of Europe by the end of the sixteenth century, it continued in England as the advocates of divorce pressed their case against a recalcitrant church. Moreover, the seventeenth century witnessed remarkable changes in England. It began with the promulgation of canon laws of the Anglican church that forbade divorce but ended with a procedure by which divorces could be obtained by circumventing the church. Moreover, it was in the seventeenth century that some of the English colonists in North America legalized divorce. The present chapter will examine this watershed period in England, old and New.

An emphasis on marriage and divorce in the seventeenth century is hardly inappropriate, for the family was one of the great moral, social, and political issues that preoccupied theologians, social critics, and other intellectuals of the time. The evidence lies in the hundreds of conduct-books, sermons, tracts, treatises, and theses devoted to all aspects of the family: marriage, divorce, parent–child relations, the status of women, family government, property, sexuality, and the duties of fathers, mothers, husbands, wives, and children. The family was portrayed as the basic unit of society, and order within the family was the guarantor of social and political order. This vast literature aimed to ensure that individuals understood their individual and integral roles within a smoothly functioning family and to emphasize the importance of marital and family stability for society and polity. Fundamental to these considerations was religion, for marriage was ordained by God and familial relationships were prescribed by God, so that any behavior that ran counter to harmony in marriage or the family not only threatened social stability but was contrary to divine commandments.

28

Given these perspectives, it is hardly surprising that seventeenth-century commentators regarded stress and conflict within marriage – or worse, marriage breakdown – with the greatest apprehension. The failure of any family members to perform their obligations (such as the failure of children to obey their parents) was bad enough, but the collapse of marriage was particularly alarming because the married couple was the fundamental relationship of any household. Second, the relationship between husband and wife was more closely regulated than others because the spouses, by marrying, had entered a relationship ordained by God. Some writers, indeed, represented marriage as a triad, uniting God, husband, and wife (in that order) in an indissoluble union. Third, the maintenance of the conjugal relationship was regarded as especially important because husband and wife were regarded as exemplars to other members of the family: If they could not manage *their* relationship, what hope had the rest?

The religious dimension of marital harmony cannot be underestimated, and many seventeenth-century writers stressed that conflict between wife and husband was a symptom of the chaos that the Fall had caused in social and political relations. Robert Abbot, later bishop of Salisbury, insisted that "the first government that ever was in this world was in a family; and the first disorder that ever was in the world was in a family; and all the disorders that ever fell out since, sprung from Families." The notions of order and government expressed in the conduct-books and other seventeenth-century writings comprised not only the obligations of sexual fidelity and cohabitation, but also the duties of the husband to love, guide, and assist his wife, and of the wife to love, comfort, and obey her husband. Marriage failure, then, included not only adultery and desertion, but conflict and the failure of one or both partners to fulfill any of his or her varied duties.

What is more – and it gives the seventeenth-century writing a sense of urgency – there was a prevailing belief that wives and husbands were ignoring their obligations on a grand scale, and that marriage failure was a widespread and increasing occurrence. In 1608 Robert Abbot concluded a wedding sermon with a reference to the "lamentable ruptures and divisions betwixt husband and wife [that] are everywhere to be seene amongst us." In midcentury another clergyman deplored the extent of separations: "A deserted Lady, or Gentlewoman is become a common notion. As one sayd, now the dogs bark at the Masters of the family, when they return, as if they were absolute strangers." Yet later in the century Richard Allestree wrote: "We see every day the slightest disgust nowadays too strong for the matrimonial love." Love, he went on, often lasts no longer than a month, and "it is every bodies admiration" to see it last a year.

The overall sense conveyed in this corpus of writing was that marriage and the family were on the brink of destruction, a situation reflecting the moral malaise of the times. As one clergyman wrote, "it now adaies falleth out in the corruption of our time of sinne, that the merry estate of marriage is altogether amongst most, marred." This was not simply a reference to human society after the Fall, for the writers believed that marriage and the family could be retrieved from the brink of disaster on which they were poised. To this end they sought the causes of marriage problems and breakdown and proposed methods of solving them. In doing so they were necessarily forced to confront the issue of divorce.

Among the suggested causes of marriage problems, sexual offenses ranked high. Fornication, which generally meant premarital sexual intercourse, was said to be rife and was portrayed as leading to adultery. As John Dod, a lecturer at Banbury, put it, premarital sex poisons the body and lingers within it, ready to break out in adultery after marriage: "An olde fornicator shall be a new adulterer." Many writers expressed disappointment that adultery was no longer a capital offense and warned that God would punish the whole society that permitted adulterers to pursue their filthy activities with impunity. This was part of a tradition that would lead to the 1650 Adultery Act, which made some kinds of adultery punishable by death.

Adultery was viewed with horror not only because it was forbidden by divine law, but because it could result in a married woman's bearing a child that was not her husband's. Such a spurious child might take its place in the family and effectively cheat the legitimate children of their inheritance. One work calling for the death penalty for adultery described the effects of adultery thus: "a Spurious issue that robs the Husband by wholesale of his Estate, of all his own and his Ancestors Acquisition, is brought into his family. The Crime is then a Complication of all the Wickedness in Lust, Breach of Faith and Robbery." Beyond the purely material concerns, the personal effects of adultery were described in graphic detail as "a diseased body, a poore estate, a blemished name, and damned soule, and the drawing and murdering of another soul."

Beyond the offense of adultery the seventeenth-century commentators identified other problems in marriages. God had intended wife and husband to be companions, but too often they were indifferent – or worse, hostile – toward each other. Robert Crofts was not alone in lauding the benefits of marital love while lamenting its absence among his contemporaries:

Nuptiall Love and society sweetens all our Actions, discourse; all other pleasures, felicities, and even in all respects, Encreases true Joy and happiness . . .

[but] after Marriage it is strange to thinke, what Jealousies, Contentions, Feares, Sorrowes, strange actions, gestures, lookes, bitter words, outrages and debates, are between men and their wives for want of true love and discretion.

Failure to live together, sexual infidelity, lack of love and companionship: these were the main areas of trouble within marriage that were identified. They are readily recognizable as desertion or separation, adultery, and incompatibility. What lay beneath these manifestations of discord was vigorously discussed, and there was a ready consensus that marital discord of any kind was the devil's work. Marriage was, after all, one of God's institutions, and it was a prime target for his wrecking rival. As one wedding sermon put it: "For then did God create the world, first he made things, then he machd [matched] them; first he created, and then he coupled them; of man and woman he made one in marriage . . . but then came the devil upon the stage, and his part was again to divide what God had united." Given mankind's propensity to sin, and therefore for marriages to fall far short of replicating heavenly bliss on earth, the challenge for writers on marriage was to advise men and women as to how they could maximize the chances of having a good marriage.

The first approach was to give advice to the unmarried. Most of the works in this genre were directed at young men who, it was assumed, would take the initiative in courting and choosing a mate. They were warned to marry for the right reasons, for although God had provided marriage as a hedge against fornication, sex was not the most important part of a marital relationship. A man could become subjugated to a woman's sexuality, "rendering him subject to slavery, that was born free, and Her to command, who ought in righter reason to serve and obey." One warning against the dangers of women's sexuality was expressed graphically thus: "I have heard a well-built woman compared in her motion to a ship under saile; yet I would advise no wise man to be her owner, if her Fraught [freight] be nothing but what she carries between wind and water."

Once a young man had decided to marry, he was advised to give the greatest attention to traits such as piety and personality, than to appearance, charm, and wealth, which were transient qualities at best: "If it [marriage] be built upon beautie, Riches, Wealth and such like vanishing and changeable things, it cannot endure, but faileth when the foundation is taken away." In general, men and women should marry partners similar to themselves in age, quality, and wealth. Anything more than a moderate disparity of age, for example, could, by itself, have appalling consequences: "An old woman," wrote one commentator, "is a very unfit and unpleasing companion for a young man, and for an old man to dote upon young wenches is very unseemely hurtful ... and commonly much strife, suspicion, jealousy, discontents and miseryes ensue such marriages." Observance of a handful of basic precepts in choosing a spouse, it was thought, would minimize the likelihood of discord within marriage.

But it was clear that too many people married unwisely or, once married, failed to observe the rules of matrimony. The rules were few and clear: Husbands were to love, guide, protect, and provide for their wives, and wives were to love, honor, and obey their husbands and look after their households. But did they? No, chorused the commentators. Women were particularly criticized for failing in their obligations. Some writers referred to "the very sloth and incapacity of women now adays ... even to a contempt of Huswifery." Women nagged their husbands, were materialistic, and disobedient. Indeed, a number of writers suggested that it was women's faults that drove their husbands from the path of righteous behavior. The words "we wives may doe much either in making or marring our husbands," were put in the mouth of a character in one marriage guide that was written in the form of a dialogue. Other commentators, however, blamed husbands for marital disharmony because they were dominant in marriages. It was a precept in law that a husband was accountable for his wife's actions, just as a master was accountable for his servant's. Within marriage this principle justified the notion that a husband had the right to punish his wife physically, but although this right was debated vigorously (see Chapter 5), there was little argument that men ought to wield the authority within marriage.

The examination of the state of marriage, the extent of conflict and breakdown, and their causes and solutions compelled seventeenth-century writers to confront the issue of divorce. Many suggested that divorce should be allowed under certain circumstances, but none (at least until John Milton in the 1640s) went further than recognizing grounds other than adultery or desertion. Many, indeed, did not go this far and forbade divorce under any circumstances. Alexander Niccholes, for one, insisted that "this knot [marriage] can neither bee cut nor loosed, but by death." He, like others of his persuasion, recommended that unhappy spouses should simply face the reality that they were bound to each other for life and learn to live with it. Even when faced with adultery, wrote Richard Allestree, "a patient submission" was a wife's best response: "They are therefore far in the wrong, who in case of this injury pursue their husbands with virulencies and reproches."

But there were others who thought that there were limits to the behavior that spouses ought to have to tolerate with patience and charity. Those who thought that divorce should be permitted, however, found the Church of England unreceptive to the idea. As we have seen, the reform of Anglican canon law that was drafted in the 1550s (the *Reformatio Legum Ecclesiasticarum*) proved too liberal, and when the Church's canon laws were promulgated in 1604 they expressly forbade divorces. Separations would be allowed, but it was specified that separated spouses could not remarry while both were still living. As security, separated spouses had to pay a bond to the court, "that they will not in any way break or transgress the said restraint or prohibition." Even so, the issue was not settled in absolute terms. When bigamy was made a felony in England for the first time in 1604, the law stipulated that a person who had separated before contracting a second (bigamous) marriage would be treated more leniently than a person who married twice without having obtained a separation from the first spouse. The bigamy law responded to the 1602 case of Hercules Foljambe, which had been heard by the Court of Star Chamber. Foljambe had been granted a separation from his wife, then had married again; and although his marriage was voided, he argued that many theologians considered remarriage permissible after a formal separation. The qualification in the bigamy law seemed to acknowledge that there was at least a gray area.

Foljambe was frustrated in his marital ambitions, but he was right to argue that "divers divines and civilians of great account and learning" agreed that divorce ought to be permitted. The retention of the principle of marital indissolubility was a source of great annoyance to many clerical and lay members of the Church of England. There are some indications that the leaders of the church, including John Whitgift when he was archbishop of Canterbury, attempted to suppress debate on such a contentious issue, but there is ample evidence, in the form of many works on divorce, that such attempts failed.

The first two decades of the seventeenth century saw a number of closely argued works in defense of the Anglican church's ban on divorce. John Dove, a London vicar, published a sermon against divorce in 1601, and the next year John Howson, later to be successively bishop of Oxford and Durham, defended a University of Oxford thesis against the notion that divorce was permissible for reason of adultery. The thesis was published in 1606. In 1610 there were two more works that argued against divorce on purely theological grounds. It is notable that the opponents of divorce included a significant number of bishops. In fact, no bishop, archbishop or incumbent of high Anglican office in the first half of the seventeenth century supported the legalization of divorce.

At the lower levels of clergy, this antidivorce position was defended by men of many positions on the spectrum that the Anglican church spanned. Puritans and non-Puritans alike rejected divorce, and there is little to be said for the notion that "Puritans" supported divorce while "Anglicans" opposed it. (Apart from anything else, this formulation sets up a false dichotomy between Puritans and Anglicans, for Puritans were Anglicans.) One Puritan who opposed divorce was Thomas Gataker, rector of Rotherhithe in Surrey, who was in 1643 named a member of the Westminster Assembly of Divines. For Gataker, marriage was "a bond knot by God," and he advised couples: "Art thou married? seek not to be loosed: abide in the calling God hath called thee in... for if cohabitation be of God, then the contrary unto it is of Satan."

One characteristic of the antidivorce literature of the first half of the seventeenth century is that it appealed almost entirely to scriptural interpretation. There were long discussions of the biblical texts and other ecclesiastical authorities, but there was virtually none of the social theology of the prodivorce writers, who tended to give more emphasis to conceptions of justice and the right ordering of morality and society. In the 1640s John Milton would dismiss the antidivorce arguments as "resting on the meere element of the Text," as distinct from the prodivorce arguments that "consult[ed] with charitie, the interpreter and guide of our faith."

One of the most interesting works in favor of divorce was *A Bride-Bush*, published in 1617 by William Whately, who was a Puritan vicar in Banbury (near Oxford) from 1610 until his death in 1639. In this work, "describing the duties of married Persons, by performing whereof, Marriage shall be to them a great Helpe, which now find it a little Hell," Whately proposed allowing divorce when the two "principal duties" of marriage – sexual fidelity and cohabitation – were breached. This made Whately an advocate of divorce for adultery or desertion, and thus no more liberal than many other Anglicans, but after a second edition of *A Bride-Bush* was published in 1619, he was summoned to appear before the Court of High Commission to explain himself. Whately retracted his advocacy of divorce, though somewhat ambiguously, and in his next major work, *A Care-Cloth* (1621), went to lengths to advise unmarried men and women to stay that way. If divorce were not permitted, Whately seemed to be saying, it is better not to enter a marriage where one risked having to stay with an adulterous partner or remain linked to a spouse who had deserted. Even in other marriages, Whately wrote, things were seldom satisfactory: Wives were spendthrifts and nagging, men were tyrannical and selfish, and children were disobedient and the bane of their parents' lives. Whately's rather jaundiced view of marriage might well have informed his premarital counseling, for it is notable that while he was vicar at Banbury the number of marriages in the parish declined.

Whateley was a Puritan, but, as we have noted, support for divorce was not characteristic of the Puritan movement in England. This was highlighted during the conflicts between King Charles I and his parliaments that led to civil war in 1642. The metaphor of marriage was often used by both sides in the conflict, in the debate whether in the case of a tyrannical husband (the king at the constitutional level), the wife (the kingdom) could rebel, and finally divorce by repudiating the union between them. On the royalist side, as we would expect, it was argued that the contract between a king and his subjects was binding and indissoluble, like a marriage. But no matter how useful the principle of divorce would have been to the parliamentary polemicists, most of them shrank from it.

The essential conservatism or moderation of the divorce doctrines espoused across the Puritan and non-Puritan Anglican spectrum was highlighted by the intervention in the divorce debate by John Milton. In the early Civil War period Milton published four tracts on divorce: *The Doctrine and Discipline of Divorce* (1643, with further editions in 1644 and 1645), *The Judgement of Martin Bucer, concerning Divorce* (1644), *Tetrachordon* (1645), and *Colasterion* (1645). This burst of publishing, which has earned Milton tenure in the history of divorce, coincided with the period in which Milton's young wife had left him: She had ostensibly gone to visit her parents, but did not return for three years. There can be little doubt that Milton was spurred into print on the subject of divorce by his wife's absence, and he ceased writing on the subject when she returned in 1645.

Yet there was more to Milton's writing than self-interest. Had he had only his own circumstances in mind, he would have needed to advocate divorce for reason of desertion, a common enough position. Milton, however, went much further and adopted a doctrine on marriage and divorce close to that articulated by Martin Bucer a century earlier. Milton argued that the essence of marriage was "the apt and cheerful conversation of man with woman, to comfort and refresh him against the evill of solitary life." The idea that marriage was essentially for procreative or sexual purposes (the Roman Catholic and predominant Anglican doctrine), Milton found "a grosse and boorish opinion, how common soever."

Milton carefully related the purpose of marriage to the circumstances that would warrant divorce. Sexual fidelity he thought least important (adultery was "but a transient injury," an act "soon repented, soon amended"), but when a couple were no longer compatible, when they ceased giving each other solace and love, they were no longer married in God's eyes. In such a case, wrote Milton, "there [is] no power above their own consent to hinder them form unjoyning.... Neither can it be said properly that such twain were even divorc't, but onely parted from each other, as two persons unconjuntive and marriable together." According to these principles, divorce seemed to follow automatically

35

from incompatibility or falling out of love, although there was clearly a bias in favor of men. Women were made for men, according to Milton, and incompatibility was generally the failure of the wife to conform to her husband's expectations and to satisfy his needs. Even with this qualification, often overlooked by commentators on Milton, the doctrine stood out as radically divergent from the Anglican pro-divorce writings in terms of the grounds for divorce and in respect to divorce's being portrayed as an automatic consequence of certain conditions within a marriage.

There was some support for very liberal divorce doctrines such as Milton's, particularly among some of the religious sects, such as Baptists, Quakers, Ranters, and Muggletonians, that proliferated during the Civil War in England. Some adopted principles of free love, divorce, and polygamy, although it is often difficult to distinguish between their actual beliefs and those that were ascribed to them by their opponents in order to discredit them. Milton's *Doctrine and Discipline of Divorce* sold well, although that does not necessarily indicate that its ideas were popular. The book was, indeed, criticized and condemned, and there were calls in Parliament for action against the book and its author, not only because of the contents of the work, but because it had been published without a license.

For the most part, however, the attacks on Milton's divorce doctrines reflected the dominant view that marriage should remain indissoluble. It is notable that no divorce law was passed under Oliver Cromwell's government, although changes were made to other parts of matrimonial law. In 1653 civil marriage was legalized, and in 1650 an act made adultery by a married woman, or by a married man with a married woman, a capital offense. (Adultery by a married man with an unmarried woman or with a woman he said he believed was unmarried was punished by imprisonment.) Yet while the death penalty for some forms of adultery removed the need for divorce in those cases, the issue of divorce was not seriously addressed. The continuing resistance to divorce was exemplified in 1654 when one of the arguments against a proposal that Jews be permitted to live in England was that Jewish law permitted divorce, and that it would be "of very evil Example amongst us."

By the accession of King Charles II in 1660, then, no progress had been made toward the legalization of divorce in England. The pro-divorce cause seemed doomed, not only because the Church of England was as resolutely opposed to divorce as ever, but also because the new king veered toward Roman Catholicism (and did in fact convert to that faith on his deathbed). Yet by 1670 a divorce had been permitted in England, and it provided a precedent for hundreds of others in the next two centuries. It was not so much that the barriers to divorce were overcome, however, as that they were circumvented. Nor was it that the principle of a right to divorce was established, but rather that one man, determined to escape his marriage, found a way that he himself could do so.

The man was John Manners, Lord Roos, who had separated from his wife because of her adultery, and who had subsequently had her bastard children illegitimated so that they would have no claim on his title or estate. In 1669 Roos introduced a bill into the House of Lords to have his marriage dissolved and to permit him to marry again (so that he might produce a legitimate heir). He was fortunate in that the timing of his bill coincided with Charles II's concern that his own marriage had produced no offspring. Charles was advised by some at court to divorce his wife and saw in Lord Roos's case a possible precedent. So keen was the king on the idea that he attended the debates on Lord Roos's bill in the Lords, and his known support contributed to its passing in 1670. Although Charles II soon abandoned his own divorce project, Lord Roos's success later enabled other men to divorce their adulterous wives, albeit by the cumbersome and expensive means of obtaining a private Act of Parliament.

If Lord Roos had been forced to take a circuitous route to get his divorce, others took a longer route – to North America. It was the conservatism of the Church of England in retaining Roman Catholic doctrine in matters like divorce that persuaded some Puritans to leave England for more congenial theological climates. One group traveled first to Holland in 1606 before sailing to North America in 1621 where they founded Plymouth Colony and other New England settlements. Although the charters of the various colonies prohibited them from enacting legislation repugnant to the prevailing laws of England, matrimonial rules in the colonies diverged markedly from Anglican doctrine. Marriage was declared to be a civil contract, and only civil magistrates, not ministers of the church, were permitted to solemnize marriages.

More important for our purposes is that some of the colonies made ad hoc provisions (later laws) for divorce that drew on both Continental Protestant divorce laws and on the Anglican canon law relating to separations. In most of the colonies divorce was permitted on the grounds of adultery and desertion. This was so in Plymouth Colony, where in the first years of settlement adultery also was punished by death when committed by a married woman or by a man with a married or betrothed woman. (These were similar to the terms of the later 1650 Adultery Act in England.) Plymouth Colony also allowed separations in other circumstances, such as violence and severe incompatibility. The colony's courts tried for two years to reconcile one couple (the husband was charged with "harsh and abusive carriages" against his wife), but eventually gave up when faced with a welter of

37

allegations concerning his impotence and her promiscuity, and granted a separation.

In Massachusetts Bay Colony divorce could be obtained from the civil court from 1629 on the grounds of the wife's adultery, the desertion of either spouse, and "the cruel usage of the husband." The double standard in respect of adultery persisted until the second half of the eighteenth century, although before that time some women managed to divorce their husbands guilty of both adultery and another offense. As for "cruel usage," it had to be extreme to warrant a wife's suing for a divorce. Despite some pressure to liberalize divorce law – including the abandonment of the double standard of adultery – the only modifications to the colony's divorce provisions were changes in 1695 and 1698 that allowed one spouse to remarry if the other was presumed lost at sea. A waiting period of seven years was imposed in 1695, but it was reduced to three years in 1698.

Other New England colonies pursued their own divorce policies. New Hampshire's was virtually identical to that of Massachusetts, but in Rhode Island there was a different pattern of development. There a 1650 law introduced divorce on the sole ground of adultery, but five years later desertion was recognized, and in 1685 the grounds were expanded by the addition of absence for five years and neglect. Divorce was also available in the town of New Haven before it was incorporated into Connecticut. From 1655 New Haven divorce law recognized as grounds adultery, desertion, and the husband's failure in his conjugal duties, and in 1663 seven years' absence was added.

Of all the New England colonies it was Connecticut that had the most liberal provisions for divorce. A 1640 law warned that "many persons intangle themselves by rash and inconsiderate contracts for their future joining in Marriage Covenant," and in recognition of this the colony made informal provision for divorce. For example, when in 1665 Rebecca Smith complained to the court that her husband Samuel had deserted her, he was warned that if he did not return to her the court would consider granting her "a release or divorce." Samuel Smith did return, but when he deserted again the court granted his wife a divorce. Between 1655 and 1667 other divorces were obtained in Connecticut on such grounds as impotence, desertion, adultery, and refusal of sexual intercourse. In 1666 jurisdiction over divorce was granted to the Court of Assistants (later to become the Superior Court) and the recognized grounds for divorce set down in law: adultery, desertion, fraudulent contract, or seven years' absence. In addition there was provision for divorces on other grounds to be sought from the colony's legislature. One, obtained in 1677, was a successful action by Elizabeth Rogers on the ground of her husband's heretical opinions and "hard usage," or violence.

The New England colonies, then, broke with English legal tradition and adopted doctrines and laws of marriage and divorce more akin to the Continental churches. Still, as in Europe, there was no great stampede to the divorce courts. As we shall see in Chapter 4, only Massachusetts and Connecticut produced significant numbers of divorces in the seventeenth century. In Massachusetts from 1636 to 1698 there were fifty-four petitions for divorce and annulment, of which forty-four are known to have succeeded. There were forty successful petitions in Connecticut (including New Haven) between 1655 and 1699. As in Europe, divorce in early colonial New England was a rarity, although the judges seem to have been more willing to grant divorces there than their European Protestant counterparts were.

Elsewhere in America the history of divorce reflected specific colonial conditions. In New Netherlands (later New York) the Dutch authorities introduced divorce on the Calvinist principles in force in Holland, and there are records of three divorces between 1655 and 1664. In 1664 the colony passed to English control under the duke of York, and in the following year a codification of legislation (the Duke's Laws) included a reference to circumstances under which "it shall not be punishable to remarry." They included the conviction of one spouse for falsifying an oath, one spouse's having died away from New York, and absence in "forraigne parts" without news for five years. These were not really grounds for divorce, being references to bigamy, widowhood, and presumed death, respectively. Moreover an amendment specified that adultery justified only a separation, not a divorce.

Despite these provisions some of the English governors of New York authorized divorces between 1664 and 1675, some for reason of adultery by a wife. In 1672, for example, Thomas Pettit obtained a divorce from his wife for her "defiling the marriage bed and committing adultery with several persons." Governor Lovelace granted the divorce as conforming with the laws of England, but he was entirely wrong, and the absence of divorces in the colony after 1675 suggests that the authorities were reminded that divorce (Lord Roos's recent achievement notwithstanding) was repugnant to English law and practice.

The colonial authorities in London certainly made their displeasure of divorce known to the administration of Pennsylvania Colony. In 1682 divorce was allowed there, on the sole ground of adultery, under William Penn's Great Law. In 1700 divorce was extended in the context of other offenses. A law dealing with sodomy and bestiality specified that if the offender were a married man he should be castrated "and the injured wife [sic!] shall have a divorce if required." Another 1700 law, this one on bigamy, provided for imprisonment with hard labor for the offender and for his or her first spouse to have a divorce if it were desired. Both the 1700 laws were disallowed by the English government, but even so divorce for reason of adultery remained on the colony's books.

Divorce law in the Middle Colonies – notably New York, Pennsylvania, and New Jersey (where there were some divorces in the seventeenth century) – was less coherent than its counterpart in New England. Divorces were also far less common. Yet even these limited provisions (sometimes limited by the English authorities) went further than the law enacted in the southern colonies. Maryland was a special case because its government was dominated by Roman Catholics, but in the other southern colonies, too, divorce was not introduced until the 1790s at the earliest: Georgia, for example, legalized divorce in 1798, but North Carolina waited until 1814, and South Carolina delayed until 1868.

Looked at as a whole, the English colonies in seventeenth-century North America constituted a patchwork of different divorce laws and policies. The variety is not surprising, given that each colony's authorities took responsibility for regulating marriage formation, annulment, and dissolution. This was not the intention of the English government, of course, and the charters of the colonies forbade passing laws that varied significantly from English law or were repugnant to it. Clearly some colonies obeyed the injunction while others ignored it, and we should attempt to explain the different responses.

One explanation of the different divorce policies of the southern and northern colonies was advanced by William O'Neill, who focused on the degree of cohesion in colonial family types and the importance attributed to the family as a source of social stability. He suggested that "when families are large and loose, arouse few expectations, and make few demands, there is no need for divorce." Divorce becomes a safety valve, however, when families are the center of social organization and place unbearable demands and excessively high expectations on individuals. Individuals who are frustrated and oppressed by the system can divorce, so that divorce is "not an anomaly or a flaw in the system, but an essential feature of it." In general, however, this is an anachronistic explanation of divorce patterns in the seventeenth century because divorce was not available to those who were oppressed by a suffocating family system, but, at best, to those whose spouses had committed adultery or had deserted. On the other hand there were differences in family systems between the northern colonies (especially New England), systematically colonized by family groups, and the southern colonies, where early settlement was dominated by adult males. But these demographic distinctions represented ideological differences because the settlement of New England by family units was a deliberate policy or strategy of social organization. Puritan ideology placed the family at the center of the social order at the first rank of social control.

It was this very belief, expressed so well in contemporary English writing on the family, that motivated colonies such as Massachusetts, Connecticut, and Plymouth to prohibit the practice of living alone. There were numerous convictions for the offense, such as that of John Littleale, punished in Essex County, Massachusetts, because "he lay in a house by himself contrary to the law of the country, whereby he is subject to much sin and iniquity, which ordinarily are the consequences of a solitary life." Laws against living alone – the original "solitary vice" – were not passed in the South, for obvious reasons.

The whole ideology of the Puritan authorities of New England reflected the emphasis on the social, political, and spiritual importance of marriage that was made in contemporary England. Marriage was the fundamental social institution, and the family was to be organized and ordered on Christian principles in which each member knew and fulfilled his or her obligations. Divorce, then, can be seen as a remedy to the moral or physical disintegration of marriage and, by extension, the family. When granted in circumstances of long absence or desertion, divorce enabled the deserted spouse to enter a new marriage, that most desirable institution, and form a new family.

Adultery was a different case in that a marriage could continue in spite of it. (Many did so, in fact, for although 147 Massachusetts men and women were convicted of adultery, only 15 divorces in the colony included that ground; in Connecticut there were 56 convictions and only 12 related divorces.) But the colonial governments counted it a heinous crime and punished it accordingly. Massachusetts, Connecticut, Plymouth, and New Haven made adultery by or with a married or betrothed woman a capital offense until the late 1600s, and even the more lenient penalties applied thereafter were harsh, including branding and whipping. A 1683 sentence in Massachusetts gives an idea of the severity of the law in practice. Joshua Rice, convicted of adultery, was ordered

to be taken out of the prison and with a rope around your neck Conveyed through the Town to the Gallows and there to be set upon a ladder and stand on a full hour with your Rope turned over the Gallows and then to be taken down and . . . severly [sic] whipped with thirty stripes through the streets to the Gaol and there left till you discharge the Charge of your trial, prison and court fees.

His accomplice was ordered to suffer the same punishments. The sheer horror of adultery, together with the explicit reference to it in the Bible as a ground for divorce, explains its inclusion in the divorce laws of the northern colonies, just as it does in the divorce laws of Protestant Europe.

In the final analysis the variety of policies on divorce in the early American colonies is explicable by religious and general ideological predispositions. The divergent divorce policies that distinguished Lutheran Germany from Calvinist Holland and Anglican England are to be explained not in terms of demographic, economic, or social structure, but in terms of religious orientation, and we should understand the American colonies in the same way. The patchwork of divorce policies in early colonial America was, indeed, part of the inheritance that the New World received from the Old.

Yet although the New England colonies in particular had, from the very beginning, adopted matrimonial policies at odds with English law, there was resentment at persistent, if sporadic, interference in colonial legislation. The English government, as we have seen, disallowed some Pennsylvania laws in 1700, and later in the century it attempted to assert its control in one of the Canadian colonies, Nova Scotia. In 1750, a year after the colony was founded, the governor of Nova Scotia and his council (composed of army officers) granted a divorce to a lieutenant for reason of his wife's adultery. The divorce was promptly overturned by the British authorities, and in 1758 a newly formed assembly passed legislation that would allow divorce on the grounds of impotence, marriage within the prohibited degrees, adultery, and desertion while withholding maintenance for three years. The British promptly disallowed this act too, but then, quite inconsistently, assented to a 1761 law that allowed divorce for impotence, precontract, adultery, and cruelty.

Attempts by other colonies to legalize divorce or grant individual divorces in the late 1760s and early 1770s were closely watched by the British government. One of the first was a decision by the Pennsylvania General Assembly to dissolve the marriage of Curtis and Anne Grubb for reason of her adultery. The British government was advised, by a lawyer it referred the matter to, that this divorce was not repugnant to English practice because it was essentially the same as the parliamentary divorces being granted in England at that time: It was a divorce granted to an individual man, by special act of the legislature, for reason of his wife's adultery. At the same time, concern was expressed at the exercise of matrimonial jurisdiction by the colonial legislatures. Just as the British feared, Grubb's divorce, assented to by George III, seems to have encouraged other Pennsylvanians, and in 1772 and 1773 there were four more divorce petitions. The General Assembly rejected two of them, and the governor declined to assent to the third. The fourth, a straightforward case of a wife's adultery, was passed and sent on to London for assent. There, however, it was turned down because Pennsylvania's divorce procedures did not comply precisely with those in force in England, this notwithstanding the fact that the Grubb case had been identical in its form. It must have been not only the refusal of the British to allow these divorces that irked the colonists, but also the lack of consistency in the government's decisions.

Other colonies had similar experiences in the same period. A 1772 act of the New Jersey legislature dissolving a marriage was disallowed in London, and two New Hampshire bills, one from 1771 and the other from 1773, were refused assent. No doubt as a response to this rash of divorce bills appearing from the American colonies, the British government tried to deal with the problem systematically rather than on an ad hoc basis. In 1773 the governors of Britain's American colonies were instructed not to approve any colonial law that would divorce "persons joined together in Holy Marriage."

This instruction did not affect the increasing number of divorces in Massachusetts and Connecticut, because the divorces were granted by the courts and did not require the assent of the colonies' governors, but it did interfere with legislatures in other colonies. And, as Nelson Blake comments: "What embarrassments were thus caused by upsetting divorces two or three years after the event, we can only imagine." Such actions by the British government can only have contributed – no matter how marginally – to the resentment of the American colonies to British rule. The first specific grievance cited by Thomas Jefferson against King George III was that he had "refused his Assent to Laws, the most wholesome and necessary to the public good." While it is obvious that Jefferson was referring to more than divorce laws, he himself was familiar with the specific problem: In 1771–2 Jefferson was engaged in the preparation of a divorce bill on behalf of a Williamsburg doctor, and his research notes for the case reveal extensive knowledge of the theological and political aspects of divorce.

Divorce might not have been Jefferson's or the colonists' major grievance against the British, but the speed with which many of the colonies legalized divorce, after they began to act independently in 1776, suggests that British policy had frustrated the general desire for broadly available divorce. Pennsylvania led the way, perhaps appropriately, given the number of its matrimonial laws struck down in London. Between 1777 and 1785, thirty-five petitions were lodged with the state's legislature, and eleven – most based on adultery – were approved. Only seven were rejected definitively and the remainder lapsed for various reasons. The list of state legislatures that either passed divorce laws or began to dissolve individual marriages by individual statutes is impressive. In addition to the beginning of legislative divorce in Pennsylvania in 1777, the list includes Pennsylvania (new statute, 1785), Massachusetts (1786), New York (1787), Maryland (1790), New Hampshire (1791), New Jersey (1794), North Carolina (1794), Georgia (1798), Vermont (1798), Rhode Island (1798), and Tennessee (1799). In the first decade of the nineteenth century many more states introduced divorce.

The surge of divorce-related legislation and the spread of divorce throughout almost all the United States at the end of the eighteenth century took various forms. Most of the northeastern states put colonial practice into legislative form, and some took the opportunity to liberalize their policies beyond the commonly accepted grounds of adultery and desertion. New Hampshire's 1791 law recognized impotence, adultery, extreme cruelty, and three years' absence by either spouse, and also allowed a wife to file for divorce if her husband abandoned her and failed to provide for her over a period of three years. In Rhode Island not only were specific matrimonial offenses grounds for divorce, but the courts were granted discretion to permit divorce in cases of "gross misbehavior and wickedness in either of the parties, repugnant to and in violation of the marriage covenant."

This law reflected a general trend toward giving control over divorce to the states' highest courts. Gradually the legislatures surrendered jurisdiction over divorce, sometimes because they were simply overwhelmed by divorce suits. Divorces filed with Pennsylvania's General Assembly, for example, underwent two full readings, together with a lengthy judicial procedure to hear witnesses, determine the facts, and reach a decision. So time-consuming was it, and so much did it deflect the legislators from other business, that in 1785 jurisdiction over divorce was transferred to the state's supreme court. Moreover the 1785 law expanded the grounds for divorce and made provision for the legislature to grant divorces in compelling circumstances not covered by the statute. Between 1795 and 1874 the legislature approved 291 divorces under this rubric, an average of almost four legislative divorces a year. Pennsylvania's 1785 law also contained a residency requirement of one year to prevent out-of-state residents taking advantage of its liberal divorce policy. Such requirements were to become common in American divorce laws.

The trend in the northern states, then, was toward more liberal and judicial divorce. In the South, where there had been no divorce before independence, policy was initially more cautious. In Maryland the legislature granted a divorce in 1790 to a man whose wife had committed adultery and given birth to a mulatto child, and although other legislative divorces followed, jurisdiction was not turned over to the

44

courts until 1842. In North Carolina the legislature controlled divorces from 1794 until 1814, when the procedure was shared with the courts, and it was not until 1835 that the courts gained full jurisdiction over divorce.

A state-by-state account of the spread of divorce provisions in the United States is, however, unnecessary. What is notable about the first decades of independence is the spread itself, despite the residual distinctions between a more liberal North and more conservative South, as each region drew upon its preindependence traditions. Equally important is the broader, Atlantic perspective. As we have seen, the early colonial divorce laws in America represented a rejection of the doctrine of marital indissolubility that held sway in contemporary England. English practice made up some ground by the middle of the eighteenth century when divorces, as we shall see in Chapter 4, were regularly (if rarely) being granted in England by Act of Parliament. Not long afterwards, however, the American colonies sloughed off British rule and British constraints on divorce and developed policies that were utterly repugnant to the traditions of English law and practice. The difference was that by the 1780s it no longer mattered.

Suggestions for further reading

Blake, Nelson, *The Road to Reno: A History of Divorce in the United States* (New York, 1962).

Davies, Kathleen M., " 'The Sacred Condition of Equality' – How Original Were Puritan Doctrines of Marriage?" *Social History* 5 (1977), 563–80.

Demos, John, *A Little Commonwealth: Family Life in Plymouth Colony* (London, 1970).

Dewey, Frank L., "Thomas Jefferson's Notes on Divorce," *William and Mary Quarterly*, 3rd. ser., 39 (1982), 212–23.

Fraser, Antonia, *The Weaker Vessel: Woman's Lot in Seventeenth-Century England* (London, 1984).

Halkett, John, *Milton and the Idea of Matrimony: A Study of the Divorce Tracts and "Paradise Lost"* (New Haven, 1970).

Howard, George E., *A History of Matrimonial Institutions* (3 vols., Chicago, 1904).

Johnson, James Turner, *A Society Ordained by God: English Puritan Marriage Doctrine in the First Half of the Seventeenth Century* (Nashville, N.Y., 1970).

Koehler, Lyle S., *A Search for Power: The "Weaker Sex" in Seventeenth-Century New England* (Urbana, Ill., 1980).

Morgan, Edmund S., *The Puritan Family: Religion and Domestic Relations in Seventeenth-Century New England* (Boston, 1944, repr. New York, 1966).

O'Neill, William L., *Divorce in the Progressive Era* (New York, 1977).

Thomas, Keith, "The Puritans and Adultery: The Act of 1650 Reconsidered," in Donald Pennington and Keith Thomas (eds.), *Puritans and Revolutionaries: Essays in Seventeenth-Century History Presented to Christopher Hill* (Oxford, 1978), 257–82.

3

~~~~~~

Secularization, the Enlightenment and the French Revolution

One of the most important long-term changes in Western society since the Middle Ages has been the general progress of secularization. It is a process that had a marked effect on marriage and divorce in various respects: Over time, doctrines of marriage and divorce shed their exclusively theological characteristics in favor of secular considerations. At the institutional level marriage ceased to be regulated by ecclesiastical laws enforced in church courts and became a matter for civil law, with litigation and enforcement in the secular courts. This is not to deny the continuing role of religion in modern marriage, where individuals may be guided by religious precepts to a greater or lesser degree, and where spiritual courts may still play a marginal role, but it is to point to a marked decline in the influence that religion plays in the making, regulating, and undoing of marriages in modern Western society.

Secularization was the means by which divorce developed in a critical period between about 1600 and 1800. Before 1600 matrimonial policy was, as we have seen, largely a matter for theological debate, and divorce laws conformed closely to interpretations of the Bible. After 1800, when there was a period of dramatic liberalization and expansion of divorce throughout the Western world, policies, doctrines, and laws were generally determined by secular criteria. The 200 intervening years were thus a transitional period that demands some understanding. The issues and their implications are discussed in this chapter, and particular emphasis is given to divorce during the Enlightenment and the French Revolution, both of which exemplified, among other things, the process of secularization.

As it affected marriage and divorce, secularization took two main forms. The first was institutional, the transfer of functions from religious institutions, usually the established church in a given state, to secular or lay bodies. Social, political, and economic tasks involving education, health services, social welfare, and the keeping of vital records were primarily the responsibility of the churches, but over time they were surrendered to the state. The second principal sphere of

47

secularization was ideological: Political, social, and legal theories shed their theological points of reference in favor of secular considerations based on social, moral, or individual criteria. With institutions and ideologies, there was often a mingling of the secular and the religious at any given time, but the balance incontestably shifted toward the secular.

The secularization of divorce is most easily discernible in the increased involvement of secular legislative and judicial institutions in dissolving marriages. As we have noted, by the Middle Ages formal legislation and jurisdiction over matrimony fell almost entirely to the Roman Catholic church, notwithstanding the persistence of secular, customary traditions in many parts of Europe. (We should recall that the church's authority in this respect resulted from a process we might call "desecularization," in which the church's canon law had replaced secular laws on marriage and divorce.)

The view that the spiritual power should monopolize matrimonial law was challenged effectively by the Protestant Reformers, who stressed that although marriage was ordained by God, it was essentially a civil contract and that jurisdiction over it fell properly to the secular authorities. Luther, for one, described marriage as a "worldly thing" and insisted that it was the duty of the government to regulate it by marriage and divorce laws.

But this stress on the civil aspects of marriage did not lead to the immediate establishment in Protestant states of purely secular laws and civil courts to deal with matrimonial issues. In most, in fact – in Germany, Switzerland, Scandinavia, and the Netherlands – the sixteenth-century marriage and divorce laws were issued in the form of church ordinances. Although this arrangement conflicted with a strict interpretation of the Protestant doctrines, it was defensible in practical terms. Under the Roman Catholic regimes matrimony had been regulated by the church, and the Protestant ordinances provided a continuity. Nor was it supposed that a secular law would differ in any essential point from the doctrine of the state's dominant church.

If the marriage and divorce laws of Protestant Europe continued to emanate from the spiritual authorities, there was at least a change in the judiciaries enforcing them. For the most part the marriage tribunals in Reformed states had both clerical and lay members, and the latter tended to predominate. The *Ehegericht* of Basel consisted of seven members, five drawn from the city's legislative bodies and two from the clergy, while the marriage court of Zurich comprised four lay and two clerical judges. In Sweden ecclesiastical and secular judges cooperated in divorce sequentially. The church courts acted as courts of first instance, but because their primary task was to attempt to reconcile the spouses, the clerical judges acted in a pastoral as much as a purely

48

judicial capacity. But if a case proved intractable and divorce was considered, it was referred to the secular judges.

Just as the convenience of tradition and continuity might explain the persistence of church laws on marriage, so it does in respect to the continuing participation of clerical judges in courts deciding matrimonial issues. In Scotland, for example, the bishops' courts were suppressed in 1560, but it was not until 1563 that the Church of Scotland's judicial system was properly organized, and in the interim the individual kirk sessions provided judicial services. In Iceland, there was a delay of decades between the application of the basic Reformatory Church Order, which reformed the church, and the systematic reform of marriage law. Not surprisingly, bishops tended to provide jurisdiction in marriage cases in the interim, although many decisions were apparently made by "half-courts," tribunals composed equally of clerical and secular judges, all sitting under the presidency of a bishop. England was, in this question of jurisdiction, a special case, for matrimonial law continued to be applied predominantly by ecclesiastical courts.

Overall, the effect of the Reformation was to reduce the authority of the ecclesiastical authorities without giving the secular authorities complete control. There emerged a close partnership between churches and states based on what was, in the short term at least, a virtual identity of views as to what the content of matrimonial law ought to be. Yet this very partnership marked the beginning of secularization, and in the course of the seventeenth century the process continued, not so much by the secular authorities' reducing the functions of the churches, but by the development of parallel secular institutions that provided alternatives to the clerical or mixed clerical–secular institutions. The net effect, of course, was to reduce further the significance of the churches' roles in the overall pattern of matrimonial regulation.

Sweden is an example of this process at work. Divorce law was established by church ordinances of 1572 and 1686, both of which limited the grounds to adultery and desertion. From the 1630s on, however, the Swedish kings began dissolving marriages by royal dispensation. Initially such dispensations added flexibility to the church's laws, granting divorces in cases where, for example, adultery had almost certainly taken place, but where it could not be proved beyond the shadow of a doubt. Royal intervention brought an element of equity to divorce that, in itself, testified to the rigorous demands of church and secular judges in their application of church divorce law. Gradually, however, the Swedish kings began to grant divorces in circumstances not covered by ecclesiastical law. Divorces were allowed on grounds such as ill-treatment, drunkenness, and "hatred and bitterness between the spouses" (tantamount to serious incompatibility), imprisonment for a serious crime, a serious illness such as leprosy, mental illness, and incurable insanity. By expanding the grounds in this way, the monarchy created an avenue for divorce that rivaled, rather than complemented, the church's law. Incompatibility was recognized as a ground for eventual divorce (there was a long procedure) in the Swedish Civil Code of 1734, but the other grounds remained available at the monarch's discretion until 1810, when secular divorce legislation was passed, replacing the ecclesiastical laws.

Other European monarchs also granted divorces. In Denmark the kings granted dispensations from the restrictive church divorce laws and, from the 1790s on, dissolved marriages when spouses had lived separate for a fixed period of time (set at three years in 1796). In eighteenth-century Prussia, too, Frederick William I dissolved marriages by personal decree in circumstances not recognized by prevailing church law. His son and successor Frederick II ("the Great") withdrew from such actions, but he did issue a rescript in 1751 that permitted the Prussian courts to dissolve marriages that were affected by "deadly and notorious hostility." By 1794, the first comprehensive codification of Prussian law went beyond the Lutheran grounds (adultery and desertion) and permitted divorce by mutual consent when there were no children or at the request of either spouse when there was proof of such violence or emotional aversion that the spouses could not be reconciled or the ends of marriage achieved.

Further south, in Catholic Austria, the secularization of matrimony also proceeded apace. Under Emperor Joseph II the civil courts were given control of marriage in 1784 by an edict that declared, "marriage is considered to be a civil contract, and the rights and relationships which it implies derive their existence, their form and their definition entirely and uniquely from the civil power." Ecclesiastical judges were forbidden to take jurisdiction over any matrimonial matter. Divorce itself was introduced into the Austrian Empire when, in 1781, non-Catholics in the territories of Lombardy and Venice were granted the right to divorce.

The intervention of these monarchs in marriage and divorce law – some on an ad hoc basis, others in a more formal manner – not only added to the secular element in dissolving marriages, but extended divorce policies significantly. The grounds for divorce that were recognized throughout Europe continued to vary, but by the seventeenth century, and certainly in the eighteenth, they included more than the classic Protestant grounds of adultery and desertion, and in some cases extended to circumstances recognizable as emotional incompatibility where it was difficult to attribute fault exclusively to one spouse.

Some of the courts themselves began to expand the grounds they considered appropriate for divorce. By the middle of the eighteenth century judges of the consistorial court at Württemberg, the well-spring of Lutheranism, were exercising wide discretion when deciding divorce cases. Although the church ordinance restricted divorce to cases of adultery and desertion, marriages were dissolved on such grounds as long absence, excessive cruelty, incurable diseases (such as leprosy), insanity, impotence, and banishment or imprisonment for life. Some of these were justified under the desertion rubric of the Lutheran divorce doctrine, but others were permitted by appeal to natural law principles.

In many places, too, the courts themselves were secularized. The "half-tribunals" (mixed clerical–lay courts) of sixteenth-century Iceland gave way to exclusively secular courts during the late seventeenth century. In England the church courts continued to have jurisdiction over family matters until the mid-nineteenth century, but there were significant secular inroads. In the sixteenth century Parliament dissolved the marriage of the Marquis of Northampton, as we have seen, and in 1670 it granted a divorce to Lord Roos, an act that established a precedent for hundreds of other parliamentary divorces until a civil divorce law was passed in 1857. In such divorces the more passable secular route was used to circumvent the ecclesiastical roadblocks to divorce. Marriage law was also secularized in England to some extent. Although Cromwell's marriage law of 1653 lapsed with the Restoration, in 1753 a new Marriage Act (Lord Hardwicke's) established the procedures and preconditions of a valid marriage in England, matters that until then had been regulated by the church.

In many jurisdictions, then, the dominant role of the church in marriage law and regulation gave way to a partnership of church and state or a dominant state role. Rarely was this accomplished without a struggle: Joseph II's reforms in Austria provoked a visit from the pope, while the bishops who sat in England's House of Lords vainly resisted the passage of individual divorce bills. In France, marriage was one of the most sensitive issues in a broad-based struggle between church and monarchy for authority. From the sixteenth century the royal courts developed an action called the *appel comme d'abus*, based on the notion that a court hearing a case was acting beyond its jurisdiction and that the matter belonged in the royal courts. Over time the monarchs used this means either to transfer the gamut of matrimonial litigation – the marriage of minors, bigamy, impediments, broken engagements, and property questions – from the ecclesiastical to the royal courts or to force the ecclesiastical courts to apply secular laws. By the late eighteenth century the legal regulation of marriage had effectively passed from the church to the royal or other secular authorities. This is not to suggest that there were necessarily conflicts between the content of the ecclesiastical and royal laws of marriage, for in general both upheld the principle of indissolubility: Louis XIV, for example, forbade the Lutheran magistrates of Alsace (annexed to France in 1680) to dissolve marriages. Nonetheless the secularization of law had begun in France, and it established the foundation for the complete laicization of family law during the French Revolution, which is discussed later in this chapter.

On the other side of the Atlantic, in the British American colonies, secularization took a different course. Most of the New England colonies began with an almost purely civil perspective and forbade the clergy to perform marriages. What changes there were, in fact, ran counter to secularization, for in the late seventeenth century Massachusetts and Connecticut began to permit ministers to perform marriages in the towns where they lived. Divorce, however, remained under the exclusive control of the secular judges, and ecclesiastical courts were not established. This was so in the southern colonies, too, for although matrimony there was regulated by the Anglican church, there were no ecclesiastical courts, and matrimonial litigation was heard by the civil magistrates.

The American cases were exceptional in many ways, not least because the colonies were founded, and their institutions established, at a time of transition in Europe. The constant threat of interference from England – the country where the secularization of marriage was most ambiguous – must also have skewed the organic development of American law and institutions.

The final form of secularization that is important in this period is the secularization of attitudes toward, and doctrines of, divorce as political and legal philosophers shook off the theological assumptions they had inherited from the medieval period. One important school that had immense influence in expanding doctrines of divorce beyond the biblical limits established by the sixteenth-century Reformers was the natural law school. Hugo Grotius, a founder of modern natural law theory, described the law of nature as "a dictate of right reason, which points out that an act, according as it is or is not in conformity with rational nature, has in it a quality of moral baseness or moral necessity." Such an act would be forbidden or enjoined by God, Grotius went on, but the law of nature is not contingent upon God, for it would be the same if God did not exist. Natural law theorists stressed, in addition to this secular character of natural law, the principle of contract: That in order to be really binding, an obligation had to be freely entered into by the parties and that the contract might be dissolved if its conditions were not fulfilled. These two legal precepts were readily brought to bear upon marriage to strengthen the notion that marriage was essentially a civil contract.

Needless to say, natural law theorists were far from unanimous in the conclusions they reached about divorce. Grotius, for one, attempted to bring divine and natural law into harmony. He had no difficulty in establishing that divorce was permitted in natural law, and focused his efforts on reconciling this with the biblical texts. This he achieved by interpreting "adultery" in the Bible as a generic term covering a broad range of offenses that effectively ruptured the marriage bond: Among them he listed sexual infidelity, threats of death, apparent adultery, and infanticide. Samuel Pufendorf, another natural law theorist, left his readers to decide what grounds should justify divorce, but he suggested they might include violation of the marriage contract, sterility, crimes against nature, incompatibility of temperament, and even mutual consent. Like Grotius, Pufendorf considered procreation the main purpose of marriage, but he explained it as not only a divine injunction but also a pact made by the wife and husband at marriage. A marriage could be dissolved, then, when the conduct of one of the spouses made that goal unattainable. Such conduct included adultery, malicious desertion, and obstinate and voluntary refusal of intercourse.

Pufendorf interpreted the biblical divorce texts in terms of the principle of contract. Adultery and desertion were singled out not as the sole exceptions to the rule of indissolubility, he argued, but as examples of the rule that "when one party does not abide by the agreements, the other is no longer bound by them." Yet there were limits to Pufendorf's divorce doctrines. He decided, for example, that a husband's being "unreasonably" severe was not a reason for divorce, for it did not interfere with the prime purpose of marriage, namely procreation. This placed him at odds with his contemporary, John Milton, who stressed the companionate aspects of marriage. Suggesting that perhaps Milton was so concerned about divorce "because [he was] irritated by his own domestic infelicity," Pufendorf argued that emphasis on the social aspects of marriage at the expense of the sexual might just as well result in marriage between individuals of the same sex.

During the eighteenth century natural law theorists gave a great deal of attention to marriage and divorce, and most were led to embrace liberal divorce doctrines. Johann Heineccius, a professor of philosophy, concluded that because marriage was a contract entered into for procreation, the inability to procreate or to live together (a precondition of procreation) permitted the dissolution of the contract by divorce. Among others who adopted similar positions were the father and son, Heinrich and Samuel Cocceji. The latter argued for divorce by mutual consent in order to stress that "it belongs to no one to intervene and force spouses to live together against their will," and also suggested that specific offenses such as adultery, desertion, deadly hatred, and having a venereal disease should warrant a divorce. Samuel Cocceji was especially important because he was minister of justice, and later chancellor, of Prussia in the mid-eighteenth century, and influenced the liberalization of Prussia's divorce law in 1751.

One interesting development within the natural rights and contract theorists' writing on divorce was a new emphasis on children. Earlier works had stressed children in terms of procreation, but in some of this literature greater consideration was given to the social obligations conferred by parenthood. This emphasis was entirely appropriate to a century which has been described by a number of historians as having "discovered" childhood.

Moreover, even the injunction to procreate was secularized in this period. In the seventeenth and eighteenth centuries procreation was not only the accepted reason for marriage, but was also increasingly stated as the justification for allowing divorce. Unhappy couples do not have sexual intercourse, it was argued or implied, and the continuation of their marriages therefore impedes population growth. Divorce, in this view of things, enabled the unhappily married to escape their bonds, remarry, and have children. This argument lay behind Frederick William II's 1783 cabinet order to judges that "in matters of divorce one ought not to be so easy going as to further abase; but one should not be too difficult either, because that would impede population." Pronatalist aims lay behind proposals for divorce in Austria and France as well, and in 1769 the governor of New York (where divorce was not available) suggested that access to divorce in New England was partly responsible for greater population growth of the colonies there. In this period, in short, the state co-opted the biblical injunction that people should go forth and multiply; by the eighteenth century the aim was not to increase the faithful but to provide the demographic basis of robust and strong states.

Eighteenth-century France is an example of the processes of secularization at work in the ideology, institutions, and law of marriage and divorce. It is by no means typical, however, not least because the tendencies we can follow through the century culminated in the French Revolution, which, in 1792, legalized divorce in the most liberal form of any contemporary Western jurisdiction. This very liberal divorce policy not only differed from the still restrictive (if liberalizing) policies of Protestant Europe, but it broke radically with the French legal and social tradition that had ruled out divorce entirely before 1792.

Under the Old Regime in France the Roman Catholic doctrine of marital indissolubility had been maintained by the Gallican (French Catholic) church and the state. Separations (*séparations de corps et d'habitation*, or separations of body and dwelling) were granted, and by the eighteenth century jurisdiction had generally shifted to the civil courts because of the property considerations that figured so prominently in such cases. There was a general expectation that separations would be sought mainly by women because women needed the assistance of the law against tyrannical husbands. In fact, the grounds usually accepted for separations in France described circumstances where the wife was thought to be in physical or moral danger: ill-treatment by the husband, being falsely accused by him of adultery, his insanity, his attempting to murder her, or the husband's conceiving a "deadly hatred" of her. In other cases women had little recourse. The customary law of Normandy, for example, specified that a woman whose husband committed adultery could do nothing but be patient unless he brought his accomplice into the marital domicile. Only then was it thought that her sensitivity was so offended that she might file for a separation.

Separations seem to have been quite rare in France under the Old Regime. In the Norman city of Rouen (population 85,000) there is evidence of only thirty-three petitions between 1780 and 1789, and of these a mere four appear to have succeeded. In the diocese of Cambrai in northern France, which had a population five times that of Rouen, there were about seven separations a year during the eighteenth century. There, however, the church courts retained jurisdiction and permitted husbands as well as wives to sue for separations. In the period 1737–74, 76% of the separations were sought by women, 13% by men, and 11% jointly.

Separations seem to have been far from common in eighteenth-century France, and the comparative popularity of divorces after 1792 suggests that the rarity of separations reflected their failure to respond to the needs of women in particular. A separation certainly allowed a woman to live independent of her oppressive spouse, but it did not permit her to remarry. Nor did a separation help a woman who had been deserted by her husband.

The shortcomings of separations were highlighted throughout the eighteenth century in a body of literature that condemned the principle of marital indissolubility and called for the legalization of divorce. Divorce was one of the subjects taken up in this century of the Enlightenment, when all aspects of the family – marriage, inheritance, paternal authority, marital authority, and the roles of church and state – were analyzed and criticized in the light of reason, natural law, liberty, and natural rights. Even so, it is notable that the better-known philosophers and social commentators of the time, men such as Voltaire, Rousseau, Diderot, Condorcet and Helvétius, wrote about divorce in a cursory and often frustratingly vague way. It was left to others, minor writers, some of whom wrote only on family issues, to develop coherent critiques of Old Regime matrimonial law and practice. Nonetheless the criticism of Roman Catholic doctrines and the role of the church, and the advocacy of reforms, were trenchant and unambiguous.

A prime line of argument was that marital indissolubility was contrary to human nature. Men and women, it was argued, were too fickle and changeable to be able to engage themselves to others for life. "Natural law," wrote Jean Charles Lavie, "gives man the right to flee from unhappiness and to free himself of it . . . the perpetuity of marriage is thus contrary to the intention of nature." The "natural right" to divorce was discovered in the past and present and projected into the future. Divorce, most advocates pointed out, had been permitted in classical times, among the Jews, among the Visigoths and Franks, and in the early Christian church. It was only the despotism of the medieval church that had deprived people of this liberty. The proof that divorce was of the natural order of things was displayed by Diderot in his *Supplément au voyage de Bougainville,* a fictional account of the contact between Europeans and the South Sea cultures. In a dialogue between Orou, a Tahitian who represents natural man, and a French priest, Diderot portrays Orou as shaken to learn that in civilized Catholic states husbands and wives are united until death:

These strange precepts I find contrary to nature, contrary to reason. . . . In fact does anything seem to you more senseless than a precept that denies the change that is within us; which commands a constancy which cannot be there, and which violates the nature and freedom of male and female, in chaining them forever, one to the other.

Much was made, too, of the fact that divorce was available throughout much of contemporary Europe. The Protestant states allowed divorce, and England (the least liberal of all, for it allowed divorce only by private Act of Parliament) was often cited with particular approval. In 1784 the duc de la Rochefoucauld noted that "English husbands have an advantage over us of which they sometimes avail themselves, namely divorce," while in 1789 a nationalistic tone entered the debate in Albert Hennet's influential *Du Divorce*: "The English have adopted divorce, but in a defective form: our glory is not only to imitate but to surpass them."

Simple emulation of others was not reason enough to introduce divorce, however, and although the principles of restoring natural rights and bringing law into line with nature were powerful arguments in the eighteenth century, utilitarian reasons were also advanced. Divorce was portrayed as conferring three main benefits on society: It would promote population growth, regenerate morality, and increase happiness and harmony within families.

The demographic argument for divorce, already alluded to in this chapter, was made early in the century by Montesquieu, who suggested in his *Lettres persanes* that the higher birthrate among non-Christian populations was a result of their permitting divorce. Being able to divorce, he suggested, men were more ready to marry and produce children. This argument was taken up and embellished throughout the eighteenth century, for despite the fact that France's population increased by a healthy 30% or more between 1700 and 1800, there was a persistent belief (until the 1770s, at least), that France was experiencing a demographic decline. The most imaginative scenario was produced by Cerfvol (a pseudonym), whose rate of divorce tract production rivaled John Milton's: Cerfvol published five works on divorce between 1768 and 1770. The most important of them was his *Mémoire sur la population* (1768) in which he published detailed (though largely spurious) statistics to prove that celibacy was increasing in France at each generation, that generations were failing to reproduce themselves, and that the logical conclusion would be the utter depopulation of France.

The principal way to arrest this galloping celibacy and the attendant decline of population, Cerfvol wrote, was to legalize divorce. He recognized other factors at work in population decline – among them incontinence, unequal and excessive taxation, the use of wet nurses, and women's wearing corsets – but, he wrote: "Let us seek the true cause of depopulation nowhere else than in the indissolubility of marriage. All the other causes are derived from this." If men were only able to divorce, they would no longer fear marriage; paradoxically, divorce would encourage marriage, cure all immorality, and give France the large and robust population it needed to become the economically, politically, and militarily strong state it had been in the past.

Divorce found a place in almost all the depopulationist literature of the eighteenth century, though it was understandably of less interest to French demographers in the last decades of the Old Regime who appreciated that their country's population was increasing, not falling. One of the most prominent, Moheau, thought that divorce would harm population by weakening marital and family bonds. Others suggested that the children that might be produced as a result of blissful remarriages would do no more than compensate for the children that would not be born as a result of dissolving marriages.

It was not only reproduction but also regeneration – moral regeneration – that concerned the commentators of the Enlightenment. The evidence of immorality was plain for all to see in the poverty, illegitimacy, child abandonment, the emphasis on luxury, and celibacy that were rife in the Old Regime, and philosophers like Condorcet and Helvétius were among those who thought that divorce would help to improve things. Both argued that the lack of divorce was the main cause of adultery and illegitimacy, because unhappily married men were forced to prey on unmarried women. Divorce would also make marriages happier, and the judgment of Montesquieu on divorce among the pagans was often cited:

Nothing contributed more to mutual affection than the ability to divorce; a husband and wife were led patiently to tolerate domestic difficulties, knowing that they were able to put an end to them, and they often held this power in their hands all their lives without using it, for the single reason that they were free to do so.

A subtheme of the promotion of domestic happiness was that divorce would be particularly useful for women, who could use it (or the threat of it) as a counterweight to the authority that their husbands wielded within marriage. Montesquieu proposed that only women should be able to divorce, for it would be abused by men. D'Holbach echoed the sentiment, arguing that divorce would enable women to

rebel against tyranny, tiresome emotions, against the continued bad-temper of a spouse, life together with whom had become intolerable. This tyrant should lose the rights which he has so badly abused; the law should wrench his authority away from him; the spouses should be separated forever.

For all that these and the many other writers on divorce often expressed a jaundiced view of marriage, they regarded it as a laudable and necessary institution. As an integral part of the society of the Old Regime, it had been corrupted, not least by the imposition of the Roman Catholic doctrine of the indissolubility of divorce. Jean Lavie put it this way:

Marriage offers the most sweet and the most bitter fruits; when tenderness, which is less impetuous than love but deeper than friendship, unites the two spouses, it is the source of the most pleasant and most constant happiness. On the other hand there is no hatred as strong as that which takes root in an indissoluble marriage.

Once the oppressive laws and practices of marriage were reformed, they thought, it would become the beautiful institution it should be, and play its essential role in the regeneration of the nation's morality and population.

The writing on divorce before the French Revolution was disparate and cast rather generally. Because the main aim of the prodivorce writers was simply to establish the case for the legalization of divorce, they rarely went into detail on the circumstances that should justify divorce. Looked at in an aggregate sense there were references to matrimonial offenses (especially adultery and ill-treatment) as well as to emotional incompatibility. The differences between the sixteenth-century Protestant advocates and those of the Enlightenment are striking evidence of secularization. In the later period references to the Bible and church authorities were used to establish the legitimate history of divorce before its prohibition by the medieval papacy, but the actual arguments in favor of divorce were framed in terms of natural rights and social utility.

Only with the burst of social comment and criticism that heralded the end of the Old Regime in 1789 did there appear a sustained proposal for a divorce law for France. In his *Du Divorce* (1789), Albert Hennet suggested that divorce should be permitted when the spouses were temperamentally incompatible or in one of eleven other circumstances, including one's spouse's being sentenced to a long term of imprisonment, incurable illness, exile or disappearance, insanity, and adultery. Hennet devised precise procedures including, in some circumstances, an assembly of relatives that would decide on divorce petitions. Divorces would not be obtained quickly, and there were provisions for the custody of children.

Hennet's book was not only popular (the first edition sold out immediately), but it also proved influential; the divorce law that was eventually passed in September 1792 followed Hennet's proposal closely. Even so, more than three years intervened between the beginning of the revolution and the legalization of divorce, largely because more important issues occupied the attention of France's new legislators. The low priority attached to divorce was prefigured by its virtual absence as an issue in the *cahiers de doléances*, the grievance lists drawn up throughout France in early 1789 and often used by historians as an indicator of public opinion on the eve of the revolution. Divorce was mentioned in a handful of the *cahiers*, but more opposed its legalization than supported it. The parish of Aulnay-les-Bondis (close to Paris), for example, seized on the moral consequences of divorce to argue that "it would be the greatest danger to admit divorce, which would cause general turmoil in France and would be the cause of the greatest scandal." Others, like the Third Estate (commoners) of one Paris district, called for the legalization of divorce "because an indissoluble contract is contrary to the changing character of man," but overall in 1789 the debate on divorce was buried in the rubble of the Bastille and by later events.

Divorce did emerge as an issue from time to time between 1789 and 1792. It was referred to in debates on the reorganization of the judiciary and it was included in lists of demands that petitioners, many of them women, presented to the legislatures from time to time. The most important event, however, was an article in the Constitution of 1791 reading: "The law considers marriage to be only a civil contract." Until this time (and, indeed, for a year afterward), the law of marriage remained as it had been under the Old Regime: celebrated by the clergy, subject to canon law, and indissoluble. With the declaration of marriage as a civil contract, however, pressure began to develop outside and inside the Assembly for a comprehensive reform of matrimonial law that would include the legalization of divorce. In some parts of France mayors and justices of the peace conducted civil marriages and even dissolved marriages in the belief that they were justified under the terms of the constitution. Such acts and the legal confusion they caused added to the pressure, and by March 1792 a Paris newspaper reported: "From all sides there are demands for a divorce law, and the National Assembly appears to be on the verge of considering it."

Action was finally taken in August 1792. On the tenth of that month the monarchy was suspended and many conservative deputies abandoned the Assembly, so that when a petition in favor of divorce was read on the twentieth it received a rather more positive reception than it might have earlier. The legislative committee was instructed to produce a draft divorce law, and after lengthy discussion it was passed on September 20, 1792. The law abolished separations and introduced divorce by mutual consent, on the ground of incompatibility of temperament, and for several specific reasons: madness, condemnation to certain degrading punishments, cruelty or ill-treatment, notoriously dissolute morals, desertion for at least two years, absence without news for at least five years, and emigration. Emigration, a political crime, was the only sign that this was a revolutionary law; the Assembly defeated a motion that divorce should be allowed when one spouse was unpatriotic. In 1794, separation for six months or longer was made a ground for divorce, but this addition was repealed in 1796, partly because of claims that it had been abused by women who had used it to divorce their husbands who were absent on military service.

Even without the additional ground, the 1792 divorce law was far more liberal than any contemporary legislation in Western society. Any couple who could agree enough to petition jointly for divorce could obtain one by mutual consent, and a spouse who claimed incompatibility as a ground did not have to present evidence. In both cases, however, there was a lengthy procedure and a requirement that the parties had to appear on three occasions before an assembly of their relatives (*assemblée de famille*) who were required to try to reconcile the couple. But if the petitioner (or petitioners) persisted in the divorce suit, they could not be refused. As for unilateral divorces based on one of the specific grounds, the evidence was evaluated by a family court (*tribunal de famille*, a different institution), composed of relatives, friends, or neighbors, that acted as a regular court and delivered a decision. Even if a petition failed in a family court, however, a divorce could still be obtained for reason of incompatibility, so that no husband or wife in France who wanted a divorce could be denied one.

The 1792 law was very egalitarian in that it made divorce available to women and men equally, and (until 1796, at least) gave jurisdiction to informal family assemblies and courts that made divorce virtually free of costs. The law was also very modern in its appearance and made provision for the custody of children, division of property, and alimony. If custody could not be decided amicably by the divorcing couple, sons were to be looked after by their father and daughters by their mother. Divorced women were to recoup the property and any dowry they had brought to the marriage, and alimony was to be granted to either spouse on the basis of need and the ability of the better-off spouse to pay.

This divorce law was part of a broad reform of family law, passed at the same time, that made the family secular and more individualistic. The responsibility of registering vital events (births, marriages, and deaths and now divorce) was transferred from the church to the state. The rules of marriage (including impediments and the forms of consent) were secularized, and marriage was to be a civil ceremony. The age of majority was lowered to 21 years for men and women (from the 25 or 30 years common in the Old Regime), and married women were given property rights.

Added to earlier reforms in family law, such as the abolition of primogeniture, equality of inheritance, and the weakening of the father's power over his children, the marriage and divorce laws of September 20, 1792, represented an attempt to remodel the French family on the bases of liberty and equality. Echoing the complaints of the Enlightenment, the revolutionary legislators of 1789–92 tried to regenerate family relationships by creating a legal structure in which there would be justice, not arbitrary authority, harmony, and equality of rights. Divorce was an integral part of these reforms in that it aimed to protect men and women from oppressive marriages, and to make marriage a voluntary relationship, not one from which there was no escape. Divorce was seen, however, as a last resort, and other means, such as regular festivals of marriage (*fêtes des époux*), were employed to remind citizens of the social, political, and personal advantages of a happy family life. At the festival held in Rouen in 1798 one speaker proclaimed:

It is morality that constitutes the strength of states, and it is domestic virtues, it is happy marriages, that principally constitute good morals. The festival of virtuous spouses ... is thus one of the most important national festivals in its object; it is, perhaps, the most essentially republican of all our festivals.

There is no sign here of the burning desire, which has often been alleged, to use divorce to destroy morality and the family. At the time, of course, divorce was opposed by the church, although some clergy suggested that the faithful might divorce as long as they did not remarry, thus using divorce as a kind of separation. As we shall see, there were large numbers of divorces in the first years of the law, particularly in the larger cities. In Rouen, where there had been only four separations from 1780 to 1789, there were more than 100 divorces in the first year divorce was permitted, and almost 200 in each of the following two years. Such statistics – they were echoed in other cities – produced a reaction against divorce, and calls for restrictions and even the repeal of the law.

It was not until the Napoleonic period, however, that the 1792 divorce law was replaced. In 1803 a new and far more restrictive law was introduced. Divorce for reason of incompatibility was abolished, divorce by mutual consent was retained, and the specific grounds were reduced to cruelty, adultery, and condemnation to certain degrading punishments. Beyond the simple grounds, however, divorce was more difficult to obtain. The procedures were long and expensive and women were discriminated against in the matter of adultery just as they had been under the Old Regime: Under the Napoleonic divorce law a husband could divorce his adulterous wife, but a wife could divorce her adulterous husband only if he committed adultery in their common dwelling. The overall effect of the 1803 divorce law was to reduce the number of divorces to a trickle. The trickle itself disappeared in 1816 when, under the restored French monarchy, divorce was abolished "in the interest of religion, of morality, of the monarchy, of families."

In the matter of divorce, as of so many things, France experienced a great deal in the revolutionary period, and as far as divorce was concerned, it was no more available in 1816 than it had been in 1789. Revolutionary divorce had many facets, being part of a broad attempt to regenerate and reform the family as part of a remaking of French society more generally. But the divorce law of the revolution, whatever else it did, embodied in a particularly stark form the process of secularization that is detectable throughout Western society between 1600 and 1800. The process was not linear, its pace was irregular, and it was more evident in some places than others. Its existence, however, is undeniable, and it was exceptionally important in the history of divorce, for it was secularization that enabled divorce doctrines, policies, laws, and practices to shed more conclusively the theological shackles that the Reformation had loosened.

Suggestions for further reading

Bonnecase, Julien, *La Philosophie du Code Napoléon appliquée au droit de la famille* (Paris, 1928).

Dufour, Albert, *Le Mariage dans l'école allemande du droit naturel moderne au XVIIIe siècle* (Paris, 1972).

Garaud, Michel, *La Révolution française et la famille* (Paris, 1975).

Gaudemet, J., "Législation canonique et attitudes séculières à l'égard du lien matrimonial au XVIIe siècle," *XVIIe siècle* 102–103 (1974), 15–30.

Gillis, John, *For Better, For Worse: British Marriages, 1600 to the Present* (New York, 1985).

Howard, George E., *A History of Matrimonial Institutions* (3 vols., Chicago, 1904).

Lottin, Alain, *La désunion du couple sous l'Ancien Régime: l'exemple du Nord* (Paris, 1975).

Outhwaite, R. B. (ed.), *Marriage and Society: Studies in the Social History of Marriage* (London, 1981).

Phillips, Roderick, *Family Breakdown in Late Eighteenth-Century France: Divorces in Rouen, 1792–1803* (Oxford, 1980).

Traer, James F., *Marriage and the Family in Eighteenth-Century France* (Ithaca, 1980).

Tucker, Richard, *Natural Rights Theories: Their Origin and Development* (Cambridge, 1981).

4

Formal and informal divorce in early modern society

As we have seen, divorce was legalized in various parts of the Western world between the sixteenth and eighteenth centuries. This chapter focuses on three particular case studies to show what use was made of divorce, who divorced, why, and what the divorces can tell us about wider issues of marriage and the family. The cases studied here are divorces by private Act of Parliament in England from 1670 to 1857, divorces in the British American colonies in the seventeenth and eighteenth centuries, and divorces in France under the revolutionary and Napoleonic laws (1792–1816).

As we can appreciate, however, the laws in most jurisdictions in this general period were quite restrictive, and divorce was inaccessible to many groups and social strata of their populations. If men and women in such groups were to escape their marriages, they had to find alternatives to formal divorce, and the second half of this chapter discusses the most common categories of informal "divorce": murder, desertion, bigamy, and wife sale, among them. For the most part it is impossible to measure the extent of such behavior, but it is important to understand, as we look at the following case studies, that formal divorce was only one solution to severe matrimonial problems.

Divorces in England by Act of Parliament, 1670–1857

The dissolution of individual marriages in England by private Act of Parliament was the means by which the Anglican church's opposition to divorce was circumvented. Following the success of Lord Roos's divorce bill, other men introduced bills into the House of Lords, and by the middle of the eighteenth century such divorces were becoming regular occurrences, even if they were not very common (see Table 4.1). Despite the expense, the length of the procedure, and the limitations (only adultery was accepted as a ground), parliamentary divorce remained the only means of legally dissolving a marriage in England until the country's first divorce law came into effect in 1858.

The passage of a private divorce act was only the last of a series of

Table 4.1. *Divorce Acts of Parliament, England, 1670–1857*

Period	Divorce acts	Period	Divorce acts
(1670, 1698)	2	1780–9	12
1700–9	3	1790–9	42
1710–19	2	1800–9	23
1720–9	3	1810–19	27
1730–9	2	1820–9	25
1740–9	4	1830–9	35
1750–9	15	1840–9	54
1760–9	13	1850–7	29
1770–9	34		

procedures a petitioner had to go through. First, he had to obtain a separation from a church court for reason of his wife's adultery. Second, the aggrieved husband had to obtain damages from his wife's accomplice in her adultery. The damages, for an offense known as "criminal conversation" (illicit sexual intercourse), were based on the principle that a married woman was her husband's property, and that by having intercourse with her, any other man trespassed on the husband's property and owed him damages. The amount of damages awarded in such actions varied from £20,000 to nominal sums like a shilling or a farthing. The precise sum reflected several considerations: the ability of the defendant to pay, the status of the wife, and the perceived happiness of the marriage before the adultery (the happier the husband had been, the greater his loss caused by the adultery). A parliamentary divorce was, then, a three-stage process: a separation, a successful suit for damages, and only then the parliamentary dissolution of marriage with the right to remarry.

Under these conditions divorce was a privilege of the wealthy, and specifically of wealthy men. Parliamentary divorces typically cost between £200 and £300, far beyond the means of ordinary folk, and some cost thousands of pounds. If some men of quite modest means divorced, they did so only after saving for years. In 1840, for example, one Jonathon Warr, a slate merchant from Bolton in Lancashire, introduced a bill to divorce his wife, from whom he had separated in 1827 and who had given birth to a child two years later. Warr stated in his petition that when he discovered his wife's adultery he was only a journeyman slater, "and was not in circumstances of sufficient affluence to enable him to bear the expense of any legal proceedings, but [he] ... has since that time by industry and frugality improved his circumstances and condition in life," and lodged a petition as soon as he was able to. Men of the working class, and in fact any man who did not have several hundred pounds of disposable income, simply could not avail themselves of divorce. Divorce was little other than another privilege for those already privileged in English society.

If there was a desire to keep the number of divorces low and out of the hands of the masses, it succeeded. During the whole period from 1670 to 1857, when parliamentary divorces were available, there were only 325 divorces in England, an average of one or two a year. Of the 325, only 4 were obtained by women, and these only in the nineteenth century when women were given access to this kind of divorce if they could prove their husbands guilty of aggravated adultery, that is, adultery aggravated by some additional offense such as incest or bigamy. Not only were divorces rare and almost entirely (99%) monopolized by men, but in the earliest years they seemed positively aristocratic. After the 1670 act dissolving the marriage of Lord Roos, the next parliamentary divorces were obtained by the Earl of Macclesfield (1698) and the Duke of Norfolk (1700). But even when commoners entered the divorce lists, there was no great rush to divorce, and by 1750 only sixteen divorces had been approved by Parliament. Table 4.1 shows the number of divorces by decade. Other petitions were lodged and then withdrawn or, in some cases, rejected. Six bills were rejected between 1714 and 1779, and ten between 1780 and 1819.

The limited social constituency of divorce under parliamentary rules is indicated by the rank or occupation given in 242 divorce acts passed between 1770 and 1850. Sixteen (7%) of the petitioners were peers of the realm, and if we add together all men with titles (most who were not peers were baronets), they account for 12% of the total. The largest single group (40%) was made up of men described as "gentlemen" or "esquires," vague designations but usually implying property owners. The military contributed a significant 21% of divorced men (their high representation is explained below), and the clergy made up a surprisingly high 7%. The remaining 20% were mainly from the professions (especially doctors), commerce (merchants), and white-collar occupations, but there was also a piano-maker, a riding master, and a butcher. Little is revealed of the social origins of the four women who obtained divorces, except that in one case the adulterous husband was a merchant and in another he was a gentleman (in terms of social rank, at least).

It is interesting to compare this limited social spectrum of divorce petitioners with the social derivation of their wives' accomplices. In broad terms they were from similar groups, but the corespondents were somewhat more diverse, and sometimes exotic. Fifteen percent of the corespondents were titled, and they included an Italian count, a Spanish marquis, an Austrian prince, and a son of the ex-Caliph of Constantina. But if titled men were slightly more common as corespondents than as petitioners, "gentlemen" and clergymen were less common as known adulterers, accounting for 23% and 5%, respectively. On the other hand, men in the miltary (29% of corespondents), and in professions and commerce (20%), were more common as corespondents than as petitioners.

When we look at individual cases, we find frequent relationships between the occupations of husbands and their wives' accomplices. The wife of a civil engineer eloped with a civil engineer, the wife of a chemist committed adultery with another chemist, and the wife of a surgeon slept with another surgeon. Other married women committed adultery with their or their husbands' employees: the wife of an attorney slept with his clerk, the wife of a gentleman eloped to France with one of his servants, and one wife committed adultery with the steward of her husband's estates.

A far more striking pattern in the divorces between 1770 and 1850 was the Indian connection, for nearly one in five (18%) had an association with the subcontinent. The recurrent pattern was of a couple marrying in England and then moving to India where the husband was a civilian or military employee of the East India Company. In many instances the wife returned to England after a few years, either to recover from ill-health brought on by living in India or to accompany children returning to England for their education. En route to England, or once there, the wife committed adultery, and when this was discovered by the husband, still in India, he introduced a bill for dissolution of the marriage.

One example was provided by Thomas Weston, a major in the 96th Regiment of Foot, who married Frances Lenn in England in 1787. The following year he was ordered to India, where the couple lived until April 1794, when Frances returned to England for health reasons. The English air clearly did her a world of good, for she soon began a sexual relationship with Hector Weir, an officer in the South Devon militia, lived with him from 1796, and bore him two children. In another case James Allardyce married his wife Dorothy in England in 1813. They later moved, with four children, to Madras, where James was a surgeon with the 34th Infantry, and in 1820 Dorothy and the children returned to England, partly for her health, partly for the children's education. On board the ship back to England she committed adultery with Alexander Johnson, a soldier with the East India Company. When James Allardyce obtained a divorce in 1823, Dorothy and Alexander were living together in France. So common did the Indian connection become after 1800 (it was a feature of almost a third of the divorces between 1800 and 1850) that in 1820 Parliament passed an act permitting witnesses in divorce cases to be examined in India and Ceylon, so as to avoid their having to travel to London to give evidence in person.

Clearly, mobility and independence were important factors in the adultery of women who left their husbands in India. Women also gained a measure of autonomy when their husbands were absent, and the American and European wars of the late eighteenth and early nineteenth centuries created such circumstances. Examples are scattered through the divorce records. Henry Sheridan's wife committed adultery while he was serving in America in 1776. While Admiral Sir Hyde Parker commanded H.M.S. *Victory* in the Mediterranean from 1793, his wife conceived "a base-born child" with the assistance of an army officer. Finally, the Honorable Pownoll Bastard Pellew's wife committed adultery (but did not conceive a child) while her husband was at sea in command of H.M.S. *Impregnable*.

Military service, together with the apparently divorce-prone servants of the empire in India, helped to push up the number of parliamentary divorces from the late eighteenth century. It is not that war created social instability, but that the common and lengthy separations of husbands and wives gave each the opportunities to form transient or permanent sexual relationships with others. We should not assume, however, that the adultery described in the divorce acts – almost always by the wife – accurately reflected the pattern of adultery. It was easier to detect the adultery of the sedentary (or supine) spouse – in these cases, the wife – and, we must remember, it was adultery by the wife that was a ground for a parliamentary divorce.

Not all divorces can be explained in terms of the forced separation of husband and wife, of course. In many the circumstances were what we might dare call banal: a wife tired of her husband and attracted to another man. A number of these cases led to the couple's eloping abroad. In two divorces youthfulness at marriage was pleaded as a factor. In one of these Edward Cripps married in 1842 at the age of nineteen, without his father's knowledge or consent. Cripps lived with his wife only seventeen days before being persuaded by his elder brother that she was "a person of immoral habits." The marriage was soon dissolved.

Of the four parliamentary divorces obtained by women, all between 1801 and 1850, two involved incestuous adultery between the husband and his wife's sister, and the others were based on adultery aggravated by bigamy. In one of the bigamy cases there had clearly been marital problems before the offense, for Ann Battersby, the petitioner, noted that she and her husband had lived together for less than a month after their 1826 marriage:

Within a few Days of the said Marriage the said Arthur Battersby began to treat [her]... with Neglect and Harshness, and frequently left her at Night and went abroad and remained until late Hours in the company of common Prostitutes, and with the said Prostitutes carried on an adulterous Intercourse and Connexion.

Not only was Arthur Battersby's first marriage dissolved, but he was sentenced to seven years' transportation for bigamy.

Beyond the specific offenses in individual cases, it has been suggested that divorces by Act of Parliament served the purpose of allowing men, especially peers, to remarry younger women when their wives had failed to provide them with a male heir. This might indeed have been true in some cases: It was a factor in Lord Roos's divorce, although matters were complicated there because his wife was producing bastard children. But of the twenty-three peers and baronets who divorced, and on whom information is readily available, eight definitely had sons living at the time of the divorce, and a further three might have (they had children, but their sex is not stated). Divorce as a strategy for remarriage so as to produce an heir is not a satisfactory explanation, then, not only because there is little evidence of it, but also because a husband thus motivated would also have to persuade his wife to commit adultery or would have to connive in it in some way.

Divorce by Act of Parliament was a fundamentally unsatisfactory compromise between marital indissolubility and a divorce law. Perhaps the most surprising aspect of it is that it lasted so long, and perhaps it did so because any pressure to liberalize divorce was effectively balanced by influential opinion (including the Church of England) that thought any form of divorce to be unacceptable.

Divorces in the New England colonies

Divorces in the early modern Western world were so uncommon that, for the most part, it is hardly worth expressing them as rates: There were 130 parliamentary divorces in England in the eighteenth century, and the country had a population of nine million people by 1800. We do not have to calculate precisely the rate per unit of population to see that Britain's North American subjects had a higher divorce rate, for Connecticut and Massachusetts together, with a far smaller population, produced almost a thousand divorces in the second half of the century alone. Was it that marriages were more fragile in the colonial context or were there other reasons for the greater propensity for the American colonists to divorce, a propensity that has underlain the high divorce rates in the United States ever since?

Divorce in the New England colonies, which alone had enough divorces to warrant discussing, went through three broad phases: Divorces were relatively rare up to the middle of the eighteenth century, rose from midcentury to the 1770s, and rose again – dramatically, this time – in the revolutionary period.

The precise number of divorces in the early period is unknown because of the variety of institutions that dissolved marriages. Courts, governors, councils, and legislatures were used by the different colonies, and not all their records have survived. The most comprehensive search for formal terminations of marriages in the New England colonies, by Lyle Koehler, turned up 128 petitions, but if we subtract annulments, separations, and a few idiosyncratic actions called "self-divorce" and "common-law marriage split up," we are left with 103 divorce actions between 1620 and 1699. Massachusetts provided 40 of them, Connecticut 38, Rhode Island 15, Plymouth Colony (later part of Massachusetts) 8, and New Hampshire 2. The numbers are so small that it would be hazardous to make much of the differences among the colonies. Massachusetts and Connecticut were the most populous, but even so Massachusetts had twice Connecticut's population by 1700, and that was not reflected in the number of divorces.

Two-thirds (65%) of the divorce actions were initiated by women, 30% by men, and 5% jointly. Because of the divorce laws in force in New England, adultery and desertion were the most common grounds, comprising 77% of the total. Women more often divorced for reason of desertion (60%) than simple adultery (13%), and women often (22% of cases) combined adultery with desertion or cruelty to justify a divorce. This gives the impression that women were tolerant of adultery unless it was aggravated, an echo of the principle applied in English parliamentary divorce rules. Men in New England, however, divorced more often for simple adultery (29% of petitions), desertion (23%), and adultery and desertion combined (23%). The other grounds invoked in these New England divorces included such offenses as cruelty, threats to life, incest, refusal of intercourse, heretical opinions, and a wife's refusal to accompany her husband when he moved to another town.

We should be careful not to read divorce statistics as necessarily indicative of general social realities. The divorce suits suggest that women were more likely to commit adultery, but records of convictions for adultery in New England courts show that of 308 convictions, 174 (56.5%) were of men and 134 (43.5%) were of women. Only in seventeenth-century Maine did men comprise fewer than half the convicted adulterers: 30 of the 61 were men. What the divorce statistics suggest (this point is developed in the next chapter) is that married men and women, who had to initiate divorces (unlike prosecutions, which were generally initiated by the community or public authorities), were generally tolerant of adultery. After all, 174 men were convicted of adultery, but only 23 divorces included this offense, and we must conclude that 151 adulterous husbands (87%) continued to live with wives who had the legal right to divorce. A similar proportion of women convicted of adultery apparently continued to live with their husbands: 134 women were convicted, but only 17 divorces initiated by men (13%) referred to adultery.

Desertion, too, was no doubt more common than the divorce records suggest, and generally the divorces only hint at other aspects of marital behavior. Only five petitions referred to cruelty, although we should expect, from the evidence of other sources, that violence – wife beating especially – was common in seventeenth-century marriages. Between 1630 and 1699, 128 men and 57 women were prosecuted in New England courts for physically abusing their spouses, and 5 men were tried for killing their wives.

Not all matrimonial offenses could have been translated into divorces, even if the aggrieved spouses had wanted, because of the limitation of prevailing divorce laws. All the other factors that inhibit divorce must also have come into play: financial dependence, religious scruples, social pressure, and the individual decision that a specific offense was not so severe as to warrant a divorce. We must remember that even if divorce was permitted in colonial New England, it was regarded as scandalous and shameful. On one occasion a divorced woman and her new husband complained to the Massachusetts authorities that some people had insulted them "in most reviling speeches," accusing them of adultery because of the wife's having been divorced.

It is possible that attitudes were somewhat more tolerant in other colonies. One commentator on Connecticut described the Indians in the colony as changing husbands and wives "on ye least dislike or fickle humor . . . [and] saying stand away to one another is a sufficient divorce." She suggested that the colonists had gleefully adopted similar behavior: "And indeed those uncomely Stand aways are too much in Vogue among the English in this Indulgent Colony as their Records plentifully prove." Connecticut did, as we have seen, have a higher ratio of divorces per population than Massachusetts. But it is debatable whether this should be attributed to more "indulgent" attitudes or to factors such as that Connecticut judges rode circuit, bringing justice (and cheaper divorce) to the outlying populations, whereas petitioners in Massachusetts had to attend court in Boston.

During the first third of the eighteenth century, indeed, the difference between the Connecticut and Massachusetts divorce rates widened. The number of petitions in Massachusetts ranged between four and nine a decade right up to the 1730s, so that if anything, the colony's divorce rate fell, when placed in the context of a rising population. In Connecticut, however, the average one petition a year in the seventeenth century grew to two or three a year, on average, in the period 1700–50. In both colonies, however, divorces rose sharply toward the end of the century, and especially in the period of the revolution. From an average seven per decade from 1636 to 1634, divorces in Massachusetts rose to twenty-nine per decade between 1735 and 1774, and there were eighty-six in the ten years from 1775, the period of the American war of independence. Successful petitions rose from four to seventeen to sixty-one in these periods, respectively. Population growth explains only part of the increase, and there was no liberalization of divorce law, so we should look to other factors for an explanation.

Connecticut experienced an even more astonishing surge in divorces. From 10 petitions per decade in the seventeenth century (45 in the period 1655–99), the colony produced 25 per decade in the period 1700–49 (123 petitions), and a staggering 175 per decade in the second half of the century (839 petitions between 1750 and 1797). In Connecticut, too, population grew rapidly in the eighteenth century (it doubled between 1750 and 1800), but this accounts for only a small part of the increase in divorces.

The large number of divorces in eighteenth-century Massachusetts and Connecticut, the only American colonies to produce significant numbers, allows us to make some generalizations about the use of divorce there. Unlike parliamentary divorce in contemporary England, judicial divorce in these colonies was generally accessible to groups beyond the wealthy. In Connecticut, successful petitioners ranged from Colonel Henry Beekman Livingston, a member of a prominent New York family, to James, a Norwich slave. Each divorced his wife for reason of desertion. As for the Massachusetts divorces, they came mainly from the middling classes. A third of the husbands involved as petitioners or defendants were artisans or traders, 22% were husbandmen or yeomen, another 22% were fishermen or mariners, and 17% had high social rank, being professionals, ships' captains, merchants, gentlemen, or militia officers. Only 7% derived from the lower end of the social scale: truckmen, laborers, servants, and the like.

In both colonies women predominated as petitioners in divorce cases. In Connecticut they accounted for 69–91% of petitions, depending on the period. In Massachusetts the proportion of women's petitions was lower, at 56%, although it tended to increase during the century. As in the preceding century, women's petitions tended to cite desertion more frequently than men's. In Connecticut 54% of all women's petitions were based solely on desertion, and in Massachusetts desertion was an element in 41% of the grounds cited by women.

Desertion, fostered by the mobility of colonial life, often left women destitute. Mary Dewey, of Colchester in Connecticut, reported that her husband's desertion had forced her to go "begging from house to house for support for her and her infant child." For such women divorce provided an opportunity for remarriage and survival.

Adultery was the other main ground invoked in eighteenth-century divorce cases. Between 1692 and 1764, 78% of men's petitions referred to adultery, as did 40% of women's petitions. From 1765 to 1774, the figures were 94% and 50%, and from 1775 to 1786, 91% and 79%. Adultery, then, alone or in combination with other offenses, became the most common matrimonial misdeed cited in Massachusetts divorce suits. This might indicate that women were becoming less tolerant of their husbands' adultery, and, if that is so, it is also possible that the judges shared their views, for the success rate of women's petitions based on husbands' adultery rose from 49 to 70% between 1692–1774 and 1775–86.

There is little exceptional in the accounts of adultery in the eighteenth-century divorce records. There were the usual stories of men on the move, taking advantage of their independence: Jeremiah Beckwith, the captain of a trading schooner, was divorced when his wife discovered that he had had sexual relationships in four different New York ports on one voyage. For their part women used their husbands' absences to their own advantage, some bearing children a year or more after their husbands had gone away.

Other signs of marital trouble were generally excluded from the divorce records because of the prevailing laws. Not one woman in Massachusetts obtained a divorce on the ground of cruelty, although the courts did permit separations in such circumstances. In Connecticut more than 10% of women's petitions cited verbal or physical violence. But only one woman was granted a divorce for reason of cruelty alone, and that was a particularly tragic case in which the husband not only assaulted his wife, but also killed his infant son and the wife and child of a neighbor who were visiting at the time.

The general patterns of divorce, and the circumstances of individual divorces in Connecticut and Massachusetts, can be described easily enough, but it is difficult to explain such changes as the rise in the number of divorces and the shifting ratio of petitioners in favor of women. In her studies of Massachusetts divorces, Nancy Cott has proposed a connection between the political ideologies of the revolutionary era and a more egalitarian notion of sexual justice. The rejection of British "vice" and "corruption" implied a moral regeneration and a "critique of the traditionally loose sexual standards for men of the British ruling class." The idea of a transfer between political ideology and attitudes toward sexuality and family government is provocative, but difficult to prove. It is reinforced, however, by Cohen's finding that in Connecticut the word *tyranny*, a popular description of British rule, was applied to marital oppression in women's divorce petitions of the wartime and postwar periods. The 1788 petition of Abigail Strong was as clear an example as one could want: She applied for divorce "being fully convinced that she is under no obligation to live with him [her husband] any longer or submit to his cruelty, for even Kings may forfeit or discharge the allegiance of their Subjects."

The intrusion of revolutionary or egalitarian ideologies into marriage might well partially explain such features of eighteenth-century American divorce as the increase in women's petitions (which pushed up the total number). It is probably more useful, however, to understand trends in these divorces in the broader Western contexts that are set out later in this book.

Divorces in revolutionary and Napoleonic France, 1792–1816

The third of these three case studies, divorces in revolutionary and Napoleonic France, presents us with the first example of mass divorce in the history of Western society. Divorce, as we have seen, was legalized for the first time in France in 1792, and people in the cities warmed to it immediately. Although precise global figures are not available, there were almost 20,000 divorces between 1792 and 1803 in the nine largest cities. Paris led easily with some 13,200 divorces, Lyon and Rouen each had more than a thousand, and cities like Marseilles, Strasbourg, and Bordeaux each produced more than 500 divorces in the twelve-year period.

While these figures might not seem astonishing in late twentieth-century terms, we have only to compare contemporary England and the American colonies to see why the French experience was exceptional. In one city, Rouen, with a population of 85,000 at the end of the eighteenth century, there were more divorces in the 1790s than there were in Connecticut between 1750 and 1800, and many times more than in England during the whole eighteenth century. The presence of divorce in revolutionary France can also be gauged when divorces are expressed as a ratio to marriages: In Paris there was one divorce for four marriages after 1792, in Rouen one for eight, and in Lyon, Marseilles, and Toulouse one for every ten to thirteen.

As Figure 4.1 shows, divorces were not distributed evenly throughout the twelve-year life of the 1792 law, but tended to bunch in the first three years. In Rouen, for instance, the first years witnessed 108, 185, and 191 divorces, respectively (an average of 161 a year, 1792–5), but from 1795 the annual average fell to 67. Divorces in the first

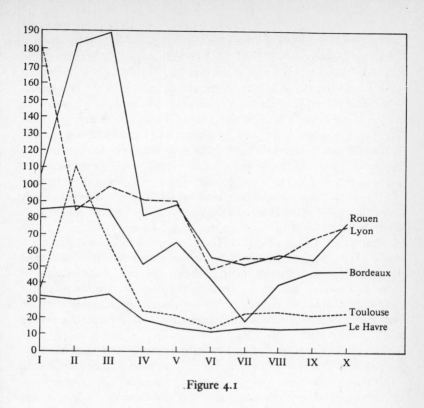

190
180
170
160
150
140
130
120
110
100
90
80
70
60
50
40
30
20
10
0

I II III IV V VI VII VIII IX X

Rouen
Lyon
Bordeaux
Toulouse
Le Havre

Figure 4.1

three years accounted for almost half the divorces between 1792 and 1803, a pattern that has been recorded in various French cities, as the diagram indicates. (Figure 4.1 is expressed in terms of the French Revolutionary calendar; see p. 84.)

We should not think of the sudden rush to divorce as indicating the sudden breakdown of thousands of marriages, even though it has often been suggested that the divorces in these years reflected social instability and a crisis in the family brought on by the radical, anti-Catholic phase of the French Revolution. Rather, we should recognize that a large proportion of the divorces in the years following the legalization of divorce dissolved marriages that had ended in reality years earlier. One of the first divorces in Rouen was obtained in December 1792 by Marie Piedeleu, a sixty-six-year-old woman who divorced her husband who had left home more than thirty years earlier to serve in the Seven Years' War. Sixteen days after her divorce, Marie Piedeleu married a man whose address was the same as hers. Her divorce and remarriage evidently did no more than put on a legal footing an arrangement that might have been years or decades old. No doubt many divorces in the early period of divorce served this purpose, for a large proportion was sought by women on the grounds of their husbands' long-term absence or desertion. Once this backlog of divorces-in-waiting was cleared, the number of divorces declined. It was simply coincidental that the period of many divorces coincided with the radical period of the revolution, and that the decline of divorces coincided with the more conservative period of the Directories, but the coincidence has quite wrongly made for a positive relationship between divorce and radical political activity.

Apart from its skewed distribution over time, divorces in revolutionary France had two prime characteristics: Most were sought by women, and they were far more common in the cities and towns than in rural areas. The association of women with divorce emerges clearly from all local studies. If we consider only those divorces sought unilaterally (that is, not by mutual agreement), women obtained 71% in Rouen, 73% in Metz, 64% in Toulouse, 71% in Nancy, and 72% in Le Havre. Although women tended to outnumber men in almost all categories of unilateral divorce, they were most preponderant in divorces based on desertion, absence, and ill-treatment. Significantly (bearing in mind the figures in Massachusetts and Connecticut) the only category where men were predominant was divorces for reason of "notorious immorality."

It is not difficult to explain why more women than men used the divorce law. In eighteenth-century society men were more mobile than women and were more likely to desert or be absent, leaving their wives at home to fend for themselves and their children. When divorce was legalized, with desertion and absence recognized as grounds, women were more likely to wish to take advantage of it. Even when a couple lived together, it was women who were likely to resort to divorce when they were dissatisfied with their marriages. Husbands, in theory and in practice, could enforce their will over their wives by physical coercion if necessary, for Old Regime law recognized the right of "moderate correction," the right of a husband to use "moderate" physical force on his wife when he judged it necessary. During the revolution a law was passed that provided for heavy penalties on men who assaulted women, but in practice the judiciary were reluctant to allow wives to prosecute their husbands. In one Rouen case the judges told a wife that because she "is under the authority of her husband, is not divorced and has not started divorce proceedings," she could not prosecute her husband for beating her. The woman in question started divorce proceedings within a week.

The divorce court records of the revolutionary period in France provide a rare window into eighteenth-century marriages, though we must always remember that it enables us to see more of the unhappy than the happy scenes of marriage. Still, even evidence in divorce cases can give us negative evidence about expectations of marriages and can shed incidental light on aspects not directly related to divorce.

The most consistent image divorces revealed was the dominance of husbands over wives. Dominance took many forms, though its starkest manifestation was violence. The case of Marie Vasse is simply exemplary. In May 1793 her husband

without reason or excuse ... seized the fire shovel which was by the chimney, and dealt his said wife three blows with it, hurled himself upon her like a madman, dealt her various blows to the head and to the body, threw her to the ground, and tore at her hair while she was on the ground, while threatening to break her arm or leg if she should have the misfortune to cry out.

Some women were so badly injured in such attacks that they fled from their homes or were rescued by neighbors. Women neighbors often provided first aid, refuge, and in at least one case in Rouen put a beaten woman up at an inn and cared for her there.

Men exercised control not only by violence but by evicting their wives, often with their children, at all hours of day and night, leaving them in the street without resources. Other men incarcerated their wives, locking them inside their homes, often in order to prevent them from having contact with their families.

Desertion was yet another recourse that men had in case of dissatisfaction. Men were more mobile than women and seem more readily to have abandoned their families. Many men disappeared during economic depression, leaving ostensibly to find work in another region of France, and never returning. Others left for purely marital reasons, and many took advantage of the revolutionary conditions to join the armies. In 1792, for example, Louis Poussolle "without telling [his wife] ... left her; two days passed and, making enquiries as to what had happened to him, she learned that he had signed up to go on military service on the frontiers."

In France, as in England, military service provided the circumstances in which adultery flourished. A Rouen case was that of Marie Gruchy who bore two children while her husband was away in the army for two years, and was pregnant with a third at the time of his return home. He promptly sued for divorce, and in the course of the trial the neighborhood baker testified that he had asked Gruchy who was responsible for her pregnancies, and that she had replied "it is my husband who is away serving the Republic; he sends them to me in a letter." In France as in England, it was women's adultery that was more easily detectable, and for this reason, if for no others, husbands' petitions tended to outnumber wives' when the ground was immorality.

The French Revolution itself, as distinct from the wars and economic problems that accompanied it, impinged only marginally on divorce.

The 1792 law did allow divorce for reason of emigration, which was a political crime, and all over France women divorced their émigré husbands who had fled the revolution for refuges in England, Austria, Prussia, and elsewhere. But although some of these divorces might well have reflected marital problems, others had an ulterior motive. The properties of émigrés had been declared forfeit to the nation, but by divorcing and getting a property settlement, their wives were able to protect the properties. Moreover, the wives of émigrés were also subject to arrest, but divorced wives were exempt. Many of the divorces for reason of emigration, then, were fictive, and in some cases the spouses remarried when it was safe for the husband to return. This happened in six of the thirteen émigré divorces in Metz, but only in two of the fourteen divorces in Rouen.

Overall, the preponderance of women's petitions in the divorce lists of revolutionary France is easy to understand. Ill-treatment, desertion, and absence were the most common offenses cited, and women were more likely to be the aggrieved party. Women also sought most divorces for reason of incompatibility of temperament and that too can be explained, for this ground, where no evidence was required, was designed to prevent the scandal of having to describe sordid and embarrassing episodes to outsiders. The evidence suggests that these divorces involved the same range of circumstances as those for which detailed evidence is available. Wives appear to have taken the initiative in most divorces by mutual consent, too.

The French Revolution was exceptional in making divorce equally available to women and to men. It also attempted to make divorce accessible to all social groups by establishing informal family courts and assemblies to hear divorce petitions. Each party in a divorce nominated relatives, friends, or neighbors to constitute a court, where evidence was heard, witnesses examined, and verdicts rendered. The result was that family justice was accessible, cheap (lawyers were not required), intimate, and rapid. No doubt this goes some way to explaining the social composition of the divorced. In Rouen almost three-quarters (72%) of women petitioners were working women, most in the city's textile industry. Of the rest, about half had private means (women divorcing émigrés swelled this group), and others were small merchants such as fish sellers and merchant bonnet-makers. The male petitioners were also mainly (69%) working men and artisans, with the remainder being merchants and some professionals and entrepreneurs.

If the divorced men and women were roughly representative of the married population (the indigent tended to be in neither group), they were exceptional in one respect, and that is the size of their families. Couples divorcing by mutual consent had to state the number of children they had (childless couples could divorce more rapidly), and in Rouen almost two-thirds (64%) had no children at all, an extraordinarily high rate. Fifteen percent had one child, and 20% had two or more children. Nor was Rouen aberrant, for of the thirteen couples in Le Havre on which there is adequate information, twelve had no children. Childlessness was one characteristic of divorce in revolutionary France, and so was youthfulness at marriage. In Rouen the average age at marriage of men and women who later divorced was three years below that of men and women who did not divorce. For women the critical difference was located in the very young ages, for fully 40% of women who eventually divorced had married before reaching the age of twenty-one, a percentage twice that of women who did not divorce.

These demographic traits aside, the second dominant characteristic of divorce in the French Revolution was its concentration in the cities. There were 374 divorces in Toulouse between 1792 and 1803, and the number decreased the further one went from the city. In the Moselle region, the city of Metz (population 35,000) had 257 divorces, but the eight next towns in terms of size (with a combined population of 80,000) had a total of only 80 divorces. Two facilities associated with large towns probably enabled people there, especially women, to divorce more readily than their rural counterparts. First, cities had accommodation. The first requirement of a divorcing spouse is somewhere to live, and the shortage of alternatives in the rural areas was highlighted in a case in a village near Rouen, where a wife moved into a cowshed. Second, cities had a more extensive labor market, a necessity for an independent life. In the rural areas work was done in family units – agriculture and domestic production – and there were few employment opportunities for a divorced woman. Evidence that urban conditions favored women seeking divorce lies in the fact that women sought 71% of divorces in the city of Rouen, but only 42% of divorces in the surrounding communes. Rural divorce, then, was not dominated by women as urban divorce was. The lack of opportunities in the rural areas is further suggested by the fact that most women who divorced in these areas soon took up residence in Rouen.

Awareness of the consequences of divorce must always have influenced the readiness of men and women to dissolve their marriages, and the revolutionary law can only have facilitated divorce. First there was provision for alimony, in that the financially better-off spouse had to contribute to the other. Payments were based on need and the ability to pay, and in some cases alimony was awarded to men. Second, the custody of children was carefully regulated. Unless the couple could arrange custody amicably, a simple formula was applied such that sons lived with their father, and daughters with their mother, except that sons lived with the mother until the age of seven. In some cases there were disputes over the fitness of a parent to have custody. In Rouen, Nicolas Bernard objected to his wife's claim for custody of their two youngest children because, he alleged, she had shown little care for them, "letting them go to bed without undressing, [and] by neglecting to comb their hair or dress them properly."

The divorce records of this period have a very modern ring to them, just as the revolutionary law itself has more in common with late twentieth-century legislation than with contemporary codes. In one respect at least, however, divorces in France in the 1790s were quite unlike their modern counterparts, and that is the rarity of remarriages. By 1820 only 28% of men and 25% of women divorced in Rouen had remarried in the city. True, others must have married elsewhere, just as men and women divorced in other parts of France married in Rouen. Even so, it is unlikely that they made much difference to the remarriage rates.

Finally, let us look briefly at divorce in the Napoleonic era, when the law was far more restrictive. The immediate effect of reducing the grounds and complicating the procedure of divorce was evident in the decline in the numbers. In Rouen there had been an annual average of sixty-seven divorces from 1795 to 1803; after the Napoleonic law came into effect in 1803 divorces fell to an annual average of six. In Lyon the annual average fell from eighty-seven to seven. On the other hand, women continued to dominate Napoleonic divorce, despite the double standard that had been introduced in the 1803 law, under which a woman could divorce her adulterous husband only if he committed adultery in their home. Even so, divorce under the Napoleonic law was a mere shadow of the phenomenon it had been during the revolution, and even this shadow disappeared when divorce was abolished in 1816.

The case studies: Some conclusions

One of the most striking conclusions from the English, American, and French case studies is the importance of legislation in influencing the extent of divorce. The most restrictive divorce facility, divorces by private Act of Parliament in England, effectively excluded all but men (with four exceptions) and the well-off from divorce. Divorce in colonial New England was more liberal, and those colonies produced many more divorces. Revolutionary France had by far the most liberal and accessible divorce legislation, and the number of divorces reflected that fact. The French case is highlighted by the depressing effect on divorces of the Napoleonic law. The sex ratio of divorce petitioners was similarly influenced by the terms of legislation, as we have seen, with English practice being highly discriminatory against women, French law treating men and women equally, and New England law falling somewhere in between.

Factors other than legal considerations also came into play. Divorce was an urban phenomenon in France as we have seen, and it was similar in Massachusetts, where a quarter of the divorces emanated from Boston, which had only 6% of the colony's population. (We should remember, however, that divorce petitions could be filed only in Boston, a fact that must have favored divorces in the town.) Social pressure was no doubt important, too. Divorce was scandalous in England and New England, partly because of its associations with offenses such as adultery. In France, on the other hand, divorce was hailed as a liberty that the revolution had restored to the people, and procedures for divorce by mutual consent and for reason of incompatibility reduced its link with embarrassing misdeeds.

The three studies also shed light on broader issues related to the family. There are hints – they are clearest in New England – that adultery was often tolerated or at least not regarded as necessarily provocative of divorce. The association of male mobility and desertion emerges from the divorce records, as does a relationship between marital problems and times of military conflict. Throughout these studies, in short, there are connections between marital relationships and broader social conditions, connections that were mediated through the divorce laws themselves. The studies alert us, in short, to the need to understand these marriages and divorces in their social, economic, and cultural contexts, not as isolated from them.

Informal divorces: The alternatives

Some of the limitations of formal divorce in early modern society are evident. With the notable exception of France in the revolutionary period, divorce laws covered a very limited range of circumstances (rarely could one spouse escape an oppressive or simply unpleasant marriage unless the other had committed a specific matrimonial offense), they were often discriminatory against women in principle or practice, and they all required the intervention of formal authorities and lengthy procedures, frequently including mandatory attempts at reconciliation. The marriages that broke down and turned up on the divorce lists fitted the limited criteria, and the spouses who petitioned were determined enough to go through the only procedures that would legally dissolve their marriages and permit them to marry again. Common sense tells us, though, that there must have been a "dark figure" of marriage dissolution behind the formal divorces, just as there is a hidden extent of criminality not revealed by records of arrest, prosecutions, and convictions. In this section we attempt to illuminate the darkness a little so as to discern the outlines of what might be called "informal divorce."

Faced with the reality that for them divorce was unavailable, what were men and women to do when their marriages became intolerable? One answer was given in England in 1688 by Mary Hobry, "a French midwife," who was charged with killing her husband. She was reported as telling the court that her husband had beaten and abused her for years and that she had tried for a long time to find a solution to their problems:

She chose to make Tryal if she could prevail upon him to agree to a Final Separation, and pressed it upon him several times with great Earnestness; but he still refused it with Outrages of Language and Actions . . . finding herself without Remedy, in a distraction of Thoughts, and under the Affliction of Bodily Distempers, contracted by her said Husband's dissolute Course of Life, her Frailty was no longer able to resist the Temptation of dangerous Thoughts; sometimes [she] . . . was thinking to go into some other Part of the world and leave him; and other while she was tempted to think of Extremities either upon her Husband or upon her Self; and often she told her Husband plainly, That *she would kill him if he followed that course.*

One night Mary Hobry's husband came home drunk and beat and abused her. After he fell asleep, she strangled him, and later cut off his head and limbs in an unsuccessful attempt to dispose of the body. Killing her husband was a desperate act, the ultimate and most extreme of the remedies she herself outlined: mutually agreed separation, desertion, suicide, and murder. Mary Hobry was in no position to follow the precedent set by Lord Roos and seek a divorce by private Act of Parliament.

Informal separation, a solution Mary Hobry urged on her husband, but which he refused, was perhaps the most straightforward method of terminating a marriage in social terms. Each partner would live separately and independently, free of mutual social, economic, or sexual obligations. The main obstacle to it was that separation was of concern to the community and the authorities, for many legal codes required married people to live together, and the obligation was enforced when infractions came to light. In sixteenth- and seventeenth-century England, for example, the Anglican church was keen to ensure that only validly married couples lived together, and that once married they did live together, not separately or illicitly with others. Local church officials were encouraged to seek out offenders for prosecution during the periodic examinations (visitations) of individual dioceses. When John Whitgift, archbishop of Canterbury, visited the diocese of Chichester in 1585, the authorities were required to discover "whether anie married within the forbidden degrees . . . any separated [i.e., annulled] in that respect, do keep company still together; any lawfully married, which offensively live asunder, or which have married else-where; any man which has two wives, or woman two husbands." Similarly when Cardinal Pole visited the diocese of Canterbury in 1557 the investigation included: "Item. Whether any have put away their wives, being not lawfully divorced [i.e., separated]?"

To judge from the results of these two investigations, the English were an obedient people in matrimonial terms, for few irregularities were discovered. There was a better catch of matrimonial offenses, however, when Bishop Redman dragged his visitation net through the diocese of Norwich in 1597. Fourteen cases of husbands and wives not living together were prosecuted. One case, involving William and Agnes Matthew, charged that "they kepe not together, and he have absented himselfe from her companie theis iij [3] or iiij [4] years last past." Both were excommunicated for the offense. Another married man, Robert Crickner, was charged "for that he hath not kepte with Anne his wife by the space of theis foure yeares past, beinge lawfullie married to her." In his defense Crickner pleaded "that he have not kept with her for feare of his life," but despite this the couple were ordered to resume cohabitation.

It was an offense for couples not to live together in seventeenth-century New England, too. One protracted case involved Mary and Hugh Drury, who were hauled before the Suffolk County (Massachusetts) court in November 1676, where Mary was charged with "leaving the fellowship of her husband." Each alleged that the other had been guilty of matrimonial misdemeanors, and they were fined fifty shillings and placed under a thirty-pound bond of good behavior. In July of the following year they were back in court, where Mary was again charged with living apart from her husband. Although she argued that she found life with him intolerable – she alleged that he had been unable to consummate their marriage – she was fined five pounds and they were ordered to live together. Later that year Mary Drury applied to the Massachusetts superior court for a divorce, but she was turned down and the court "enjoyne[d] them both to live together according to the ordinance of God as man and wife."

How common mutually acceptable separations were, we cannot tell, for the only evidence we have of them is sporadic, and prosecutions depended on the diligence of communities and local officials in rooting them out. They were certainly a minor part of matrimonial enforcement. Even the 48 cases identified by one study of the Anglican church's investigations in Yorkshire, Chesire, Suffolk, and Somerset constituted only 2% of the individuals prosecuted, and they certainly paled against the 778 prosecutions for sexual immorality.

Separation is frequently difficult to distinguish from desertion, as the case of Mary and Hugh Drury shows. Did they separate or did she desert? The fact that the court initially fined both suggests that the offense was shared. It is often difficult to differentiate between absence and desertion, for many men's occupations, in particular, led to their being absent from home for months at a time; this was true of hawkers, pedlars, ships' crews, soldiers, coachmen, fishermen, merchants, and seasonal migrant workers. A traveling sieve salesman in Normandy, seeking a marriage dispensation in 1788, declared that his work required him to be away from home eight months of the year. Fishermen were often away for months, as were men who fought in the various wars of the early modern period. Who knew whether the men who never returned had died or had been detained against their will or whether they had simply decided not to return to their wives?

One source of information on desertion or separations is marriage registers that provide the address of the parents of the man and woman marrying. The civil marriage registers of revolutionary France required this information and reveal the number of cases in which the mother and father of a bride or groom had different addresses. The registers of Rouen in two sample years, the Year II (September 1793–September 1794) and the Year XII (September 1803–September 1804) [a new calendar, starting with the foundation of the French Republic in September 1792, was used in France until it was abandoned in 1806], show that of cases where both parents were still alive when their child married, a small percentage were living apart. In the Year II they accounted for 2%, in the Year XII, 7%. In most cases the address of one of the spouses was simply not known. In the Year XII, for instance, six fathers and one mother were absent, their whereabouts a mystery. Notations generally took the form "absent for ten years, address unknown" or, more simply, "absent for several years." Sometimes the military connection was explicit, as in the case of a man who "left this town in the Tenth Seine Inférieure battalion in October 1793" and had not returned when his daughter married in 1803.

Censuses also throw light on desertion when the enumerators note those who were *not* present in a household as well as those who were. A 1570 Norwich (England) census of the poor included listings such as this:

Jone, the wyf of a William Cayn, paynter, that was nott with hyr this 2 yeres, which Jone is of 40 yere, and spyn while warpe, and 3 childrene, 2 of them spyn, the other a yong son, and have dwelt here ever.

In the 1587 census of Warwick, twelve (14%) of the households defined as poor were headed by women who had been abandoned by their husbands.

In some places desertions were not discovered by census takers but announced to the community. In eighteenth-century America, for example, it was common for men whose wives had left them to advertise the fact in newspapers, with the warning that the husband would not be responsible for any debts the wife incurred. Some advertisements went into great detail:

Catherine Treen, the wife of the subscriber [advertiser] having, in violation of her solemn vow, behaved herself in the most disgraceful manner, by leaving her own place of abode, and living in a criminal state with a certain *William Collins*, a plaisterer ... her much injured husband, therefore, in justice to himself, thinks it absolutely necessary to forewarn all persons from trusting her on his account, being determined, after such flagrant proof of her prostitution, to pay no debts of her contracting.

A study by Herman Lantz located some 3,500 such advertisements in eighteenth-century newspapers, and he suggests that a study of all newspapers would find more than twice that number. Such a body of evidence illuminates the extent of marriage termination (assuming there were few reconciliations) behind the relatively small number of divorces in eighteenth-century America.

Separation, absence, and desertion were informal means of terminating a marriage in social and economic terms, and there is no evidence of any ritual to mark them. To this extent the English practice of wife sale was quite different for it involved a public ritual that notified the community that one relationship had ended and another had begun. The procedure was as the term *wife sale* suggests, that is, the selling of a wife by her husband to another man. The sale took the form of an auction and frequently took place at a place of economic exchange, especially a market place or fair, although taverns became increasingly popular in the nineteenth century. The fact that many accounts of wife sales describe the wife's being brought to market with a halter around her neck, like cattle brought for sale, has tended to reinforce the notion that wives were regarded as mere chattels to be disposed of by their husbands at will.

The first firmly recorded wife sale in England occurred in 1533, and there were sporadic reports in the seventeenth century. By the eighteenth century, however, there were 83 newspaper reports of them, and in the nineteenth century another 268 separate accounts. In all there is evidence of 387 wife sales in England (and other cases in Scotland, Wales, Ireland, France, and Nova Scotia), and although that is not a large number, we should bear in mind that there were as many wife sales as there were divorces by Act of Parliament in England between the mid-eighteenth and mid-nineteenth centuries.

Beneath the apparently simple commercial exchange of a woman from her husband to a new "owner," there were other currents. Although the sale was in the form of an auction, the wife going to the highest bidder, it is clear that in many cases the purchaser was determined in advance with the consent of the wife. Some of these cases were clearly associated with the wife's adultery – with her purchaser – so that the "sale" marked her transfer from her husband to her lover. (In a number of cases the woman had been living with her purchaser as his "housekeeper" before the sale.) If this were so, some of the other rituals associated with wife sales take on a quite different meaning. The purchase price might well be understood as being damages for the adultery, a popular equivalent of the settlements for criminal conversation described in the preceding chapter. As for the halter worn around the wife's neck, it might well have signified not that she was a commodity for sale, but that she had committed adultery. The halter in these cases was really a noose that symbolized the death penalty for adultery: In the seventeenth century punishments for adultery included whipping, branding, and being forced to wear a noose around the neck.

Some of the cases make it clear that wife sale was this form of transfer, not a commercial sale. In his study of wife selling, Menefee cites the example of a London shopkeeper who discovered a stranger in his wife's bedchamber: "After some altercation on the subject of this *rencontre*, the gallant [lover] proposed to purchase the wife, if she was offered for sale, in due form, in Smithfield market. To this the husband readily agreed." In other cases the consent of the wife to the sale is clear, even though there is no explicit evidence of a prior relationship to her purchaser. One husband, auctioning his wife, declared: "It is her wish as well as mine to part forever. I took her for my comfort and the good of my house, but she has become my tormentor, a domestic curse, a night invasion, and a daily devil." This does not seem to be the most effective way of getting a good price – or any sale at all, for that matter – and one cannot help but wonder if the husband did not allow himself the luxury of this patter because he was secure in the knowledge that it would not deter the purchaser in the crowd.

In some cases, there is no doubt, women were sold against their will, and in other cases no bids were received at all, evidence that the term *wife sale* includes a variety of phenomena. It could, however, be a form of popular divorce that publicly announced a rearrangement of cohabitation, a ceremony drawing the community's attention to a de facto "divorce" and "remarriage." The use of a halter and payment fit within this scenario, while the venues – markets and fairs – were just the sorts of places for public announcements to be made. Traditionally, marriages were of community interest and were public events, after all. The movement of wife sales into taverns in the course of the nineteenth century might have reflected the decline of such public celebrations or the preference for a more exclusively male audience; there is evidence of growing hostility by women toward wife sales. In the end, however, too little is known about wife sales to enable us to draw firm conclusions, and they remain an intriguing example of the alternatives resorted to in the absence of, or in preference to, formal divorce.

Wife sale was one form of customary divorce, perhaps the most notorious because it seemed to reduce the wife so dramatically to the status of a commodity to be sold and bought on the open market. Other forms of customary divorce were sanctioned in parts of the Western world, involving not contractual representations but rituals denoting the undoing of marriages. One form was the "besom divorce," a reversal of the "besom marriage" found in parts of Wales, America, and England. A besom, or broom, made of branches was placed aslant in the doorway of a house and, in the presence of witnesses, the couple intending to marry jumped over it. If both did so successfully, thus overcoming an obstacle and entering the house together (the husband first), they were deemed by the community to be married. If, within a year of marriage, they wanted to separate, the procedure was reversed. One account of a besom divorce runs as follows:

By jumping backwards over the besom the marriage was broken. The wife had the right to jump back, too. But this step had to be taken within the first year. Both of them, afterward, were free to marry again. If there was a child the father was responsible for its upkeep. In jumping backwards to break a marriage, as well as in jumping forward to make a marriage, if any part of the body touched the besom or the door post the effort was in vain. There were witnesses there to watch.

Appropriately, it is more difficult to negotiate a besom backward than it is forward. The custom thus reflected the historical reality that it is easier to enter matrimony than to exit from it.

Other communally recognized forms of divorce also involved reversals of marriage. In parts of England and Wales there was a belief that if a man failed to support his wife, she could return his ring and be free to marry again. But once we leave ritualized forms of coupling and uncoupling, we enter the world of consensual cohabitation and separation. Examples surfaced in the church courts and in various other sources, but they tend to appear random and patternless. If there was a common culture of cohabitation punctuated or interrupted by separations, it has largely eluded the historical record.

One form of informal divorce and remarriage that did attract the consistent attention of the authorities was bigamy, having two wives or husbands at once. In most jurisdictions bigamy was an offense in ecclesiastical, civil, or criminal law, although it was often treated quite leniently. We have seen that in some contexts bigamy was actually preferred to divorce followed by remarriage, and that it was recommended to Henry VIII instead of annulment. Under English church law, bigamy was punished by excommunication, the same penalty meted out to those who persistently failed to attend church or who, although married, refused to live together. Bigamy became a felony in England only in 1604.

Bigamy might well have been a common occurrence in traditional societies where there was no centralized registration of vital events and no ready access to marriage registers in different parts of one country, let alone those in other countries. But if bigamy was common, as some historians have suggested, it was either rarely discovered or, if discovered, was sufficiently sanctioned by local communities and authorities that they did not take action. Bigamists rarely appeared in judicial records. During an episcopal visitation of the diocese of Norwich in 1597, there were five prosecutions for bigamy, and a sixth man was hauled into court as being "suspected to have two wives." In one of the cases a woman was charged with aggravated bigamy: She had married two men but refused to live with either of them.

Yet bigamy could often be difficult to define. In some places it was customary to permit a remarriage when one spouse had been absent, without news, for seven years. The presumption was that a man (less often it involved a woman) who had been gone for so long was dead, although there was always some likelihood that he was alive, so that a remarriage would be bigamous. One woman in Ravenstone, Kent, who was charged with bigamy defended herself by saying that her husband had left her seven years earlier. In another case, this time in Somerset in 1807, a rector agreed to call the banns for a woman whose husband had left her to do military service in the East Indies and had not been heard of since that time. This case did not work out particularly well, for after the woman's remarriage, the first husband returned home and reclaimed his wife. She returned to live with him but continued to frequent her second husband, and this so disgusted the first that he again deserted his wife. He himself was reported to have married again soon afterward. Such cases reveal the potential complexity of matrimonial and quasi-matrimonial relationships when they were not clearly regulated by marriage and divorce laws that conferred the certainty of marital status.

The difficulties of detecting bigamy were compounded by the geographical mobility of people during periods of colonization and emigration. Bigamy was perceived as a problem in the American colonies, which attracted some married men who tried, and in some instances succeeded, to pass themselves off as bachelors. In 1680 Elizabeth

Stevens divorced her husband in Plymouth Colony after it was discovered that he had three wives in addition to her: one in Boston, one in Barbados, and another in an unspecified town in England. One migrant from England was caught before he could commit bigamy: John Tipping, a cordwainer, was prosecuted in Suffolk County (Massachusetts) "for making sute to some maids or women in order to marriage, hee having a wife in London." Tipping admitted being married, and although he denied courting or proposing to any woman in Massachusetts, the judges ordered him "to depart to his wife by next opportunity of Shipping," under penalty of twenty pounds if he failed to leave. In another case before the same court, one Henry Jackman was presented "for lying in saying hee was a single man and attempting marriage with severall, who hath since confessed hee had a wife in England."

The English men who migrated to America to start a new life and a new family might evoke some sympathy. They were unable to divorce in England, and their marriages there might well have been intolerable. Even so, bigamy could coexist with the most liberal divorce policies, as revolutionary France shows. Despite the ease of divorce there, and the fact that anyone who wanted to divorce could do so, bigamy persisted, as shown by an 1800 case from Yvetot, in Normandy. It involved Marie Grenier, a trader in brandy and cotton, who married Jean Menu in 1787. They separated informally several years later when Menu discovered that she had committed adultery, then were reconciled for a year until he learned that she was again being unfaithful to him. After divorce was legalized in 1792, Menu asked Grenier to agree to a divorce, but she refused. When he traveled to Yvetot in 1799, to ask her again to agree to a divorce, he found that she had been married for two years. She had spread the word that her first husband was dead, and so his arrival in the town aroused some interest and finally led to her arrest. The prosecutor pointed out that her crime was "all the more reprehensible in that this woman had only to agree to the divorce which her husband had constantly asked for. But as she knew that his intention was to remarry she refused out of pure perversity." Whether the crime was reprehensible or not, it was certainly incomprehensible, something on which Marie Grenier had time to reflect as she served a prison sentence for committing bigamy with criminal intent.

While Marie Grenier claimed that her first husband had died, other women and men went a step further and killed their spouses. Spouse murder was one of the most drastic alternatives to divorce; like divorce it was an effective way of terminating a marriage, and it reflected a high degree of dissatisfaction with married life. It was a rarely used alternative, however, not only because of the very character of the crime, but also because the probability of detection was high and the penalties harsh. Of eighteen men convicted of murdering members of their families in seventeenth-century Essex, twelve were executed, five were branded, and another suffered an unspecified penalty. In the area around Toulouse, in southwest France, where spouse murders represented between 7 and 26% of all homicides in the seventeenth and eighteenth centuries, husbands were generally hanged and wives burned to death, although some (where there were extenuating circumstances) were sentenced to life in the galleys or banished from the region.

Men predominated as spouse killers almost everywhere. In thirteenth-century England, wives outnumbered husbands as victims by more than two to one, and wives were more often the victims in seventeenth-century Essex as well. In the area around Toulouse in the eighteenth century, however, women were the perpetrators in three-quarters of the marital homicides, although in Toulouse itself husbands were the murderers in 60% of the cases. In Paris in the second half of the eighteenth century, wives were the victims in three out of four spouse murders. The general predominance of men in these crimes should be understood in terms of the general level of violence carried out by husbands against wives.

What circumstances provoked this ultimate response? In some cases the motive was financial. In 1738 Gill Smith, a Kentish apothecary, killed his wife for her insurance money. In other cases the reason was punishment for adultery – this was the motive in most of the murders in the Toulouse region. In general, however, the motives for murdering a spouse were as varied as the motives for divorce. Murder could be a substitute for divorce, as an American feminist magazine editorialized in 1868:

There is no hope for two people shackled in the manacles of an unhappy marriage, but a release by death; and no wonder each desires deliverance, and longs for the death of the other.... Wife murders are so common that one can scarcely take up a newspaper without finding one or more instances of this worst of all sins; and none but God can know how many men and women are murderers at heart.

If there was one response to marital unhappiness that was more desperate than murder, it was suicide. With murder there was always the possibility of escaping detection or that a plea of provocation or some other defense might be accepted. Not only did the suicide take his or her own life, but for Christians there were additional consequences. Suicides could not be buried in consecrated ground, and in France the bodies of suicides might be dragged through the streets, exposed by being hung up by the feet, then either buried in an unmarked grave or burned and the ashes thrown to the winds. Suicide might put an end to the misery of mundane matrimonial life, but it placed the soul in the greatest jeopardy.

It is impossible to know how many suicides were motivated by marital despair. A third of the suicides fished out of the Seine in Paris at the end of the eighteenth century were married, but there is simply not enough information on them for us to draw conclusions about the quality of their marriages. Reports of suicides in eighteenth- and nineteenth-century English periodicals suggest that only 68 out of some 1,500 suicides reported (4 or 5%) were motivated by matrimonial difficulties. One 1790 report concerned a London pork butcher who sent his wife and a friend on a day trip into the country. The couple took the opportunity to abscond together, and when the husband learned what had happened, he drowned himself in a tub.

Suicide and murder were desperate acts in their own way; prayer for deliverance from a brutal or oppressive spouse was another form of desperation. While it is likely that many husbands and wives, devout or not, sometimes found themselves invoking divine intercession for the removal of a spouse, only married women had a patron saint dedicated to that end. Saint Wilgefortis (known as Saint Uncumber in England, and Sainte Livrade in France) was the patron saint of women who wanted to get rid of their husbands. Wilgefortis was the daughter of a king of Portugal, and against her will she was ordered by her father to marry the king of Sicily. Wilgefortis prayed to become unattractive and as a result grew a moustache and beard. When the king of Sicily refused to marry her because of her hirsute condition, her father had her crucified to punish her for her disobedience. While she was on the cross she prayed that all those who remembered her suffering should be liberated (hence Livrade, from the Latin word "liberata") from all marital encumbrances (hence Uncumber). It became customary for women who wanted to be free of their husbands to make an offering of oats, perhaps, as Thomas More suggested, "because she should provide a horse for an evil husband to ride to the devil on."

Prayer, murder, suicide, bigamy, separation, jumping backward over a besom, desertion, wife sale, all were alternatives to formal divorce. We should not think of these as actions taken for want of access to legal divorce, not least because they coexisted in the past (and coexist today) with readily available divorce. Some husbands and wives, no doubt, would have preferred to divorce than to be driven to the extremes of murder and suicide. Other husbands and wives doubtless found these alternatives (or some of them, like customary divorces and mutually agreed separations) perfectly acceptable. While there is no way of measuring the extent of these alternatives (except in the relatively rare form of murder), we should be aware of their existence and of their diversity. They are a reminder that the formal divorces that are the focus of this book represent only one dimension of marital dissolutions in the past.

Suggestions for further reading

Anderson, Stuart, "Legislative Divorce – Law for the Aristocracy?" in G. R. Rubin and David Sugarman (eds.), *Law, Economy and Society: Essays in the History of English Law* (London, 1984), 412–44.

Cohen, Sheldon S., " 'To Parts of the World Unknown': The Circumstances of Divorce in Connecticut, 1750–1797," *Canadian Review of American Studies* 11 (1980), 257–93.

Cott, Nancy, "Divorce and the Changing Status of Women in Eighteenth-Century Massachusetts," *William and Mary Quarterly*, 3rd. ser., 33 (1976), 586–614.

Gillis, John, *For Better, For Worse: British Marriages 1600 to the Present* (New York, 1985).

Koehler, Lyle S., *A Search for Power: The "Weaker Sex" in Seventeenth-Century New England* (Urbana, Ill., 1980).

Lantz, Herman R., *Marital Incompatibility and Social Change in Early America* (Beverly Hills, 1976).

Menefee, Samuel Pyeatt, *Wives for Sale* (Oxford, 1981).

Phillips, Roderick, *Family Breakdown in Late Eighteenth-Century France: Divorces in Rouen, 1792–1803* (Oxford, 1980).

Sharpe, J. A., "Domestic Homicide in Early Modern England," *The Historical Journal* 24 (1981), 29–48.

Stone, Lawrence, *The Family, Marriage and Sex in England, 1500–1800* (London, 1977).

5

The meaning and context of marriage breakdown

So far this book has concentrated on a limited range of aspects of divorce: the evolution of attitudes, changes in divorce policies, and the development of law. Throughout, divorce law has been a constant point of reference, for justifiable reasons. Divorce is fundamentally a legal process. Marriages may be terminated by desertion, even dissolved informally, but we do not consider a couple divorced unless the dissolution of their marriage has been sanctioned by law. Not only that, but the law has historically had an influence on the extent of divorce at any given time. There is, of course, no divorce if there is no provision for it: There is no divorce in the Republic of Ireland, for example. Changes in divorce law, moreover, have affected divorce rates. When the liberal French divorce law of 1792 was replaced by the restrictive Napoleonic divorce code in 1803, the number of divorces fell appreciably: In Rouen, for example, there were sixty-seven divorces a year between 1795 and 1803, but only six a year between 1804 and 1816. Liberalizations of legislation, which have been much more common, have generally led to short-term as well as sustained increases in the divorce rate. When English law recognized grounds other than adultery for divorce in 1937, for instance, divorces quickly increased: There had been 5,044 in 1937, but by 1939 there were 8,248, an increase of 64%, almost all of which can be attributed simply to the legal change.

The state of legislation is only one of the variables that contribute to the incidence of divorce, however. Divorce is not an isolated legal event that is unrelated to other personal, familial, and social actions and circumstances, but is the final stage of a marital process. In crude and schematic terms the main stages of the process are marriage, marriage breakdown, the decision by one or both spouses to terminate the marriage, and finally its legal dissolution by divorce. Needless to say, far from all marriages experience this process; only a minority do so, as the divorce statistics attest. Some, however, might go to the point of breakdown without any manifestation of it in social or legal terms. Yet other broken marriages are terminated socially, the spouses living apart and independently without the intervention or imprimatur of the law. At each stage of the process, then, a proportion of the total population of marriages goes no further. Many marriages never break down (the concept of marriage breakdown is discussed later), others break down but show no outward sign of it, others break down and terminate informally. Finally other couples – those that contribute to the divorce rate – experience breakdown, decide to terminate the marriage, and can, and eventually do, divorce.

It is clear that divorces reflect only a proportion of marriages that break down, and that marriage breakdown and divorce, although intimately related, must be treated quite distinctly. All marriages have the potential to break down, but only broken-down marriages have the possibility of being dissolved by divorce. (We may exclude the minority of divorces "of convenience" that take place for fiscal, political, or other reasons.) Yet marriage breakdown and divorce are often confused, and there has long been an assumption that the rising divorce rate is indicative of an increasing incidence of marriage breakdown.

Much of the writing on divorce in modern society assumes one of two historical relationships between marriage breakdown and divorce. They are set out graphically in Figure 5.1. In the first model both marriage breakdown and divorce are depicted as increasing over time, such that the divorce trend more or less accurately reflects the trend of divorce. This was the model favored by late nineteenth-century conservatives who interpreted the rising divorce rate to mean that marriage breakdown was spreading. In the second model depicted in Figure 5.1 the incidence of marriage breakdown is stationary while divorces increase, with the effect that over time the divorce rate more and more closely resembles the extent of marriage breakdown in society. This is the view that was adopted by more liberal commentators whose point was that there was no need to be afraid of rising divorce rates because they were little more than an increasingly honest reflection of an existing situation: extensive marriage breakdown. Variations on the two models are possible, perhaps the most viable being a hybrid: An increase in both rates, with the divorce rate increasing faster than the rate of marriage breakdown.

The difficulty with these models is that although the divorce rates can be plotted with certainty, the extent of marriage breakdown at any point in time, and thus changes in its incidence over time, cannot. Unlike other sociodemographic variables, like fertility, marriage breakdown needs leave no historical record at all, let alone a systematic historical record that would enable changes over time and variations over space to be measured. True, some manifestations of marriage breakdown, such as bigamy, desertion, and the refusal of one or both spouses to cohabit, were offenses under ecclesiastical (and sometimes civil and criminal) law in England, America, and elsewhere. But the

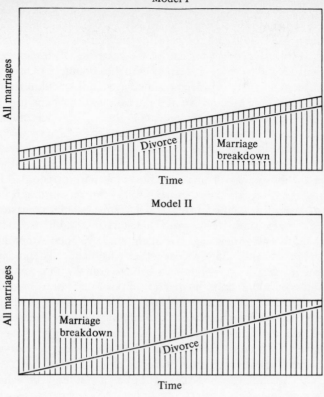

Figure 5.1

decision to prosecute offenders, and hence the likelihood of offenders' being recorded, depended on the discretion and zeal of the community, local officials, and magistrates.

There is an additional problem in determining the extent of marriage breakdown in the past, and that is the question of definition. For the most part marriage breakdown is not a matter of objectively defined conditions, circumstances, or behavior that can be determined by an outsider to a marriage. Rather, the decision whether an individual marriage has broken down is made by one or both the spouses involved. There are, it is true, some conditions or circumstances that we can reasonably argue implied marriage breakdown, independently of the perception of the spouses involved. The most important of these were discussed in the previous chapter, where types of informal divorce were discussed. Some of these, such as desertion and de facto separation at the agreement of both parties, were surely indicative of marriage breakdown, if the term is to have any meaning at all. Forms of popular divorce, such as wife sale, to take another example, hardly suggest that the vendor and the object of the transaction had a viable marriage. Little more need be said of the remedies of desperation – spouse murder and suicide – as responses to the conditions of marriage. Whether they were carefully premeditated acts and the culmination of years of misery or the impulsive and impassioned reactions to a particular situation in marriage, they reflected the will and determination to terminate the intolerable. In the perverse way of the historical record, these extreme solutions were also the most rare and the most systematically documented.

Other manifestations of marriage breakdown were recorded sporadically. Desertions are documented in some census sources; refusals to cohabit were prosecuted from time to time, but not consistently. Beyond these, however, lies a broad category of conditions, circumstances, and behavior that might or might not have been symptoms of marriage breakdown. Adultery, violence, cruelty, financial depredation, emotional indifference, all might have been tolerated within some marriages and not within others, so that it is impossible to draw hard-and-fast definitions of marriage breakdown. The individual perceptions and expectations of marriage that delineate the boundary between the tolerable and the intolerable, and thus define marriage breakdown, must therefore be taken into account when we attempt to assess the extent of marriage breakdown in societies past or present.

Marriage breakdown can be thought of as a condition or behavior on the part of one spouse, which one or both spouses regard as wholly inappropriate to their marriage. More formally we might describe it as an irremediable incongruence between the marital expectations of one or both spouses and the perceived state of the marriage. At any given time there have been individual and social views as to what kind of behavior was appropriate between husband and wife, and where the limits of tolerance should be drawn. Often, however, these views were implicit, and were expressed only when one spouse behaved in an inappropriate manner. In evidence before the divorce courts of revolutionary France, women frequently complained that their husbands had not treated them *maritalement,* a word that is best described by the phrase "in a manner appropriate between married persons." Husbands in some such cases, trying to dissuade their wives from divorce, promised to act *maritalement.* Before these men and women were faced with the behavior to which they took exception (adultery, violence, eviction, mental cruelty, and so on), it is unlikely that they could have expressed explicit and precise definitions of what was acceptable within marriage. But that they had possessed inherent notions is demonstrated by their divorce actions, which are, in themselves, eloquent statements that oppressive, abusive, and offensive behavior was not tolerable.

In order to understand definitions of marriage breakdown, then, it is evident that we must appreciate the expectations of marriage that women and men had in the past. In principle, behavior that failed to meet a spouse's expectations can be read as indicating marriage breakdown, but we must also take into account the perceived gravity, the frequency, and the context of the offense. Repetition of minor offenses, like a husband's coming home drunk, might be more acceptable than one instance of a major offense, such as overt adultery and extreme violence. We must also take into account changes in expectations during the life of a marriage. Men and women might well have modified their expectations in the light of experience, as reality overwhelmed their abstract notions of married life, or as economic conditions gave them no alternative but to tolerate behavior that they might, before marriage, have thought intolerable.

As we shall see, expectations of marriage have varied widely, not only over time, but also according to class and gender, and from individual to individual. Even so, it is possible to think of several main categories into which expectations have historically fallen: an expectation of a given standard of living (in terms of habitation and diet), even if it was very low; an expectation of sexual activity and sexual exclusivity within marriage, although men seem to have been excused from this more often than women; an expectation of a minimal degree of emotional compatibility, and that any violence should not be severe; and the expectation that each spouse would fulfill her or his labor and other economic responsibilities.

In the following pages, three issues will be examined: violence, adultery, and the emotions between spouses. All three figured prominently in divorces (the last in terms of emotional incompatibility), and from this and other evidence we should expect them to have been problematic aspects of marriage in the past. The question we ask here is whether the existence of violence, adultery, and emotional conflicts should be read as indicative of marriage breakdown.

There is some debate among historians as to the extent of marital violence – most of it inflicted on the wife – in the past. Keith Wrightson, for example, has argued that in seventeenth-century England "wife-battering was certainly known," but that there is no evidence that "physical violence was an accepted feature of lower-class marriages." Edward Shorter, on the other hand, has suggested that "as a practical matter, wife-beating was universal." There are, of course, immense problems of evidence. Wife beating came to the notice of the ecclesiastical and secular courts in divorce, separation, and other kinds of cases, but there is no way of knowing how representative the couples involved were of married couples generally. If wife beating were very common, and especially if it was a socially accepted form of behavior, it would be unlikely to turn up in court cases, except incidentally (as it does) or, perhaps, when the violence was particularly severe. The absence of systematic records of wife beating, then, might indicate that it was very common or very uncommon. My assessment is that it was common, and that a moderate level of violence within marriage was expected. Moreover, to the extent that it was expected, moderate violence could be accommodated within a workable marital relationship, and was not a sign of marriage breakdown.

There is certainly plenty of evidence for the social acceptability of wife beating. Most Western legal codes allowed husbands to inflict what was termed "moderate correction" on their wives. "Moderate" was not defined precisely, but there were various guidelines. The violence should not draw blood, for example, and if a stick were used, it should be no thicker than a man's thumb. (This is the origin of the term "rule of thumb.") As for "correction," the point was that a husband might not beat his wife at random or on a whim, but only in order to correct or punish her. "Moderate correction," then, should be interpreted as a part of the husband's general ability in law to control his wife. The underlying legal justification was that because a husband could be held legally responsible for his wife's actions, he should have the right to control her actions and to punish her when necessary. Such rights were recognized by canon law and the customary laws of medieval Europe. The thirteenth-century customary law of Beauvais (France) went further than most in holding that "it is licit for the man to beat his wife, without bringing about death or disablement, when she refuses her husband anything."

Such precepts were challenged in the sixteenth and seventeenth centuries. In England a number of commentators (many of them Puritans) argued that violence was not a legitimate part of a husband's authority. William Ames, for one, wrote that "it is by no means the part of any Husband, to correct his Wife with blowes," while Nathaniel Hardy argued that "surely we may account them besotted in their minds, or possessed with a divel who lay violent hands upon their wives." This shift of attitudes was manifested in a handful of legal codes. In Calvin's Geneva spouse beating was made a crime, and between 1564 and 1569 some sixty-one men and two women were convicted of it and excommunicated. Similarly, in Puritan Massachusetts the first code of law in 1641 emancipated married women from having to tolerate "bodily correction or stripes by her husband, unless it be in his owne defence upon her assault." In 1650 the law specified fines of up to ten pounds or a whipping for a husband who struck his wife or a wife her husband.

Limitations on the right of "moderate correction" were sparse, however, and even where they were applied it is not clear how much impact they might have had on deeply entrenched beliefs about the relative power of husband and wife. While it is possible to find popular support for the view that wife beating was wrong, there is more evidence of support for the traditional power of men to control their wives by force if necessary. Against the sixteenth-century German saying that "To strike a woman brings little honour to a man," we can range proverbs such as "Don't expect any good from an ass, a nut or a woman unless you have a stick in your hand" (Languedoc), and "Good or bad, the horse gets the spur. Good or bad, the wife gets the stick" (Provence).

There were challenges to the principle of moderate correction in some eighteenth-century legal codes, such as a 1790 French law that provided heavier penalties for assaults on women than for assaults on men. But it was not until the nineteenth century that legislation and case law began systematically to criminalize wife beating or to give beaten women some kind of redress in law. A series of laws in England in the second half of the nineteenth century enabled the courts to punish wife beaters with imprisonment, fines, and floggings. In 1878 aggravated assault was made a ground for a judicial separation, although it did not become a ground for divorce until 1937. In 1891 the husband's right to moderate correction was abolished.

There was a similar trend in the United States. An 1824 Mississippi judgment limited a husband to only "moderate chastisement in cases of emergency" (it did not define a matrimonial emergency), and the general tendency was to provide penalties for wife beating, despite the concern of some judges about the involvement of the courts in what they considered private matters. Even so, it was far from easy for women to obtain legal redress against their husbands. Judges in revolutionary France often insisted that the proper course of action for beaten married women was divorce, not an action against their husbands for assault. Individual judges elsewhere explicitly or implicitly upheld the traditional power of husbands. In the 1887 Yorkshire (England) assizes, for example, Judge Edward Cox heard the case of a woman who had been knocked down by her husband and then beaten about the head with a poker until the blood flowed. Her offense had been to go to "some amusement" without first getting her husband's permission. Despite the fact that the assault went well beyond the accepted limits of "moderate," and despite recent legislation against wife beating, the judge ruled that the husband's violence was within the bounds of "reasonable chastisement" and stated that it was a "waste of time to bring these cases before the jury." Other judges, however, condemned wife beating as "barbaric," calling the perpetrators "brutes," "tyrants," and "monsters."

The number of wife-beating cases that came before the courts was small, however. If we assume that the phenomenon was widespread, we should explain the rarity of cases in terms of the absence of effective laws, the recognition that laws were applied inconsistently, and the simple domestic reality that a wife's prosecuting her husband would almost certainly worsen, rather than improve, their relationship. It is possible, too, that some cases of wife beating – the more extreme examples, perhaps – were dealt with informally. Charivaris, community expressions of displeasure or outright opposition to an individual's behavior – focused increasingly on wife beating in nineteenth-century England. In one charivari in Surrey in the 1840s, a crowd surrounded the offender's dwelling and treated him to a deafening cacophony with whistles, horns, cowbells, rattles, pans, and gongs, and an orator declaimed several salutary verses, including:

> There is a man in this place.
> Has beat his wife! (*forte. A pause.*)
> Has beat his wife! (*fortissimo*)
> It is a very great shame and disgrace
> To all who in this place
> it is indeed upon my life!!

This example should not be taken to represent broad hostility toward wife beating throughout England, let alone the rest of the Western world. In some parts of France charivaris against wife beating were limited to the month of May, a special month in which women were to be treated without violence. The implication, however, is that husbands could beat their wives (moderately, one supposes) with impunity during the other eleven months.

It is impossible to recapture the precise circumstances that led one wife beater to be condemned by the community and another apparently to be ignored entirely. It is possible that notoriety for serious and frequent violence led to repercussions, whereas sporadic or less severe assaults were overlooked. If it is true that violence against wives was so widespread as to be the norm, only cases that were abnormally severe would have attracted community attention.

Evidence presented to courts at various places at different times suggests that domestic violence was tolerated to a certain (moderate) extent. In a revealing case in Rouen in the 1790s, two men who were invited to a friend's house for dinner stood by while their host swore at his wife, beat her about the arms and breast, and grabbed her by the throat. The sole sign of their disapproval was a comment by one of them that it was not proper to ill-treat one's wife in front of friends. They seem to have been more offended by this breach of etiquette than by the violence, and it was not until their host seized a knife and threatened to kill his wife (this would have been catastrophic for the meal, one assumes), that they restrained him. One important qualification to the image of toleration of wife beating that we can construct, however, is that men were more tolerant than women. Women neighbors appear to have intervened more quickly and readily than men in episodes of domestic violence. No doubt women empathized with another woman being beaten, while men were reluctant to interfere in another man's (and by extension, their own) "right" to beat his wife.

What were the attitudes of the husbands and wives involved in violence, as distinct from the attitudes of outsiders like neighbors, judges, and social commentators? They were as varied as we might expect. Some husbands were contrite (one "admitted his wrongs, and hopes that his wife will forget them"), whereas others defended themselves ("it was true that he had ill-treated her several times, but he had right to punish her when she did wrong"). Many women, the victims in most of these cases, showed by their divorce petitions and other legal actions that they did not tolerate being assaulted. In other cases, however, women implied that violence might be justified under certain circumstances (though not in others) or took responsibility for the violence. Some 10% of prosecutions in nineteenth-century London were dismissed because women refused to give evidence against their husbands. It is not difficult to understand why a wife would be reluctant to exacerbate her relationship with a man who had already demonstrated his readiness to resort to violence.

Bearing in mind that wife beating includes a wide range of behavior, from a single and relatively mild slap to persistent vicious assaults, the overall image of the phenomenon is complex. There is evidence at all levels of society of support for the traditional husbands' right of correction and of opposition to domestic violence in any form. It remains unclear whether there were class differences in wife beating: Opposition to it was expressed by middle- and upper-class commentators and by working-class charivaris. There was a prevailing belief by the middle classes that violence was more characteristic of the lower ("dangerous") classes, but the social pervasiveness of domestic violence in modern Western society should dissuade us from accepting these earlier beliefs uncritically. Nor, in attempting to determine the extent of wife beating, should we rely too heavily on reported cases. The number of reported domestic assaults in London declined in the second half of the nineteenth century, but it is possible that the decline was a result of wife beating's having been driven into the private recesses of the Victorian household, where it was less susceptible to social surveillance. It is possible, too, that increasingly severe penalties – by 1882, magistrates could have wife beaters flogged and exposed in a public pillory – deterred women from reporting violence more than it deterred men from committing it.

Throughout several centuries of discussion and legal changes, wife beating seems to have persisted relentlessly. We may quote or cite the findings of numerous historians to support this point. In colonial New England, wife beating is described as "tacitly condoned." In eighteenth-century Languedoc it is reported that "it is common enough to hear wives express the just fear they have of being chastised and beaten by their husbands. Among those of low and modest condition it seems that such apprehensions were accepted without suggesting abnormal brutality." In late nineteenth-century London wife beating is described as "normal" when it served a disciplinary function. Some industrial districts of England and Scotland were known as "kicking districts" after the incidence of assaults on wives. In Ireland in the early twentieth century childlessness was customarily blamed on the wife and entitled the husband to "bounce a boot off her now and then for it." Obstetrical literature often mentioned in passing that women miscarried after being beaten: "The doctors were not particularly distressed by wife-beating, but mentioned it casually along with other medical details." Wife beating, in short, seems to have been a constant in Western society, sometimes criticized and perhaps increasingly so with the passage of time, but always pervasive.

To insist on the normalcy of wife beating is not to condone it, but rather to describe the continuous presence of this coarse thread of behavior in the fabric of married life. Its apparent extent and social universality, however, raises the question whether this form of violence betokened marriage breakdown. We should have to conclude that insofar as violence did not fall outside the expectations of marriage, it was not a sign of breakdown. Given their experience of family life as daughters and witnesses to other marriages, women must have expected to be struck at some time by their husbands. It was, then, only when the degree or frequency of violence was significantly greater than expected that we can think of it as indicating breakdown. Even then we must allow for changes in expectations when considerations of children, financial dependence, or other factors simply gave women no alternative but to tolerate violence. In the final analysis we must accept that marriage breakdown is a matter of individual as of social definition, and that if a couple, in their own personal and social context, were able to integrate a degree of violence into their conceptions of an acceptable and functioning marriage, it would be arrogant of historians to contradict them.

Many of the same problems of evidence and interpretation are raised by the question of adultery in the past, although it might be argued that adultery, by striking at the principle of sexual exclusivity, was a less ambiguous attack than violence on the essence of Western marriage. Historically, sexual activity has been defined as licit or illicit mainly with reference to marriage. Sexual activity was licit if it took place between a married man and woman (married to each other, that is) and illicit if it took place before or outside marriage. This criterion was hardened as marriage itself became more closely defined, and from the late Middle Ages the law could be more precise in subjecting premarital sex (fornication) and extramarital sex (adultery) to legal sanctions.

In the hierarchy of sexual offenses adultery has generally been allotted a middle-ranking position. Crimes "against nature," such as sodomy and bestiality and sometimes homosexuality, have frequently been capital offenses. Fornication, in contrast, was treated relatively leniently by the church courts in particular, which rarely prescribed penalties more severe than temporary excommunication, public penance, and social humiliation. Adultery fell somewhere in between. It was not an offense against nature, but it was a crime against marriage, it generally involved deception, and it had a victim: the adulterer's spouse. At times, it is true, the penalties for adultery have belied its moderate ranking. In ancient Jewish law an adulterous woman was to be stoned to death, and there was a theme in Western social and legal thought that this penalty, prescribed in the Bible, ought to be resuscitated. As we have seen, in some parts of Europe (sixteenth-century Scotland and Geneva and Cromwellian England) and America (seventeenth-century New England), adultery was made a capital offense, especially when it involved a married woman; a married man who committed adultery with an unmarried woman generally received a lesser penalty.

These were especially harsh penalties, however. In sixteenth-century England the ecclesiastical courts meted out punishments involving public penance: The guilty parties had to stand in white sheets in the town marketplace on market days or in church on two or three consecutive Sundays. If the woman became pregnant as a result of an adulterous relationship, however, the penalties might include a whipping and imprisonment, but in such cases the penalty reflected additional punishment for producing a child that might be a burden on the community. In France penalties for adultery varied from place to place and according to ecclesiastical and civil laws. In general, though, an adulterous woman could be imprisoned in a convent for two years, while adultery by a man was overlooked unless it were aggravated in some way. The customary law of Normandy, for example, provided no recourse for a wife unless her adulterous husband brought his accomplice into the marital home. Adultery was also actionable at civil law. It was a ground for separation in various places, as we have seen, and in England a husband could obtain damages for "criminal conversation" from his adulterous wife's accomplice.

The continuity and universality of provisions in law for action to be taken against adultery highlights its historical status as an offense against marriage. Only very recently have some revisions of family law abandoned explicit references to adultery, but even modern divorce codes that are based on no-fault principles (see Chapter 8) sometimes retain adultery as a unique fault-based ground. The endurance of this legal status of adultery might lead us to suppose that an act of adultery was almost necessarily a symptom of marriage breakdown. Yet we should also note that rarely has adultery led to mandatory divorce. In almost all codes where adultery has been a ground for divorce, the policy has been to attempt to dissuade the petitioner from pursuing the divorce. Mandatory delays for attempts at reconciliation have often been provided, giving the impression that although adultery could not be reconciled with marriage in the abstract, it could be accommodated within individual marriages.

This does not appear to have been entirely unrealistic, for we know that there were many more reported acts of adultery than there were proceedings for separation or divorce. Reported cases of adultery must, themselves, have represented only a fraction of cases known to the spouses of adulterous men and women. We must ask whether this disparity, this tendency not to take action to divorce or separate, does not indicate such a level of tolerance of adultery that it would be wrong to think of it as indicative of marriage breakdown.

It is important to recall that attitudes toward adultery have historically been qualified in various ways. Most laws embodied the double standard of morality by focusing solely or primarily on adultery by women. Adultery by a wife was thought to be more dangerous, and thus more reprehensible, because it carried the risk of pregnancy and the uncertainty as to the paternity of any child the woman bore. There were some exceptions, more even-handed approaches to adultery, to the double standard in strict legal or doctrinal terms, but even in these cases the application tended to weigh more heavily on women.

Yet even within the more punitive approach to adultery by a married woman there was room for a great deal of discretion. Women were treated more harshly when their adultery resulted in pregnancy: Here was a definite incentive for women in extramarital relationships to practice some kind of contraception. Second, notoriety seems to have provoked a more vigorous reaction. Needless to say, discreet adultery, known only to the two people involved, was safe from prosecution and public sanction, and it was also at minor risk when knowledge of it was confined to the offenders and their spouses. Even adultery that was the subject of local rumor or suspicion might escape too much attention from the authorities, because officials generally demanded hard evidence and were rarely prepared to proceed on the basis of hearsay. But blatant and public adultery, the flaunting of an illicit relationship, was perceived as a direct affront, perhaps as a challenge, to community standards, and it was likely that the challenge would be taken up. Gillis notes that adultery was usually tolerated among the popular classes in Britain in the sixteenth and seventeenth centuries, but only if it were "sufficiently discreet and caused no public scandal." The principle of scandal was incorporated in the 1792 French divorce law, which referred not to adultery as a ground but to "notorious" immorality.

The acceptability of adultery within individual marriages varied a great deal. One woman, seeking divorce in Rouen during the revolution, lived in the same house for five years with her husband, his mistress, and their children. In more than half the cases in Rouen where women divorced their husbands for reason of adultery in fact, they had lived à trois for periods of time. Such cases indicate considerable, but finite, tolerance of adultery. How many cases did not come to court we cannot tell, although figures from seventeenth-century New England are revealing. There, 308 men and women were convicted of adultery or "adulterous carriage" (which included attempted seduction), but only 40 divorces were obtained on these grounds. This means that 268 men and women [87% of cases where there was not only adultery, but publicly known adultery (because of the trial)], appeared to be able to reconcile their partners' behavior with an acceptable marriage.

The range of individual reactions to adultery is demonstrated in Quaife's study of peasant marriages in seventeenth-century Somerset (England). Some husbands attacked their wives' lovers with knives and other weapons; others banished the accomplice from the house. Some men beat their adulterous wives, others evicted them or brought them (or tried to bring them) before the church court. Others, however, did nothing or evinced little more than mild irritation. One man, "finding his workmate attempting his wife could only respond with annoyance – 'this is no good for you to call me forth to go to work and then come back to misuse my wife.' The two men then left for work." So lax were some husbands in taking formal action against their adulterous wives that the community did it for them, and many of the cases that appeared before the courts represented the attempts of the community to discipline wives whose husbands had failed to act. In such cases we are a long way from the image of the husband as the jealous defender of his ownership of his wife's body.

Were there class differences in attitudes toward adultery? There is a common view that sexual libertinism was established in the upper social strata during the seventeenth and eighteenth centuries. Lady Mary Wortley Montagu held in the eighteenth century that "the appellation of rake is as genteel in a woman as a man of quality." As if to put distance between their behavior and the adultery that had as recently as the 1650s been a capital offense, English practitioners of the adulterous arts adopted the euphemism "gallantry" to describe their activities. In itself this indicated a more tolerant, even an approving attitude, toward extramarital sexual relationships. Elsewhere, too, there were signs of growing lenience toward adultery. In New England penalties for adultery were reduced at the end of the seventeenth century, and in France and Scotland the courts imposed noticeably less severe sentences. In time there was a reaction against what were regarded as excessively permissive policies, such that in both Spain and France in the early nineteenth century, a man who discovered his wife in the act of adultery might kill her with impunity.

Legal sanctions against adultery are not necessarily a very helpful guide to behavior, however. When adultery was made a capital offense in England in 1650, an unambiguous sign of official hostility to adultery, there was a mere handful of convictions, no doubt because juries thought the penalty inappropriate to the offense and refused to convict. There is no way of gauging the extent of adultery at any given time, nor of changes in its incidence, despite the many affirmations from all periods that adultery was never more common. My own feeling is that even if most married men and women were not adulterous at some time, a substantial minority of them were, and men more often than women. Moreover, it seems that adultery was incorporated within the expectations of marriage or was tolerated when it occurred, or was discovered, on an ad hoc basis. The first marquis of Halifax advised his daughter at the end of the seventeenth century that "next to the danger of committing that fault [adultery] yourself, the greatest is that of seeing it in your husband." The message was clear: A wife should expect her husband to be unfaithful, and she should overlook it; adultery did not adversely affect a marriage.

This advice seems to have been followed, not only in England, not only in the late seventeenth century, and not only among the elites; everywhere, on the contrary, recorded actions against adultery were rare and seem to have been provoked most often by conditions that aggravated the offense, rather than by the offense alone. Like marital violence, then, adultery *could* indicate marriage breakdown, but it did not necessarily do so.

The third aspect of marital relationships we examine in terms of marriage breakdown is their emotional content: the intensity of love, passion, affection, friendship, coolness, antipathy, hatred, or sheer indifference that characterized the daily relations and social transactions between husband and wife. It is an assumption in modern Western society that love is such an essential element of marriage that its disappearance threatens the survival of a marriage, no matter how satisfactory it might be in financial, social, or other respects. The insistence on romantic love as a precondition and integral part of marriage is, however, a relatively recent development. One implication of this is that intensely emotional relationships were less important to married couples in the past, that expectations of what is today called "emotional fulfillment" were minimal, and that the emotional content of marriage had as little to do with marriage breakdown as it had with marriage formation.

There is a vigorous debate among historians about the relative importance of emotional and what are generally called "interest" factors (social status, financial security, and so on) in the formation of marriages in the past. There is general agreement, however, that over time spouses chose each other increasingly on the basis of personal qualities than in terms of the considerations of interest, and that responsibility for choosing marriage partners shifted to the individual concerned, so that others (such as their parents) played a diminishing role.

Within these general trends there is disagreement as to the timing of change and to the social class that was its leading edge. Edward Shorter, for example, has argued that young men and women of the eighteenth-century working class were critical, while Lawrence Stone's account of the rise of romantic love in England stresses the early place of the eighteenth-century gentry and squirarchy in "accept[ing] the need for affection" within marriage. Other historians, however, have challenged the notion that romantic love developed only as late as the eighteenth century. A study of a seventeenth-century English astrologer, for instance, showed that many of his clients suffered stresses in courtship and marriage and attributed them to problems arising from love.

It is important to understand the notion of the rise of romantic love not in starkly simplistic terms as a complete rejection of one set of criteria for marriage (interest) by another (love), but as movement within a spectrum of variables, a gradual shift of emphasis. Moreover, it is important to recognize that interest factors and love need not be mutually exclusive, in any case. The way in which men and women choose marriage partners is neither random nor wholly calculated, but a subtle process, conscious and unconscious, of selection and rejection in which various factors – social, economic, sexual, and emotional – interact with one another. To this extent the sharp dichotomy between interest and affective considerations is a false one.

Still, the shift of emphasis from interest to affective criteria in choosing a spouse seems established. It cannot be established by a simple accumulation of examples, because it is only too easy to find instances of marriage for love alone and marriages simply for financial gain. Series of continuous data, however, do demonstrate the direction of change. A study by Margaret Darrow of petitions for dispensations from the Catholic church's impediments to marriage showed that in Montauban (France) only 9% before 1770 cited emotional attachment as a reason for marriage, while 41% after 1770 did so. What is more the pattern was located in petitions from all social strata: peasants, workers, bourgeois, and nobles.

Even if there is no common timing of change or leading social group, the simple matter of a shift toward emphasizing emotion in choosing a spouse has important implications for an understanding of marriage breakdown. What it suggests is that as emotional compatibility and love became increasingly important, they entered expectations of marriage and in this way became a factor involved in marriage breakdown, defined as the failure to fulfill expectations. On the other hand, the further back we go in history, the less important affective factors were in marriage formation and the less likely they were to be involved in marriage breakdown. Put another way, in traditional Western society, emotions simply had a lower profile in the making and unmaking of marriages. This is an extremely crude formulation of an extremely complex process, of course, and we should constantly remember to think in terms of gradual shifts in emphasis, not in sudden and radical changes.

Sentiments within marriage tend thus to parallel violence and adultery as far as their roles in marriage breakdown in the past are concerned. It is difficult to enter the minds and share the feelings of women and men in earlier times, just as it is difficult to understand what motivates our contemporaries to enter, continue, and terminate their marriages. What is most striking about husbands and wives in traditional society is the flexibility and adaptability of their expectations of marriage. They seem to have accommodated within their definitions of marriage a wide range of conditions and behavior, such that they defined marriage breakdown in a very restrictive manner, women even more restrictively than men.

One implication of these potentially very low expectations is that marriages did not break down for trifling reasons. Husbands did not leave their wives, or wives their husbands, because of an isolated act of violence, an abusive word or two, or because the relationship was not ideal. It is difficult, however, to identify the roots of these attitudes and expectations that permitted women and men to put up with conditions that were often so far from ideal. Socialization and emulation, and the experiences of family life by participation and observation, were important, more important to the illiterate mass of the population than treatises, conduct-books, and legal commentaries. But apart from experience and ideology, a complex of material and other influences made the dissolution of marriage (de facto or formal) simply inconceivable for most men and women in traditional European society.

One of the most important of these institutions was the family or marital economy. For the mass of the population in traditional Western society, marriage was an economic partnership, the nucleus of the family economy that linked all members of a household in a network of economic and social relationships in addition to their kinship ties. In crude terms it was a small-scale economy in which members of the family – children and adults, female and male – worked together cooperatively as a unit of production. The most common form was the farming family economy in which all members of the family were expected to work, even though tasks were often allotted to them on the basis of sex and age. Adult males took responsibility for the tasks demanding the most physical strength, women's work centered on the household and its immediate environs (and included responsibilities such as baking, brewing, and milking), and children were allotted tasks within their physical and intellectual capabilities. This division and complementarity of work was common to all forms of activity, and the essence of the couple as an economic partnership was captured in a Scandinavian proverb: "No man can be a fisherman without a wife." Domestic textile production similarly required a family economic partnership, as women, men, and children prepared the raw materials (such as carding wool), spun the yarn, and wove the cloth, all as a cooperative effort.

One characteristic of the preindustrial family economy was that it was seldom a wage economy. Individuals did not receive an individual wage or other return for their work but benefited from the collective output and income of the household. This tended to reinforce the interdependence of household members, and to make individuals reliant upon the economic well-being of the group. As far as the married couple was concerned, the family economy reinforced the mutuality of their partnership. Although marriage and the family performed a wide range of functions, such as socialization, welfare, and education, and were bonded by emotional ties of varying intensity, the economic relationships were fundamental because individuals and the group alike were dependent on them for sheer survival.

The important point to note here is that the family economy acted as a deterrent to separation and the voluntary dissolution of a marriage. The consequences that followed the death of one of the spouses, the removal of an essential part of the family economy, are indicative of what would follow divorce. Olwen Hufton has described the loss of either husband or wife as "wreck[ing] the entire fabric of the family economy," and Peter Laslett has observed that the death of the husband "threatened an end to the familial undertaking as surely as the beginning of marriage meant its foundation." These perspectives enable us to understand why widows and widowers remarried so rapidly in traditional society. Widowers often married within a year of being widowed, while widows took somewhat longer: In one peasant community in eighteenth-century France, almost half the widowers had married within seven months of their wives' deaths, and more than a third of widows had remarried within eighteen months. Such rapidity is explicable in terms of the need to reconstitute the family economy as quickly as possible, particularly when there were children for which to provide.

Clearly, the disruption of a marriage by death had potentially disastrous consequences for the family economy, and we should expect similar or even worse consequences to flow from separation, particularly informal separation. A woman whose husband deserted her could not reconstitute the economy by marrying, as a widow could. Nor would there be the certainty of property ownership that the laws of inheritance provided. Indeed, the effects of absence must have been a powerful deterrent against one spouse's reporting the other to the authorities for committing an offense, such as adultery by the wife, that might lead to imprisonment. Against the satisfaction a husband might gain by having his unfaithful wife's illicit ardor cooled by a period in jail, he had to weigh the difficulties her absence would surely cause in domestic and other productive work.

If we accept that the family economy – a network of property and productive relations – could be a deterrent to separation, we might expect poor families to be more prone to marriage breakdown and separation. There is, indeed, evidence of an association of poverty and desertion, often cases where an unemployed husband and father left his family. Many of these men appear to have left in search of work, but then failed to return. Others simply abandoned their families. However, even when families were not cast into poverty, and where there were the material constraints of the family economy, men were able to desert their families when conditions favored them. In southeastern England in the eighteenth and nineteenth centuries, for example, desertion was most common in September and the harvesttime. According to K. D. M. Snell, in *Annals of the Labouring Poor*, "such seasonality owed more to favourable weather and the high wages of summer and harvest (the latter paid in September) which helped allow the man to desert." The harvest period thus provided a short-term labor market in the rural economy that acted as a financial bridge, permitting some men to free themselves from the restrictions imposed by the family economy.

The way the family economy worked to deter separation must remain schematic and somewhat speculative. To the extent that it was a barrier to separation, however, it had greater effect on wives than on husbands. A solitary woman was financially and socially far more vulnerable than a solitary man. Even if she could find work, she could expect to earn low wages, scarcely enough to support herself, and certainly not enough to support any children. A woman contemplating leaving her husband had only to look about her, at the poverty-stricken widows and deserted wives, for a glimpse of her future as a sole parent with dependent children.

The family economy also worked more effectively as a deterrent to separation in rural areas than in towns and cities. An urban environment offered something approaching a labor market where women and men might find work of some kind. Wage labor was more common in the towns than in the countryside, and towns also offered stocks of casual accommodation, unlike the rural areas where habitation was familial. Such factors must be part of our understanding of the historically higher divorce rates in cities than in the rural areas, where separation of any kind, formal or informal, involved a massive disruption in terms of domicile and occupation. Under the 1792 French divorce law, as we have seen, the few rural women who divorced quickly moved to the nearest town, which offered accommodation and employment. In the handful of divorces in Rouen where the couple had interlocked occupations, the wife was forced to change job after divorce. In one of these cases, husband and wife were candlemakers, and although the husband remained in that work after divorce, his former wife found employment in the city's textile industry.

Not only would a woman living apart from her husband in traditional society have difficulties finding work and accommodation, but she was by no means assured of being able to own property in her own right. Under most legal codes in Western society married women had very limited or no property rights, and any property they owned before marriage or brought to the marriage was transferred in title or trust to their husbands. Here was another sense in which widows were in a better position than women who left their husbands, for widows were provided for by inheritance, and might also, as we have noted, anticipate remarriage as another way of improving their economic position.

In general, then, the family economy and the associated legal circumstances of traditional society militated against separation. One spouse was unlikely to leave the other unless he or she had some viable alternative to the marriage in terms of work and accommodation – it was a matter of sheer survival. These alternatives were not readily provided by the family-based preindustrial economy, particularly in rural areas, and it was women who were particularly affected by the absence of alternatives, such that while married men and women were locked into marriage by material constraints, married women were especially so. To this extent we should expect separation to have increased as the force of the constraints weakened with the decline of the traditional family economy. As the Western world industrialized and urbanized from the late eighteenth century, and especially during the nineteenth century, the labor market grew, the wage economy penetrated most sectors of the economy, and the most fundamental deterrents to separation gradually lost their force.

We should by no means exaggerate the liberating effect of industrial and other employment for women, children, and men, but neither should we underestimate them. There were frequent complaints in the nineteenth century that employment and individual incomes were leading young people to shrug off parental authority. An investigation in midcentury England was told that "this premature independence too often induces them [children of sixteen to eighteen years] to quit their parents' houses, that they may be at liberty to follow their own inclinations." The same loosening of family ties must have affected marriages. The spread of wage labor, the labor market, and greater geographical mobility all gave husbands and wives greater opportunities to consider breaking up their marriages, deserting, or separating amicably – all of this allowing that we should not minimize the remaining economic, social, and ideological constraints, the effects of low wages, and the sense of obligation to family.

Yet while there is evidence that men increasingly turned to desertion in order to escape marriages and other relationships (such as engagements), women were deterred by other factors. Industrialization did not expand women's employment opportunities as much as it did men's. In most countries the rate of married women's employment was low (it was only about 10% in Germany throughout the nineteenth century), and in many places it even declined. In England, one in four married women was employed at midcentury, but by 1911 only one in ten was. There, as elsewhere in Western society, the great mass of women workers were young and unmarried; in late nineteenth-century New York and Chicago, no more than 5% of working-class married women had paid work outside the home. Many married women, it is true, worked at home, taking in boarders, minding children, and so on, but such sources of income, far from providing a platform for independence, depended on their staying in the home. Even so, changes in the economy and the growth of a labor market did provide greater employment opportunities during the nineteenth century. Few married women had an independent income, but the possibilities for one had increased, and it is possible that married women who had separated (or who were planning to) comprised a significant proportion of the small percentage of married women in employment.

In terms of the viability of separation, then, industrialization produced no sudden and radical transformation of the family economy. Men and women were less constrained by it, but they were still constrained, and this was especially true of women. In many rural areas, too, the limitations imposed by the traditional family economy remained strong. Two matrimonial advertisements from early twentieth-century New Zealand highlight the persistence of the notion that husband and wife were an economic partnership as much as anything. One reads: "A Respectable Man, 39, about to purchase a respectable little farm, would like to meet a Respectable Protestant woman, with view to Matrimony; an experienced country woman with a little means preferred," while the other was even more direct: "Young gentleman in business wishes to meet Lady with £500 to £1,000, view Partnership and Matrimony."

As important as the family economy was, there were other social and economic constraints in traditional society that bound husband and wife together. One that has already been alluded to was the prospect of solitary life, such as could be seen in the lot of widows and widowers who failed to remarry. High mortality rates produced a relatively high proportion of widowed men and women, and the economic conditions into which they were thrown were far from attractive, particularly for women. To be sure, some widows who did not remarry were well-off in their own right or inherited substantial or adequate resources from their husbands, and still others took over the ownership and operation of their husbands' trades and businesses. A woman who simply left her husband, however, could expect to take nothing with her, and was in the position of a widow left without resources. Such women, no matter how well they had survived in marriage, fell rapidly into the most dire poverty. Widows, especially those with children, formed a distinct group within the poor and destitute, and often ended up on the very margins of society, as criminals, vagrants, and prostitutes.

The resources widows might turn to were limited. In Scandinavia there were some customary provisions for what were in effect pensions: In fishing communities, for example, where the rate of widowhood was high because of the loss of fishermen at sea, a fisherman's widow and children were entitled to a share of the catch from other fishermen, usually from the crew of which her husband had been a member. In other places the churches and the state provided charitable relief for the poor, but although charity might be granted to a widow and her children, it was less likely to be given to a woman who had left her husband and was considered, for that reason, to have brought her distress upon herself. In seventeenth-century New England poor widows were often quite well looked after, but other needy women sometimes received no assistance until they had reached the depths of poverty, having to wear rags, sleep on straw, and eat seaweed. The plight of a woman who left her husband would have been aggravated if, as was most likely, she also had to leave the community where she had lived with him. In many parts of Europe and colonial America the authorities refused to let solitary women take up residence for fear that they would become a burden on the community; poor women were warned out of town, just as women suspected of being immoral were.

The living conditions of widows varied immensely according to their own resources and local circumstances, but in almost all cases the position of a solitary, still-married woman would have been even more desperate than that of a widow. She would have no inheritance, no legal right to resources, and no legal opportunity to marry. We must wonder at the circumstances under which any woman would opt for such a future, one whose outlines must have been clear as she considered her unhappiness within marriage. Widows were not responsible for the plight into which their husbands' deaths plunged them, but married women at least had the option of remaining in their homes, no matter how unhappy they were. It would have to have been utterly appalling for them to exchange it for a precarious extramarital existence of grinding poverty and social rejection.

One specific indication of social attitudes toward solitary women was the witch hunts of the sixteenth and seventeenth centuries. Study after study of witchcraft trials has demonstrated the association of the witch with what Peter Laslett has called "the lonely old widowed woman." In general, widowed and unmarried women were overrepresented among women accused as witches, while married women were underrepresented in terms of their proportion in the adult female population. The fact that women lived alone, outside the authority of household and husband, was perceived as making them easy targets for the devil. In addition, male suspicion and fear of female sexuality made it unthinkable that a woman could live without a sexual partner: If there was no husband present, how much more probable it was that her lover might be the devil himself. To make this association of solitary living and accusations of witchcraft is not to suggest that women consciously took it into consideration when they considered leaving their husbands, but it does highlight the perilous social status of the woman who lived alone.

In general, the alternatives to living within one's family – or within a family of some sort – were very limited, and this no doubt explains why there were so few solitary dwellers in Western societies. Only about one percent of adults lived alone in the hundred English communities (1574–1821) analyzed by Peter Laslett, and the point is highlighted by a study showing that in 1820 in Indiana, a frontier state peopled by newcomers, only 2.7% of households were occupied by a solitary dweller. Married women who left their homes might have found accommodation with other families, although it is doubtful that a married woman would be welcome as a guest or lodger. They might return to live with their parents, but we should bear in mind that the relative brevity of life before the nineteenth century meant that about half the women had lost one parent by the time they married. There was, of course, the possibility of forming an illicit, cohabiting relationship with another man, but there was still the problem of accommodation immediately after separation unless the extramarital relationship had been formed before separation. Perhaps wife sales responded to these kinds of circumstance.

Overall, there were immense practical obstacles to separating or leaving one's spouse: Apart from the pressure communities might apply against marriage breakdown, the possibility of official action to force a couple to live together, and the religious and cultural pressures to conform to marriage, the consequences in terms of sheer survival were daunting and must have been a strong deterrent to separation.

They must, too, have borne more strongly on women than men. Men were socially less vulnerable and more mobile and had opportunities, no matter how unpleasant, that were closed to women: Men could, for example, join the army or go to sea. The evidence of men's wider opportunities lies in their far higher rate of marital desertion. In terms of more strictly defined family constraints, too, women were more affected. Under most Western legal codes, the husband could control his wife's place of residence, and that meant compelling her to return home if she tried to leave. Children, too, seem to have acted more as a deterrent to desertion by women than by men.

Bearing in mind that this discussion has been general and in some places schematic, the image of the traditional family that emerges is one that quite clearly reduced to a minimum the potential for separation. We should ask, then, whether these conditions did not affect expectations of marriage and definitions of marriage breakdown. Is it not reasonable to expect that with only rare exceptions women and men, particularly women, were inclined to accept the conditions that married life offered? No doubt many marriages were acceptable in any case, but even in those cases where there was tension, conflict, and unhappiness, and even abuse and oppression, the simple absence of viable alternatives must have led to an acceptance of prevailing conditions. In this context we should recall the earlier discussion of expectations of marriage and definitions of marriage breakdown, where it was suggested that men and women had flexible and potentially very low expectations of marriage and high levels of tolerance of all manner of behavior and conditions. If we seek the origins of these expectations, surely they are to be found in the conditions of traditional society that all but excluded any alternative to married life once one had married and before one's spouse had died.

There was, in fact, a good deal of advice to the effect that unhappy husbands and wives should simply learn to live together because they had no alternative. Early in the seventeenth century Alexander Niccholes wrote that because marriage was a permanent relationship,

therefore as wise prisoners inclosed in narrow roomes sute their mindes to their limites, and not, impatient they can go no further, augment their paine by knocking their heads against the walles, so should the wisedom both of Husbands and Wives...beare [marriage] with patience and content...and not storme against that which will but the deeper plunge them into their own misery.

Prison might not be an attractive metaphor for marriage, but it at least captures the spirit of the way social, economic, and cultural conditions locked husbands and wives into their marriages. The same point, however, was made in somewhat gentler terms by David Hume in the eighteenth century. Marriages, he wrote, would be happier if divorce were not possible, for the heart of man "naturally submits to necessity, and soon loses an inclination, when there appears an absolute impossibility of gratifying it." What is suggested in this chapter is that the inclination to separate or desert dissipated in the face of the near impossibility of living outside marriage.

But did marriages not break down then, and did separations not take place? Clearly they did, but there is debate as to their extent. Olwen Hufton writes of the poor of eighteenth-century France that "the broken home was a common phenomenon," almost always because the husband and father deserted. Lawrence Stone suggests for England that desertion "must have been a not infrequent occurrence among the poor." There is, of course, a problem of evidence in that only separations that came to the notice of authorities entered the historical record, and in the end we can only guess at the real incidence of informal marital separation. Even so, several sources indicate that desertion and separation affected only a small proportion of marriages. Surveys of marriage registers in late eighteenth-century and early nineteenth-century Rouen (France) produced findings that separations occurred in 2% and 7% of marriages, respectively. In Metz, the 1806 census revealed 132 abandoned wives out of approximately 6,565 married women, or about 2%. In the southeastern counties of England in the eighteenth century, 4 or 5% of wives in the poor strata had been deserted by their husbands. A late sixteenth-century census of the poor in Norwich (England) showed that 8% of poor wives had been deserted by their husbands. Perhaps these figures indicate the kind of incidence of desertion and separation we should expect to find generally. We should note that they relate to the poorer sections of society and to periods of social and military turmoil, both of which might have increased the possibility of desertion. What is striking is that the range of 2–8%, with a concentration around 2–5%, hardly suggests that desertion or separation was common. Such figures pale against modern divorce rates and indicate that whatever the timing of change, marriage breakdown and separation was far less common in the past than it is in the present.

What changes have taken place that might explain an increase in marriage breakdown and separation in Western society? One of the most common explanations is that in traditional society marriages were soon cut short by the death of one of the spouses, and as life expectancy and the potential duration of marriage increased, divorce stepped in as a replacement for death. Lawrence Stone puts it this way:

It looks very much as if modern divorce is little more than a functional substitute for death. The decline of the adult mortality rate after the late eighteenth century, by prolonging the expected duration of marriage to unprecedented lengths, eventually forced Western society to adopt the institutional escape-hatch of divorce.

The evidence of the brevity of many marriages in the past is quite overwhelming, although it must be qualified. In some parishes in eighteenth-century Sweden, for example, the average duration of peasant and working-class marriages was between twelve and fifteen years, while in preindustrial England marriages lasted about twenty years on average before either husband or wife died. As ages at marriage have fallen and life expectancy has risen in the last two centuries, the potential duration of marriage has increased from the fifteen or twenty years of the eighteenth century to about thirty-five years in 1900 to almost fifty years today, when people marry in their early twenties and men expect to live until their early seventies. In short, marriages begun in recent years have the potential of lasting three times longer than those entered into two centuries ago.

The argument that this lengthening of marriage duration has led to an increase in marriage breakdown and divorce implies that there is some sort of period beyond which marriages tend to break down, but there is no evidence of that. It is true, of course, that the longer marriages last the longer they are at risk of breakdown, but there is also evidence that most marriages that break down and are dissolved in modern society do so in the first few years. Similarly, the average lapse of time between marriage and divorce in the cases studied in Chapter 4 was about twelve years, while the desertions studied by Snell occurred, on average, after about seven years of marriage. Marriage breakdown and divorce in both past and present, then, appear to have been concentrated in the early years of marriage, rather than in the later years of more recent times, as the death substitute explanation of modern divorce requires.

Several general conclusions may be drawn from this survey of the definitions, social context, and extent of marriage breakdown. The most important is that there was little evidence of desertion or de facto separation in traditional society. If marriages did commonly break down, the phenomenon has escaped the historical record. It is striking that the sources we might expect to provide evidence of widespread marriage breakdown – censuses of poor families, for instance – provide us with few examples. This direct evidence is reinforced by what we should expect to have been the case. That is to say, there is no incongruence between what we find in the historical record and what we should expect to find, given the social, economic, and cultural contexts of marriage and constraints on separation. Traditional society was above all familial and conjugal.

The increase in marriage breakdown, desertion, separation, and divorce in the more modern period can be explained largely by changes in marriage, the family, and society more generally. The constraints against separation were weakened with socioeconomic changes associated with industrialization and urbanization. As opportunities for life outside marriage widened, expectations of marriage rose and toleration of abuse, oppression, and sheer unhappiness fell. Marriage breakdown increased, and, as divorce laws were reformed and divorce became socially more accessible in the nineteenth century, divorce rates rose. This trend, which is discussed in more detail in Chapter 9, supports the first model of change set out in Figure 5.1. The increase in divorce over time was not simply the formal dissolution of an increasing proportion of broken marriages; according to the interpretation advanced here, both marriage breakdown and divorce have increased dramatically during the past two centuries.

Suggestions for further reading

Gillis, John R., *For Better, For Worse: British Marriages, 1600 to the Present* (New York, 1985).

Hufton, Olwen, *The Poor of Eighteenth-Century France, 1750–1789* (Oxford, 1974).

Laslett, Peter, *Family Life and Illicit Love in Earlier Generations* (Cambridge, 1977).

Macfarlane, Alan, *Marriage and Love in England, 1300–1840* (London, 1983).

Quaife, G. R., *Wanton Wenches and Wayward Wives* (London, 1979).

Snell, K. D. M., *Annals of the Labouring Poor* (Cambridge, 1985).

Stone, Lawrence, *The Family, Sex and Marriage in England, 1500–1800* (London, 1977).

6

The nineteenth century: Liberalization and reaction

In many respects divorce was transformed from 1800 to the outbreak of World War I in 1914. For one thing it spread geographically so that by 1914 only a few Catholic states in Europe, notably Spain, Italy, and Ireland, did not have provision for divorce, and they held out until late in the twentieth century. (There is still no divorce in the Republic of Ireland.) Moreover, divorce in the European tradition spread beyond the Western society of the Atlantic world. Divorce was introduced into the American states of the Midwest and West, as well as into the British colonies in Australasia, the West Indies, and Africa. By the end of the century, the Western form of divorce had global dimensions, as seemed appropriate to a period that saw a surge of European imperialism.

The geographical spread of divorce was matched by the extension of its social availability. By the end of this period, wherever divorce was available, it was almost always available from the courts. In England, for example, divorces by private Act of Parliament were abolished in 1857, and divorces were granted by the Court for Divorce and Matrimonial Causes. Similarly, the governors, councils, and legislatures of the American states surrendered jurisdiction over divorce to the regular courts. Judicial divorce tended to be less expensive, less demanding, and less daunting than executive and legislative divorce had been, and even if divorce was still beyond the reach of most married people, petitioners in the nineteenth century were socially more diverse than ever before.

There were also important changes in divorce policies. In general, laws were liberalized so as to recognize a broader range of grounds, discretionary clauses were added to many codes, and the gap between traditional church doctrines and secular divorce laws widened considerably. One influence on liberalization was the nineteenth-century ideologies of domesticity and femininity, which added matrimonial offenses, notably habitual drunkenness and the failure to perform appropriate domestic duties, such as a husband's obligation to provide for his wife.

Many laws, moreover, showed the growing pressure to remove the double standard of sexual morality from legislation.

The net effect of these changes in the nineteenth century, combined with more general social and economic developments, was a sharp increase in the number of divorces sought and obtained. In the United States there were almost 10,000 divorces in 1867, but by 1906 there were more than 72,000, a sevenfold increase that far exceeded population growth. The mere five divorces in England in 1857 (the last year of parliamentary divorce) increased to an annual average of 215 by 1870–4, and then to 590 a year by 1900–4. As we shall see, such increases, seen as more dramatic and unnerving at the time than they seem a century later, provoked a reaction against liberal divorce laws. The transformation of divorce, indeed, emerged from the clash of a number of contradictory forces. In the end, however, divorce policies expanded and liberalized in such a way that, if we think of the sixteenth century as having produced the first generation of divorce laws, the nineteenth century must be credited with having produced the second.

The century began, in fact, with the artificial extension of divorce throughout Europe with the expansion of French power. As the French armies pushed further and further into Europe after the outbreak of the revolutionary wars in 1792, they implanted French political and legal reforms, including divorce, in places such as Belgium, the Netherlands, Switzerland, and parts of Germany. Even states that were not occupied were influenced by the reforms of French matrimonial law: The Prussian civil code of 1794 showed French influences, as did the family tribunals introduced in Norway in 1797.

In the Napoleonic period divorce French style was extended more systematically, for one of the benefits conferred by the French on annexed and associated states was the Civil Code (later called the Code Napoléon), including its divorce provisions. This law was applied virtually intact throughout the French Empire, which covered about three-quarters of continental Europe. The major exception was Spain, where a concession was made to the fact that traditions and practices were opposed to divorce (although the same tradition in Italy was ignored, and divorce was legalized there).

The effects of French legal imperialism throughout Europe varied, but in general divorce was not widely used in the Empire except where it had been legal before the French conquest. Italy is an example. Divorce had been made available to non-Catholic populations in the Hapsburg territories in 1784, and a divorce law had been introduced in Piedmont in 1796. With the amalgamation of the various Italian provinces under French direction, and the introduction of the 1806 Codice Civile, based on the Code Napoléon, divorce was available to all inhabitants of the peninsula. But the Italians were unappreciative, and only nineteen divorces have been found throughout Italy between 1809 and 1815. There was, as we might expect, little opposition when divorce was abolished when the French Empire ebbed in 1813 and 1814, and Italy was again divided into a collection of independent states. Only in the Hapsburg provinces of Lombardy and Venetia was divorce retained, now under the 1811 Austrian General Civil Code, which allowed non-Catholics to divorce.

During the rest of the nineteenth century, divorce made little progress in Italy. One potentially influential development was the Piedmontese civil code issued by the reforming regime of King Carlo in the 1830s. It permitted non-Catholics in the realm to divorce, and it seemed possible that, with the unification of Italy under the leadership of Piedmont between 1859 and 1870, divorce might have become a feature of the civil law of the Italian state. In 1852, however, divorce had been abolished in Piedmont by Carlo's conservative son and successor, Victor Emmanuel II. A new Italian civil code issued in 1865 recognized civil marriage but explicitly stressed that marriage was indissoluble. Perhaps this was a gesture to the papacy, which was hostile to the unification of Italy.

Divorce was not, in fact, legalized in Italy for more than a century after the 1865 civil code, even though it remained a live political issue throughout the nineteenth century. Between 1878 and 1892 five divorce bills (some liberal, some restrictive) were introduced into the legislature, but all failed, even though a draft divorce bill was approved by the legislative commission of parliament in 1884 (the year divorce was legalized again in France). There were many reasons for the persistent failure of attempts to legalize divorce in Italy, but one of the most important was the continuing influence of the Catholic church. Confessional parties opposed divorce, and the desire to mollify the papacy (which opposed the creation of the Italian state) deterred politicians from supporting a policy that was anathema to Catholic doctrine. Even in the 1960s and 1970s it proved difficult to legalize divorce in Italy, and the country's experience in the nineteenth and twentieth centuries highlights the exceptional period when divorce was legalized under the Napoleonic regime.

Belgium and the Netherlands were also caught up in the legal contortions that were imposed on Europe by the French Revolution and Empire. Both countries had some form of divorce before 1789 – the Netherlands since the Reformation, Belgian non-Catholics since 1784 – and both were invaded by France and granted the benefits of the 1792 divorce law. In 1807 the Napoleonic divorce law was applied in Belgium by the Civil Code (thenceforth the basis of Belgian civil law), and in 1810 it was extended to the Netherlands when that country was incorporated into the French Empire.

Despite attempts to liberalize divorce policy on pre-Napoleonic principles, the Napoleonic form of divorce was retained in an expanded Netherlands, which incorporated Belgium, after the defeat of the empire in 1815. In 1816 the Dutch parliament defeated a bill to make divorce available on grounds of adultery, long-term desertion, unnatural immorality, the attempted murder by one spouse of the other, or one spouse's attempting to kill or injure the other spouse, or his or her parents or children. Four years later, another attempt to liberalize the law failed despite the sponsors' emphasis that the bill reflected "the spirit of the people," recognized "the holiness of marriage," and deplored any suggestion that divorce should be easy to obtain.

In the 1830s, however, there were major developments. Belgium seceded from the Netherlands in 1830 and, despite its predominantly Catholic population, retained the Napoleonic form of divorce. Under this law there were four divorces in 1830, twenty-six in 1840, twenty-nine in 1850, fifty-five in 1860, and eighty-one in 1870. There was a steady increase during the century, then, but even by the end of the century the number was small in absolute terms. Divorce law in the Netherlands, meanwhile, was recodified as part of the 1838 Burgerlijk Wetboek to recognize the grounds of adultery, desertion, imprisonment, and serious physical cruelty. Dutch couples could also divorce by mutual consent by obtaining a separation and then, after a minimum five-year waiting period, converting it to divorce. This law, which produced relatively few divorces, regulated divorce for most of the remainder of the nineteenth century.

The French Revolution had a long-term effect on Swedish divorce law, too, but in a rather different way. As we have seen in Chapter 1, divorce was introduced to Sweden on Lutheran principles during the Reformation, then gradually expanded by royal dispensations and the 1734 civil code. An even more liberal policy, reflecting French influences, was ushered in during the regency after the assassination of King Gustavus III in 1792. But when Gustavus IV came to the Swedish throne in 1796, a reaction set in and divorce was made more difficult to obtain. This policy ended in 1809 when he was deposed and Jean-Baptiste Bernadotte became crown prince. Bernadotte was one of the success stories of the French Revolution. A native of Gascony, he had enlisted in the French army in 1780, and by 1793 had become a general. Later he was a minister of war and one of Napoleon's marshals, but in 1810 he was elected crown prince of Sweden, partly in recognition of his release of Swedish prisoners of war in 1806. From 1828 to 1844 Bernadotte ruled Sweden as King Karl Johann.

It was a supreme irony that a revolution identified with a republic and a regicide should have catapulted a French soldier to one of the European thrones. But although Bernadotte abandoned his republicanism, he did not lose his revolutionary zeal for legal reform, and in 1810 he sponsored a reform of Swedish marriage law. It declared that marriage was a union based on the mutual respect of the spouses and that marriage ceased to exist in their consciences once the mutual respect had disappeared. That being so, divorce was permitted on a wide range of grounds, including not only those set down in the 1734 civil code, but also those generally recognized in royal dispensations (such as life imprisonment, banishment, and incurable insanity), as well as on additional grounds that included loss of honor, wasteful management of property, alcoholism, cruel temperament, and situations where the mutual hostility of spouses had turned into aversion and hatred. This legislation, allowing for both judicial and executive divorce on a flexible range of grounds, regulated divorce in Sweden for a hundred years.

But whereas the liberal divorce policy of the French Revolution persisted in Sweden, even the restrictive Napoleonic policy soon disappeared from much of the rest of Europe, as we have seen in the cases of Italy and the Netherlands. Moreover, divorce disappeared entirely from France after the collapse of Napoleon's empire and the restoration of the monarchy. In 1816 King Louis XVIII abolished divorce as harmful to religion, the family, and the state. In the legislative debates on divorce that preceded its abolition, divorce was portrayed as a weapon used by democrats to destroy political and social order and as a means by which women could rebel against the legitimate authority of their husbands.

The association of liberal divorce with the French Revolution, and even of restrictive divorce with the imperialism of Napoleon, made divorce an unappealing institution in post-Napoleonic France and Europe. This accounts in part for the reaction against divorce legislation throughout much of Europe. The reaction was temporary, however, as we shall see, and in the second half of the nineteenth century divorce was legalized in England, extended throughout Germany, and was restored to France. These developments, together with such trends as the spread of divorce to many other parts of Western society outside Europe, make 1850–1914 a period of remarkable activity in matrimonial legislation.

One of the most important features of the period was the passage of the first English divorce law in 1857. As we have seen, England's was the only Protestant church not to abandon the Catholic doctrine of marital indissolubility, and the process of divorce by private Act of Parliament had developed as a way of circumventing the Anglican church's opposition. The passage of a divorce law in 1857, despite the persistence of the church's opposition, was, among other things, indicative of the decline in the church's influence. In 1837 a marriage law had provided for civil marriage and for denominations other than the Anglican church to marry couples, and the provision of divorce seemed a logical extension of the processes of secularization and liberalism in family law.

The legalization of divorce in England was the result of a long and hard campaign, however, and there were many, inside and outside the Anglican church, who opposed divorce. The increase in parliamentary divorces – there were twice as many in the last three decades of the eighteenth century as there had been in the first seven – provoked alarm. As early as 1772 one member of Parliament referred to the "evil of divorce daily increasing," and in 1809 the archbishop of Canterbury lamented that divorce had cut such a swathe through the upper ranks of society that there was "hardly a pedigree that was not stained and broken by this sad frequency of crime." In the belief that the availability of divorce encouraged its use and also promoted adultery, a number of bills were introduced into the House of Lords from 1770 onward with the aim of prohibiting the marriage of a woman divorced for reason of adultery and her accomplice. A woman who could marry her lover, the bishop of London argued in the House of Lords in 1800, "received a reward for her misconduct: she got quit of a husband whom she disliked, and became the wife of the man whom she adored." This was clearly intolerable. Two bills to prohibit such marriages passed the House of Lords (in 1770 and 1779), but both were defeated in the Commons.

There were several attempts to criminalize adultery, the only offense that was a ground for a parliamentary divorce. One, entitled the "Adultery Prevention Bill, for the More Effectual Prevention of the Crime of Adultery," was withdrawn during one of its readings and replaced by another "for the Punishment and more effectual prevention of the Crime of Adultery." This would have not only prohibited the marriage of a divorced woman and her accomplice, but would have made adultery a crime punishable by a fine and imprisonment. Had it succeeded, the bill would have made adultery a crime for the first time since Cromwell's 1650 Adultery Act. The bill failed, however, despite vigorous support by most of the Lords, none of whom claimed any personal knowledge of the subject under discussion. No matter how naive and ill-conceived they were, such attempts to reduce the incidence of adultery and to make divorce unattractive dominated the British Parliament's approach to divorce in the late eighteenth century and in the first decade of the nineteenth. Voices defending divorce as a solution to some matrimonial problems, and defending the right of remarriage, were drowned out in the House of Lords, although they prevailed in the House of Commons.

In 1820 a sensational divorce came before the British Parliament, when a Bill of Pains and Penalties was introduced to dissolve the marriage of King George IV and Queen Caroline. George and Caroline had long been unhappy in marriage – they had separated a year after their marriage in 1795 – but it was not until he succeeded his father that George took action to divorce his wife. Even then he did so against the advice of his ministers, who quite properly feared the consequences should the bill succeed and George decide to remarry. In such a case England would have been faced with a king, the head of the Anglican church, divorcing and remarrying in the face of his church's doctrine of marital indissolubility. Not only would the church have been bound to oppose a remarriage, particularly in a church, but the legitimacy of any heir would have been questioned.

George, however, seemed more motivated by hatred of Caroline than concerned with any constitutional and dynastic implications, and pressed on with the divorce. It was grounded on Queen Caroline's alleged adultery with an Italian, Batolomeo Pergami, described in Parliament as "a foreigner of low station." (It is not clear which of these qualities was the more offensive.) Caroline, who had quit England some years earlier to tour the Continent, had appointed Pergami to manage her entourage, and the royal divorce bill charged that she had behaved toward him "with indecent and offensive familiarity and freedom, and carried on a licentious, disgraceful and adulterous intercourse ... by which conduct of her royal highness, a great scandal and dishonour have been brought upon your majesty's family and this kingdom." The bill was presented, then, as dealing with a matter of state as much as a state of matrimony.

The parliamentary debates on the royal divorce bill, which eventually passed two readings, were sensational. Witnesses testified to such matters as the sleeping arrangements on Caroline's ship during sultry nights in the Mediterranean, the sartorial inadequacies of Italian masked balls, and a maid even gave evidence of stained bedsheets in a hotel. The proceedings were relayed to an eager public through cartoons and broadsheets, but eventually the government cut off the entertainment by withdrawing the action against the queen. Despite apparently compelling evidence of her adultery, there was little sympathy for the king, whose own commitment to marital fidelity was widely known to be imperfect. It was no doubt a national embarrassment and scandal to have the queen of England floating around the Mediterranean, sleeping with a nondescript Italian and, to judge from the number of witnesses, being none too discreet about it. In the end, however, it became clear that the divorce bill would be defeated in the House of Commons, and it became too much a political liability to pursue it.

It is not clear what effect the king's attempt to divorce had upon divorce more generally, though the affair did raise popular consciousness of the sexual inequalities of the prevailing divorce policies. In the public debate on the matter, Queen Caroline was frequently portrayed as a woman wronged by a man himself guilty of matrimonial crimes, and the whole affair could only have contributed to unease about the principles underlying parliamentary divorces. An 1831 pamphlet summed the feeling up: "All parties are agreed that the proceedings connected with divorce in this country are most imperfect; all agree that our system is neither good in itself, nor beneficial in its operation." Among the "imperfections" the writer listed were: hypocrisy, in that a man planning to divorce and marry again had first to obtain a separation, which required him to promise not to remarry; the procedure's injustice to women; and its unfairness to those who could not afford a parliamentary divorce. To reinforce the argument in favor of legalizing divorce, the writer pointed out that in Scotland, where divorce was available, "the moral feeling of the population is of the highest cast," whereas in France and Italy, where divorce was prohibited, "the faithlessness of married persons is proverbial."

Pressure for divorce reform in England came from the judiciary as well. The best-known example is the often-quoted judgment of Mr. Justice Maule in 1845, when sentencing Thomas Hall, a laborer convicted of bigamy. It is a long exercise in irony that is worth quoting at length:

Prisoner at the bar, you have been convicted before me of what the law regards as a very grave and serious offence: that of going through the marriage ceremony a second time while your wife was still alive. You plead in mitigation of your conduct that she was given to dissipation and drunkenness, that she proved herself a curse to your household while she remained mistress of it, and that she had latterly deserted you; but I am not permitted to recognise any such plea. You had entered into a solemn engagement to take her for better, for worse, and if you infinitely got more of the latter, as you appear to have done, it was your duty patiently to submit. You say you took another person to become your wife because you were left with several young children . . . but the law makes no allowance for bigamists with large families. Had you taken the other female to live with you as a concubine you would never have been interfered with by the law. But your crime consists in having – to use your own language – preferred to make an honest woman of her. Another of your irrational excuses is that your wife had committed adultery, and so you thought you were relieved from treating her with any further consideration – but you were mistaken. The law in its wisdom points out a means by which you might rid yourself from further association with a woman who had dishonoured you; but you did not think proper to adopt it. I will tell you what the process is. You ought first to have brought an action against your wife's seducer if you could have discovered him; that might have cost you money, and you say you are a poor working man, but that is not the fault of the law. You would then be obliged to prove by evidence your wife's criminality in a Court of Justice, and thus obtain a verdict with damages against the defendant, who was not unlikely to turn out a pauper. But so jealous is the law (which you ought to be aware is the perfection of reason) of the sanctity of the marriage tie, that in accomplishing all this you would only have fulfilled the lighter portion of your duty. You must then have gone, with your verdict in your hand, and petitioned the House of Lords for a divorce. It would cost you perhaps five or six hundred pounds and you do not seem to be worth as many pence. But it is the boast of the law that it is impartial, and makes no difference between the rich and the poor. The wealthiest man in the kingdom would have had to pay no less than that sum for the same luxury; so that you would have no reason to complain. You would, of course, have to prove your case over again, and at the end of a year, or possibly two, you might obtain a divorce which would enable you legally to do what you have thought proper to do without it. You have thus wilfully rejected the boon the legislature offered you, and it is my duty to pass upon you such sentence as I think your offence deserves, and that sentence is, that you be imprisoned for one day; and in as much as the present assizes are three days old, the result is that you will be immediately discharged.

Parliament itself generated pressure to have the divorce system over-hauled. Within the House of Lords in particular there was growing dissatisfaction at the amount of parliamentary time consumed by each divorce bill. In 1840 a special committee of nine lords was established to hear the evidence in divorce cases, but the bills still had to be voted on by the full House before being sent to the House of Commons. Finally, in 1850, a royal commission was established to investigate the desirability of passing a divorce law. Its report, presented in 1853, became the basis of the 1857 legislation.

The substance of this law retained some of the principles embedded in parliamentary divorce. Only one ground for divorce, adultery, would be recognized, and women would have to prove their husbands guilty of aggravated adultery in order to get a divorce. The all-important change, however, was the procedure. Instead of obtaining a separation from a church court, then damages for criminal conversation, and only then a divorce from Parliament, petitioners would be able to obtain the divorce directly from a civil court. Indeed, all matrimonial litigation was transferred from the ecclesiastical to the civil courts, which were empowered to grant not only divorces for reason of adultery, but also separations on the grounds of adultery, gross cruelty, or desertion.

Although the reforms seem cautious and modest, their implications for the accessibility of divorce were quickly recognized, and they generated both support and opposition. There were criticisms that divorce would still be expensive. "The poor man has rights, has feelings, as well as the rich," wrote one pamphleteer; "Is the rich man, with his thousands a year, is he alone to enjoy the privilege of buying release from a tie which has become degrading?" Other critics focused on the need for women to have equal access to divorce. One wrote of "the thousands of noble-hearted English wives, the mothers of our great and good, the mothers of many a Crimean hero ... whose life-long existence is passed in worse than widowhood – in that utter desolation of spirit which follows the wreck of earthly happiness."

Against those who thought that the new law unduly restricted divorce were those – the Roman Catholic and Anglican clergy prominent among them – opposed to any form of divorce at all. One Anglican priest pointed out that divorces began in England in the reign of "that not particularly chaste and virtuous monarch, Charles the Second," and argued that divorce would encourage "inconsiderate and ill-assorted marriages," and would allow men to "gratify their passions" before committing adultery and getting rid of their lawful wives. As for remarriage: "The married life of persons who have been divorced, is seldom, if ever, a really happy one. There is a shadow, if not a blight, that seems to rest on such marriages."

Remarriage after divorce was especially problematic for the clergy, because it raised the question of whether divorced people could marry in church. Civil marriage had been introduced in England in 1837, but it was clear that some divorced people would want to remarry in their faith. The 1857 divorce law recognized the division of attitudes within the Anglican church and specified that if a priest refused to officiate at a marriage involving a divorced person, another priest of the diocese could perform the marriage in the unwilling priest's church. The prospect of intruder priests presiding over such immoral spectacles in their churches led the Oxford Clerical Association to consider ways of preventing it. Suggestions included locking their churches and refusing to hand over the keys and attempting to deter divorced people ("divorced adulterers") from remarriage by publicly embarrassing them in sermons and by starting proceedings to have them excommunicated.

Against the full range of attitudes against and in favor of the 1857 law, the English divorce court opened for business on January 1, 1858, and the demand soon appeared to justify those who had predicted social disaster. There had been 4 parliamentary divorces a year, on average, during the 1850s, but from 1858 there were between 200 and 300 judicial divorces a year. Although England's divorce rate was one of the lowest in the Western world in the later nineteenth century (and the number of divorces in a single year did not exceed 1,000 until 1918), the increased use of divorce because of the 1857 law is quite evident. The costs of divorce fell to £40–£60, about a fifth of the costs of a parliamentary divorce, and even though the floodgates were scarcely opened, divorce was far more accessible than it had ever been. In a sample of 101 divorces reported in the London *Times* between 1860 and 1919, the most common occupational groups were the military, trade (such as shopkeepers), workers (butlers, sailors), professionals, clerks, and men of independent means. Working men were represented, then, but they accounted for only a sixth of the husbands in these reports. The divorce lists were now dominated by middle-class couples, but of decidedly lower strata than those who had divorced by Act of Parliament.

There was a major change in the sex composition of petitioners. Whereas only 4 (1%) of the 325 parliamentary divorces had been obtained by women, women petitioned for 7,525 (42%) of the 17,952 divorces granted by the courts between 1859 and 1909. Not only that, but women's petitions had a slightly better success rate than men's. The representation of women in the divorce petitioners' lists is quite phenomenal, given that women had to prove aggravated adultery (adultery plus bigamy, incest, sodomy, desertion, cruelty, rape, or bestiality) in order to obtain a divorce. Women, we should note, were also more likely than men to be under financial stress, experienced greater social pressure to tolerate matrimonial offenses, and also risked losing their children as a result of divorce, for it was a working principle of the courts that children belonged to their father.

As restrictive as it seems, then, the first English divorce law had dramatic effects on divorce in England. Even though the rate and number of divorces appear negligible by late twentieth-century standards, they were astonishing and often alarming to contemporary commentators. As we shall see, the rise of divorce in England contributed to a general reaction throughout Western society against divorce and other trends that were seen as manifestations of social and moral decay.

Fears of national decline also underlay opposition to divorce in late nineteenth-century France, although advocates of the legalization of divorce there had to deal with an additional obstacle: the association of divorce with the French Revolution. Divorce, we should recall, was legalized for the first time in France by the very liberal law of 1792, maintained in a restricted form in the Code Napoléon, then abolished entirely under the Restoration in 1816. At several points in the following decades it seemed that divorce would be legalized again. Soon after the 1830 July revolution, bills to restore divorce on Napoleonic principles passed the Chamber of Deputies in four successive years (1831–4), but on each occasion they were defeated in the Chamber of Peers. The revolution of 1848 also seemed to offer hope for the restoration of divorce. The minister of justice of the short-lived Second Republic (1848–52) introduced a divorce bill, but it failed. The only reform passed by this regime was an 1851 measure that gave legal aid to husbands and wives suing for a legal separation. Finally, it seemed that Emperor Louis Napoleon might incorporate divorce in the civil laws of his Second Empire (1852–70). Louis Napoleon had praised his uncle's divorce law, but once in power he probably calculated that the support of the Catholic church was more important than this particular legal reform.

It remained, finally, for the legislators of the Third Republic (established in 1871) to legalize divorce once again in France. Bills were introduced into parliament regularly from 1876, but it was not until 1884 that one was successful, and French men and women were able to dissolve their marriages. That they were able to as early as 1884 was largely due to Alfred Naquet, a professor of chemistry who was elected first a deputy and then a senator, and whose persistence in the cause of divorce led to the 1884 law's being known as the "Naquet law." He first attempted, in 1876 and 1878, to pass a law based on the revolutionary legislation, but it was far too radical a move for the French parliament. In 1881 Naquet introduced a bill that was based on the Napoleonic principles of mutual consent and a few specific grounds, but even then the senate removed the mutual consent clause before passing the bill in 1884.

Debates in the French parliament showed that ease of divorce was fatally associated, almost a century after the fact, with the revolution. One senator, insisting that wisely regulated divorce did not harm the stability of the family, recalled that "divorce entered our laws with excesses and violence, accompanied by an ease which profoundly harmed the interests of society. In this law of 1792 there were many of the most dangerous conditions favoring caprice, the emotions, and the impulses to which human nature is prone." The effects of divorce on women were also vigorously debated. Supporters of divorce argued that women would benefit from the ability to free themselves and their children from oppressive marriages, while opponents insisted that if marriage was good for women, divorce must be bad for them. The religious issue came to the fore, as well, as it was bound to under a regime that was, in the 1880s, passing a body of laws to secularize French education. Divorce was offensive to Catholics, it was claimed; Catholics need not divorce if they did not want to, came the reply.

The overriding question, however, was whether legalizing divorce would lead to family and social instability in France. By the 1880s there was widespread concern about the state of the nation. France had been defeated in the 1870–1 war with Prussia, and many attributed the defeat to the fact that France's population had stagnated at about 36 million in the 1860s and 1870s. National strength was generally viewed as a function of population strength, and one reason why marriage and family breakdown inspired such alarm in some quarters was the fear that they would interrupt and depress the fertility of French marriages even further.

To answer such fears, Naquet and his fellow supporters of divorce argued that the legalization of divorce would not of itself promote marriage breakdown; they suggested that the number of divorces would probably be lower than the prevailing number of separations, about 3,000 a year at that time. Naquet pointed out that the separation rate in France was consistently higher than the divorce rate in neighboring Belgium, and he also demonstrated, pointedly, that the ratio of separations to marriages in the 1880s was 22 times higher than the ratio of divorces to marriages in 1802 when the hated 1792 divorce law was still in operation. The level of marriage breakdown did not depend solely on the availability of divorce, Naquet concluded, but on factors such as religion (Catholics divorce less than Protestants), race (populations such as Bretons and Flemings divorce less than others), socioeconomic status (city dwellers and professionals are particularly prone to divorce), and time (marriage breakdown increases as "civilization develops").

Indeed, Naquet argued, it was not divorce that was to be feared, but the consequences of not being able to divorce. The 2,870 separations granted in France in 1881 had released twice that number of men and women from some of their matrimonial obligations, such as cohabitation. Naquet unflatteringly described these separated wives and husbands as "5600 agents of corruption and of moral and social disorder," who were driven to form "illegitimate families." If that were not bad enough, some of Naquet's colleagues argued, some women who were unable to divorce were driven to the desperate lengths of murdering their spouses. Referring to the notorious 1840 case of Marie Lafarge, who was convicted of poisoning her husband, one senator exclaimed, "Let the civil code liberate the wife. She will seek the protection of the law instead of taking revenge with arsenic, sulfuric acid or a revolver."

The successful passage of a French divorce law in 1884 was anything but a foregone conclusion, but there were many indications that it was acceptable to a broad spectrum of the population. The press (except for clerical newspapers, of course) favored the legalization of divorce, politicians who supported the divorce law were reelected, and divorce was popularized sympathetically in contemporary plays and novels. As we shall see when we look at divorce trends in the nineteenth century, divorce quickly became a popular remedy to marriage breakdown in France. Against the predictions of Alfred Naquet, the number of divorces quickly rose to more than 7,000, twice the number of separations in the early 1880s. As in England and elsewhere, the increase in the number of divorces intensified opposition to divorce itself at the end of the nineteenth century.

Much the same sort of concern about divorce had been expressed in Prussia by the middle of the century. The Lutheran states of northern Germany, of which Prussia was by far the most important, had legalized divorce during the Reformation, but in the following centuries the laws had been liberalized far beyond the terms envisaged by Luther. Nineteenth-century Prussian law, for example, recognized eleven broad grounds for divorce: adultery or unnatural vices; desertion; refusal of sexual intercourse; impotence; raging insanity or madness; violence, attempted murder, or repeated and unfounded defamatory accusations; acts of felony or pursuing a disreputable occupation; leading a disorderly life; continued refusal of a husband to maintain his wife; giving up the Christian religion; and insurmountable aversion or the mutual consent to separate, where there were no children of the marriage (or, in exceptional circumstances, where there were children).

Enthusiasm for the expansion of Prussian divorce law was not universal, however, and there were attempts in the 1840s and 1850s to reduce the number of grounds. An 1857 bill, for instance, sought to abolish the grounds of refusal of intercourse, insanity, insurmountable aversion, and mutual consent, and to place restrictions on the use of other grounds. Being debated at the very same time the British Parliament was also considering divorce, the Prussian bill was supported by one British Member of Parliament who observed that divorce in Prussia was so liberal that "in point of fact there is no such thing as marriage in Prussia, nor is the [marriage] bond so binding as it has been and is in many heathen countries."

In Prussia itself the debate was many-faceted, but there was a stress on the implications of divorce for morality and social stability. Critics of the existing law pointed to the lessons of the decline of morals in the eighteenth century "which eventually brought in the French Revolution [and] reduced the law of marriage to the low state in which it is now found among us." (This was a reference to the influence of French revolutionary family law on the 1794 Prussian civil code.) There was particular concern that ease of divorce placed it within reach of the lower classes. "The upper classes are able to help themselves in some measure, through their higher cultivation," said Baron von Gerlach in the Prussian Landstag, but for the lower classes, as soon as "the sacredness of this primitive institution [marriage] is depreciated, there remains nothing but an irremediable demoralization." Women, he added, "are the chief sufferers from the laws facilitating divorce." The full horror of divorce, for the baron and those of like attitude, was illustrated by the fact that divorces were running at some 3,000

133

a year, and by the purported popularity of sayings such as "One is more cautious about buying a pig or a cow for fattening than about taking a wife," and "It is easier and costs less to get quit of a bad wife than of an unprofitable head of cattle."

The failure of the attempts to restrict Prussian divorce law in the mid-nineteenth century had important implications for the development of the law in Germany more generally. In 1871 the various German states united into an empire, but rather than being a federation of equals, it was an empire dominated by Prussia. The Prussian king became the German emperor, and Prussian institutions and personnel dominated the imperial system. This pattern extended to divorce when an imperial divorce law was passed as part of the 1875 Personal Status Act. It abolished separations and introduced divorce to all German states, including those like Bavaria and Saxony where no provision for divorce had been made up to that time. In such states, the grounds for divorce were set at the circumstances that had justified a separation, but elsewhere in the new German empire, divorce was based on the Prussian model.

The passage of an imperial divorce law in Germany in 1875 reflected several current trends. One was progress toward a standardized legal system, for although the 1875 law admitted regional variations, within twenty-five years German divorce had been unified. Second, the 1875 divorce law was enacted at the height of the *Kulturkampf,* Chancellor Bismarck's campaign against the influence of the Roman Catholic church in Germany. The consolidation of divorce by imperial legislation, together with the abolition of separations, can easily be interpreted as a slap in the face of Catholics, particularly as Pope Pius IX had expressly condemned divorce. It is notable that as the *Kulturkampf* ran its course, and the support of the Catholic church was needed by Bismarck in his struggles with the liberals and social democrats, the 1875 divorce provisions were modified to allow a kind of separation.

Overall, it makes more sense to see the 1875 German divorce law in the context of Bismarck's nationalist and anti-Catholic policy, rather than as the liberal measure it was in England and France. In fact when they reformed the 1875 law in 1900, the German legislators ran counter to the Western trend of liberalization, and made the law more restrictive. The ground of "insurmountable aversion" was abolished, as was divorce by mutual consent. Some of the other grounds (including infidelity, bigamy, desertion, and unnatural intercourse) were deemed "absolute," and proving them was enough to justify a divorce. But other grounds (including dishonorable or immoral conduct, serious neglect of marital duties, and serious maltreatment) were deemed "relative," and the court had the discretion of agreeing to or denying a divorce.

The development of divorce policy in Germany in the last decades of the nineteenth century was, then, more complex than its English and French counterparts. Not only was German divorce law not conceived in liberal terms, but the process of divorce legalization and standardization was inextricably bound up with the politics of national unification and the consolidation of the German Empire.

Elsewhere in Europe the signs of a conflict between liberalizing and conservative forces was evident in the development of divorce law and institutions. In Austria, for instance, divorce was permitted to non-Catholics under the 1811 General Civil Code, but there was a reaction after the revolution of 1848. In 1855 a concordat was signed that transferred control of marriage to the Catholic church, thus depriving all Austrians, regardless of their religious affiliation, of divorce. This in turn provoked a sufficient reaction that in 1868 those sections of the concordat dealing with marriage were abrogated. By 1870, divorce had been restored to non-Catholics in Austria, the recognized grounds including adultery, condemnation for certain crimes, willful desertion, having an infectious disease, ill-treatment, and threats. Divorce was also permitted, after a period of separation, when there was an "irremediable aversion" between the spouses. This divorce policy remained in force in Austria until the Nazi marriage law of 1938 came into effect.

In neighboring Switzerland divorce law was also reformed in the nineteenth century, with the promulgation in 1874 of the first federal legislation that supplanted the regional divorce codes. The federal law recognized a relatively small range of grounds (adultery, desertion, insanity, and being sentenced to a degrading punishment), and the restrictive character of divorce was underlined by limitations placed on remarriage. A divorced woman could not marry within 300 days of her divorce, and the guilty party – husband or wife – had to wait between one and three years to marry, depending on the seriousness of the offense that had justified the divorce.

Perhaps one of the most striking pieces of European divorce legislation before World War I was the legalization of divorce in Portugal in 1910. The country's 1867 civil code had ruled out the possibility of divorce by declaring marriage to be a "perpetual contract," and bills aiming to legalize divorce were regularly defeated, right up to 1910. In that year, however, the monarchy of King Manoel II was overthrown, and a republic, drawing much of its ideological inspiration from the French Revolution, was proclaimed. One of the first legal reforms of the new Portuguese regime was an extremely liberal law that allowed divorce by mutual consent, conversion of a separation, and ten specific grounds that included adultery, absence, desertion, ill-treatment, and addiction to gambling. Like the French revolutionary divorce legislation, the Portuguese law gave wives and husbands legal equality in respect of divorce, made civil marriage obligatory, and created a "Day of the Family," its importance marked by its being celebrated on December 25 each year.

Even where divorce was not legalized in Europe there were changes to, or attempts to change, marriage law. In Spain, for example, an 1870 law transferred control of marriage from the ecclesiastical to the secular authorities. Pressure from the church, however, led to the reinstatement in 1875 of religious marriage, except for non-Catholics, who were permitted civil marriage. Divorce was not legalized in Spain in the nineteenth century, but there was some recognition of unhappy marriages when separations were made available in the 1889 civil code. It was a modest advance, but it demonstrates that few European states did not participate in the matrimonial legislation activity that seemed characteristic of the nineteenth century.

By extending divorce throughout much of Europe, nineteenth-century reforms indirectly disseminated the European model of divorce around the world. The principal mechanism was the British Empire that by 1857, even before the final paroxysm of European imperialism at the end of the century, comprised vast and scattered territories in Canada, the West Indies, Australia, New Zealand, the Pacific, Asia, Africa, and South America. British colonies had been forbidden to enact laws that were repugnant to prevailing English law, and the necessity of royal assent to colonial laws – in practice this meant the agreement of the British government to them – was intended to be a guarantee that there would be a reasonable level of legal harmony between the colonies and the mother country.

As we have seen, the harmony was not perfect. Earlier British colonies in America, notably Massachusetts and Connecticut, had adopted relatively generous divorce policies, while others provided for divorce in more restrictive forms. Three future provinces of Canada did so as well: Nova Scotia, New Brunswick, and Prince Edward Island, all maritime (Atlantic) provinces that were closely associated with the northern American colonies. In 1761 Nova Scotia enacted a divorce law that recognized adultery and cruelty as grounds, and in 1791 New Brunswick provided for divorce for reason of adultery. Much later, in 1837 (but still two decades before the English divorce law was passed), Prince Edward Island made divorce for reason of adultery available from a court consisting of the lieutenant governor and his council. Beyond the North Atlantic coast of America, however, the colonies had generally complied, as far as divorce was concerned, with the requirement that colonial matrimonial legislation conform to English tradition and practice. Although the inhabitants of divorceless colonies could have their marriages dissolved by a private Act of the British

Parliament, all the colonial bills emanated from India or Ceylon. (One 1843 bill was introduced by a man who had lived in Australia; he cited the impossibility of getting a divorce there.) Being unable to legalize divorce, the authorities in various colonies adopted ad hoc regulations to deal with cases of marriage breakdown such as desertion. For example, an 1846 New Zealand ordinance "for the support of destitute families and illegitimate children" made it an offense for a man to "unlawfully, and without cause for doing so desert his wife or... children under the age of 14 years and... leave them without means of support." A man convicted of such an offense could be ordered to pay up to a pound a week in support. Similar legislation had been passed earlier in the Australian colonies of Tasmania and New South Wales.

With the establishment of a divorce court in England in 1857, however, the legislative restrictions on the colonies changed. Divorce was no longer repugnant to English law, and colonial governments were not only enabled to legalize divorce, but actively encouraged to do so. In 1858 the secretary of state for the colonies sent a copy of the English divorce law to colonial governors and suggested that they recommend similar legislation to the colonial legislators. Some colonies responded with breathtaking haste. In South Australia a divorce law on the English model was on the statute books within seven months. Others waited longer, however: New Zealand passed a divorce law in 1867, New South Wales in 1873, and Jamaica in 1879.

The arguments for and against divorce in the colonies generally echoed the debate that had taken place in England. Opponents insisted that divorce was not only contrary to Christian doctrine, but that it would lead to the collapse of the family and the social order. Against this, the proponents of divorce could raise the powerful arguments that the British Parliament, the mother of parliaments, had legalized divorce, and that there was no immediate evidence that English morals or society had broken down as a result. The English example gave the advocates of divorce a useful counterweight to the terrible specters of moral and social decline their opponents saw in "foreign" countries that allowed divorce. It was during the late 1860s that divorce rates in the United States began to climb after the Civil War, and America began to gain a reputation as a nation of low morals, fragile family life, and impoverished national character. In the debates on divorce in New Zealand, one Member of Parliament evoked the image of Chicago where, "when the great American railway stopped, they could hear shouted out: 'There's ten minutes allowed for divorce, and twenty minutes for refreshments'."

Otherwise the colonial debates on divorce traversed what is by now familiar ground. Divorce would be disastrous for women, who would be abandoned by their husbands at the least whim; conversely, divorce would give women some protection against their husbands' offenses and oppression. Children would suffer; children would benefit. Divorce would destroy marriage; divorce would strengthen marriage by correcting its most flagrant abuses. There were familiar configurations of opposition and support, too, with the Roman Catholic and Anglican churches opposed to the legalization of divorce, and Presbyterians, drawing on the Calvinist tradition, often to the fore in promoting it.

Throughout much of the British Empire, in the end, the result was the same as in England itself: Divorce was legalized so as to allow men to divorce their wives for reason of adultery, and women their husbands for aggravated adultery. Initially, at least, the colonial legislators resisted pressure to pass divorce laws more liberal than the English. There was a wish to ensure that laws throughout the Empire were harmonized for fear, as one New Zealand politician put it, that "a woman may be a lawful wife in one part of the Empire, and be living in immorality in another." Even so, many of the colonies did liberalize their divorce policies before England did. An 1898 New Zealand law enabled women to divorce for reason of simple adultery and added several new grounds for divorce: desertion for five or more years; the wife's drunkenness, coupled with her failure to carry out her domestic duties; and the conviction of either spouse for attempting to murder the other. Such reforms anticipated English law by decades: Women in England were given equal access to divorce for adultery only in 1923, and other grounds were not added to English law until 1937.

The Canadian colonies stood noticeably apart from the Australasian tendency to emulate, then surpass, English divorce policy. The three maritime colonies (Nova Scotia, New Brunswick, and Prince Edward Island) were to remain the only provinces with a divorce law. An 1833 bill to legalize divorce in Upper Canada (later Ontario) was withdrawn before its second reading, and from 1839 the Lower Canada (Quebec) legislature adopted the procedure of dissolving individual marriages by statute rather than legalize divorce. With the unification of Canada in 1867, legislative control of marriage passed to the dominion (federal) parliament, but because the terms of confederation were that laws in the individual provinces should stand, the three maritime provinces kept their divorce laws. As for the inhabitants of the rest of Canada, their sole recourse was a dissolution of marriage by individual Act of Parliament. The Canadian parliament, then, entered the divorce business ten years after the British Parliament had abandoned it. The sole ground that was accepted was adultery (by wife or husband), but divorces were rare enough: There were only sixty-nine (two a year) between 1867 and 1900.

Sporadic attempts to legalize divorce in Canada during the nineteenth century failed. Bills aiming to establish provincial divorce courts were defeated in 1875, 1879, and 1888, and there was even an attempt to abolish the existing provisions for divorce in New Brunswick. Part of the refusal of the federal legislators to countenance provincial divorce institutions was a fear that Canada would develop, as the United States had, a myriad of divorce laws that caused interminable problems of interjurisdictional recognition. They were given a taste of the problems when they had to deal with Canadians who, for lack of divorce at home, had their marriages dissolved in the United States and then wished to remarry in Canada. Another obstacle to a national divorce law was the province of Quebec, with its predominantly Catholic population and a powerful church adamantly opposed to the legalization of divorce. Just as England had been the only Protestant state not to legalize divorce in the sixteenth century, so Canada faltered in the nineteenth and became the only major member of the British Empire not to give its population access to judicial divorce.

For a real contrast to Canadian conservatism in divorce, however, we should look not to the other parts of the empire, which adopted the cautious English divorce policy, but to the United States. It was there that the nineteenth century witnessed a dramatic geographical spread of divorce laws, a startling liberalization of policies, and a rapid increase in the number of divorces. Despite these easy generalizations, describing and explaining the evolution of divorce laws and policies in the United States is complicated by the fact that marriage and divorce legislation fell within the control of the individual states. Because an account of divorce in each would be tedious and often repetitive, the discussion here divides the United States into three large regions: the northeast, the South, and a combined Midwest and West.

As we have seen, many of the states of the northeast passed divorce laws in the 1780s and 1790s, soon after independence was won from Britain. In the following half century they sorted out the residual confusion between legislative and judicial divorce, and most of the states liberalized their policies. Pennsylvania is an example of a state that went through these steps. After a brief period of legislative divorce from 1776 to 1785, the legislature passed a law allowing divorce on the grounds of bigamy, adultery, or malicious desertion for four years. In addition, wives who could prove their husbands guilty of extreme cruelty or some other misconduct could get a separation. Beginning in 1815, this 1785 law was extended. Desertion was reduced to two years, and two further grounds were added: cruel treatment by the husband such that the wife's life was endangered and his indignities toward his wife that made her life intolerable and forced her to leave home. (The latter is known as "constructive desertion.") In 1843 the wife's insanity was added as a ground to the state's divorce law, and in 1854 two further grounds were recognized: imprisonment of either spouse for a felony and cruel treatment by the wife toward her husband. The extension of grounds for divorce in Pennsylvania, then, was gradual and sometimes incomprehensible (why was the wife's insanity a ground for divorce, but not the husband's?), but it was steady.

Connecticut, which had established itself as having the most liberal divorce policy among the colonies, pursued the liberal course of divorce even more rapidly in the nineteenth century. Despite attempts to restrict divorce in the 1780s, Connecticut maintained its policy intact, allowing divorce for adultery, fraudulent contract, desertion for three years, and prolonged absence where there was a presumption of death. The opponents of divorce did not give up, however. One of the most prominent was Timothy Dwight, president of Yale University, who preached a sermon in 1816 condemning any divorce but that based on the biblical ground of adultery. The evil of divorce had been contained in earlier times by religion, Dwight asserted, but "at the present time, the progress of this evil is alarming and terrible": in New Haven alone there had been 50 divorces in the preceding five years, and more than 400 in the whole state. Dwight dwelt on the horrors that divorce had caused during the French Revolution (by coincidence, divorce was abolished in France the year Dwight delivered this sermon) and predicted a similar fate for Connecticut:

It is clearly evident, that the progress of divorce, though different in different countries will in all be dreadful beyond conception. Within a moderate period, the whole community will be thrown, by laws made in open opposition to the Laws of God, into a general prostitution.... Over such a country, a virtuous man, if such an one be found, will search in vain to find a virtuous wife. Wherever he wanders, nothing will meet his eye, but stalking bare-faced pollution. The realm around him has become one vast Brothel; one great province in the world of Perdition.

Connecticut's governor and legislators were in the audience as Dwight evoked this hellish specter of a society with a liberal divorce policy, but they were apparently unmoved. The state's divorce law was next reformed only in 1843, and then it was to add habitual drunkenness and intolerable cruelty to the grounds. Throughout this period, we should note, the Connecticut legislature also dissolved marriages where the circumstances were not covered by the law. In 1849 alone the committee of the legislature that tried divorce cases heard forty petitions, and advised divorce in fourteen of them for such reasons as offensive behavior, cruelty, eviction, and failure to provide. That bumper crop of divorces was the last, however, for in the same year divorce was passed entirely to the jurisdiction of the courts. At the same time the grounds were extended even further, notably to allow divorce for reason of "any such misconduct as permanently destroys the happiness of the petitioner and defeats the purpose of the marriage relation." This, known as an "omnibus clause," gave the courts wide discretion and was clearly intended to compensate for the loss of the discretionary element that legislative divorce had provided. The overall result was to give Connecticut one of the most liberal divorce codes in the United States by the middle of the nineteenth century. Conscious of this, and anxious to forestall a rush to divorce by out-of-state men and women, Connecticut law required three years' residence before a divorce could be obtained.

Not all the northeastern states consistently liberalized their divorce laws after independence, however. In 1786 Massachusetts enacted a divorce law that was more restrictive than provisions that had given the colony America's second largest number of divorces. The new law excluded desertion, and recognized as grounds only adultery, impotence, and bigamy, although cruelty was a ground for judicial separation. From this more restrictive position, however, Massachusetts liberalized its legislation and in 1811 added, as grounds for separation, the husband's desertion or his failure to provide for his wife. Later in the nineteenth century additional grounds were added to divorce: a sentence to seven years' imprisonment at hard labor (1835); malicious desertion by either spouse for five years (1838); and either spouse's leaving the other for three years or more to belong to a religious sect that believed that the sexual relationship between wife and husband was unlawful (1850).

Pennsylvania, Connecticut, and Massachusetts were examples of two general trends in the northeastern states of the United States: the transfer of divorce from legislature to judiciary and the liberalization of divorce legislation. In a number of states omnibus clauses allowing for divorce in circumstances of "intolerable hardship" and "offenses against marriage" transferred to the courts the discretion that legislators had exercised in individual cases. Without such clauses the exclusive use of judicial divorce would have reduced the availability of divorce, so that the insertion of omnibus clauses was a means of protecting liberal policies.

Other northeastern states pursued more or less liberal policies. Rhode Island, New Hampshire, and Vermont passed laws in the 1790s that recognized adultery, desertion, and cruelty among other grounds for divorce. Rhode Island also added an omnibus clause that permitted divorce where there was "gross misbehavior and wickedness in either of the parties, repugnant to and in violation of the marriage covenant." With such a clause Rhode Island might well have left its divorce law alone, but instead it added the grounds of habitual drunkenness in 1844, and desertion for five years in 1851.

The striking exception to the liberal policies of the northeast was New York. In 1787 adultery was made the sole ground for divorce, and even then it seems that the aim of the legislators was to use divorce as a punishment for adultery, rather than to provide divorce as a relief for the aggrieved spouse of an adulterer. The history of divorce in New York from 1787 until the Civil War and beyond is little more than a catalog of unsuccessful attempts to liberalize the law. It is true that there were reforms in related legislation, such as that governing separations. In 1813 women were given the right to separate if their husbands treated them cruelly or inhumanely, if cohabitation were unsafe, or if they were abandoned. And in 1824 men were given equivalent rights to separation. But as far as divorce was concerned, New York's legislators could not be moved from the single ground recognized in 1787. Nor did New York provide ready access to legislative divorce. Although many petitions were lodged with the state's assembly, only a few persistent husbands and wives succeeded. One woman lodged a petition in 1809, detailing her husband's cruelty, violence, and his false accusation that she had committed adultery with several men. Her divorce was granted two years later. The net result of the restrictive law and reluctant legislators was that the inhabitants of New York had less access to divorce than those of almost any state. Only the citizens of South Carolina, where divorce was not legal at all, might have envied New York's married couples.

South Carolina itself was as exceptional to the South as New York was to the northeast. As we have seen, the southern colonies had not provided for divorce in the colonial period, but soon after independence some of them began to make divorce available by legislative act: Maryland's legislature began to dissolve marriages in 1790, North Carolina's began in 1794, and Georgia's started in 1798. From 1799, though, divorce laws sprang up throughout the South. Tennessee led the way in 1799, and it was soon followed by Georgia (1802), Alabama Territories, which included the future Alabama and Mississippi (1803), Arkansas (1807), Kentucky (1809), North Carolina (1814), Florida (1827), Virginia (1827), Louisiana (1827), and Texas (1841). South Carolina finally legalized divorce in 1872 but then repealed the law in 1878. Throughout the South, legislatures continued to dissolve marriages even after divorce laws were passed, but in the 1830s and 1840s many states passed constitutional amendments to forbid legislative divorces.

Although the South generally lagged behind the northeastern states in making judicial provision for divorce, it would be wrong to think of the southern laws, once they were in place, as being particularly restrictive. The common association of the South with conservative social policies is certainly misleading in respect to divorce, for the southern states progressively liberalized their divorce policies throughout the nineteenth century.

The development of North Carolina's divorce policies was not typical of the South as a whole, but it is an example of the way one state's legislators wrestled with the sensitive problems divorce posed. Divorce had not been available during the colonial period, but in 1779 a petition for a dissolution of a marriage was filed with the legislature. It was turned down, as were several others after it, but eventually a legislative divorce was granted in 1794, and there were a further nine in the next six years. During this early period of statehood, then, divorce was difficult, although the courts were empowered to grant separations or alimony if a wife was forced to flee from her husband. A 1796 judgment, for example, recognized that one Margaret Spiller had been compelled to leave home on account of her husband's cruelty, and the court ordered him to pay her £100 a year for the rest of her life, together with £200 to cover her living expenses between the time she left home and the court's decision.

There was increasing pressure on the North Carolina legislature to adopt a more liberal and coherent divorce policy, and in 1808 a bill was introduced that would allow divorce for adultery, impotence, and cruelty on the part of the husband. A vigorous public debate raged, with opponents of divorce predicting social chaos if the bill passed, and the bill was finally defeated. When divorce was finally legalized in 1814, it was on more restrictive bases than the 1808 bill. The courts were empowered to grant separations and divorces, as they saw fit, in cases of adultery or natural impotence. A woman might also obtain a separation for reason of desertion, cruel treatment, being evicted from her home, or "such indignities to her person as to render her condition intolerable or life burthensome." To deter hasty or ill-considered divorces, the offensive conditions had to have lasted six months before the petition was lodged, and a final divorce decree was issued only after twelve months had elapsed from the judgment. If the petitioner survived this procedure (which effectively meant a minimum eighteen-month period between an offense and the divorce), he or she was rewarded with a divorce that enabled only the innocent party to remarry.

This system remained intact for only seven years, for in 1821 the North Carolina legislature began to dissolve marriages again and had passed fifteen when in 1827 a new law was passed giving the courts broad discretion to grant divorces "whenever they may be satisfied... of the justice of such application." The state's chief justice, however, insisted on interpreting this so narrowly that the legislators began to dissolve marriages again in 1832, and they halted the practice only in 1835 by passing an amendment to the state constitution abolishing legislative divorce. In 26 years between 1800 and 1835 (records for 10 years are missing), the North Carolina legislators had dissolved 52 marriages, agreeing to a fifth of the 266 petitions that were filed. The grounds had included "cohabitation with a Negro," adultery, separation, cruelty, prostitution, wasting property, incompatibility, drunkenness, ill-temper, and indecent conduct. To this extent the legislature had provided a useful adjunct to the courts, providing a discretionary way of liberalizing divorce policy.

As individual as this period of North Carolina's divorce history was, it shared certain characteristics with other southern states. Most abolished legislative divorce between 1834 and 1850, and from 1830 until the Civil War there was a general liberalization of policies. In some states this was achieved by accepting as grounds for divorce the grounds that had until then justified only a separation; between 1835 and 1842 this was done in Florida, Arkansas, Tennessee, and Mississippi. An 1826 Louisiana law allowed separations to be converted to divorces after a waiting period of two years (of one year after 1857). North Carolina courts finally began to use the 1827 omnibus clause from the mid-1830s, while in Virginia from 1853 the courts granted divorces on a wide range of grounds: imprisonment, adultery, impotence, desertion, conviction of an infamous offense before marriage without the knowledge of the other partner, and evidence that the wife had been a prostitute before marriage or that she had been pregnant by another man at the time of the marriage. (Divorce laws everywhere included apparently strange grounds such as these, which were codifications of particular cases with which the courts had dealt.)

The process of divorce law liberalization was not always linear and smooth, as North Carolina showed, and the examples of Georgia and Missouri confirm. The 1798 Georgia constitution provided for a two-stage procedure: a court trial to authorize the divorce, followed by an act to dissolve the marriage passed by the state legislature. An average of eight divorce acts a year was passed between 1798 and 1835. In 1835 an amendment to the constitution transferred the procedure to the courts alone, but the whole thing was thrown into doubt in 1847 when the Georgia supreme court ruled that the only grounds for divorce in the state were those of the common law. This allowed only annulment and separation (not divorce) and threatened to invalidate any marriages that had taken place as a result of a divorce in Georgia. The state legislature acted quickly to avert matrimonial chaos and in 1849 passed an act validating all remarriages. The following year it passed a new divorce law that recognized eight grounds, including adultery, desertion, and imprisonment for a morals offense.

In Missouri there was a battle for jurisdiction over divorce between the judiciary and the legislature, with dozens of unhappily married couples temporarily held hostage. The state had a divorce law, but many couples turned to the legislature when the circumstances of their marriages were not covered by it. In 1833 the governor vetoed one of these legislative divorces, arguing that such divorces might not be recognized outside the state. The legislators passed the divorce over the governor's veto, and in response the governor vetoed a collective bill that dissolved thirty-seven marriages. This too was passed over his veto, and so it went on until forty-nine marriages were dissolved by the legislature in the 1833 session, even though the governor had given his assent to only two of them. In the short term this struggle can only have caused anguish to the couples involved, whose marital status seemed to change from day to day. Over the longer term, however, the conflict produced a more liberal divorce law, and in 1835 Missouri extended the grounds for divorce, abolished separations, and relaxed the prohibition on the marriage of the guilty partner.

Divorce law liberalization was not an easy road, then, but it was traveled by almost all the southern states. Apart from South Carolina, all the states that would later form the Confederacy had by 1860 included adultery, desertion, and cruelty among the grounds for divorce. Moreover, the definition of cruelty itself was expanded beyond physical violence to encompass verbal violence and threats, particularly when they were aimed at women. An 1849 Arkansas court ruling listed the following acts as constituting a personal indignity: rudeness, vulgarity, unmerited reproach, contumely and studied neglect, intentional incivility, injury, manifest disdain, abusive language, malignant ridicule, "and every other plain manifestation of settled hate, alienation and estrangement, both of word and action." When such indignities were "habitual, continuous and permanent," they could justify a divorce. What underlay the widening definition of cruelty was a belief that women, especially women of the upper classes, were as sensitive to verbal abuse as they were to physical violence. Whereas women of the lower classes might be expected to put up with domestic violence and crude language, one southern judge argued, "between persons of education, refinement and delicacy, the slightest blow in anger may be cruelty." It was but a short step to include nonphysical violence.

The overall image of divorce in the American South in the first half of the nineteenth century is more complex than this short survey suggests. It is clear, however, that even though the southern colonies did not permit divorce, and the southern states lagged behind the northeast in abandoning legislative divorce, there was a comparable trend of liberalization of law and policy. By the outbreak of the Civil War, in fact, divorce policies in the southern states were about as liberal as those in the northeast. South Carolina, it is true, was recalcitrant, but it was no more typical of the South as a whole than the restrictive policy of New York was typical of the northeastern states.

If the South little deserved its reputation of conservatism in divorce policies, what is to be said for the association of the West of the United States with matrimonial libertarianism? As the American West opened up during the nineteenth century, the territories, then the states that were formed from them, quickly gained notoriety for divorce laws that were wide-ranging in their grounds, lax in their operation, and whose minimal residency requirements seemed to invite migrants in search of divorce. The notion of "The West" conjured up an image of a rough, violent, transient society of men and horses that was hardly conducive to the formation and survival of stable marriages and families. This popular image of the "wild" West, however, has misrepresented the essentially traditional character of social structure and relationships in the western states where, as elsewhere, marriage and the family were important and fundamental social institutions. One study showed that 90% of women who traveled west in the mid-nineteenth century had married by the age of twenty-five and that 80% of men had done so by the age of thirty. Gunsmoke from the clashes of independent men has too often obscured the dominant reality of family life in the little house on the prairie, in the hills, and on the Pacific coast.

The fact does remain that divorce laws in the West, varying though they did from state to state, tended to be more liberal than elsewhere and that these laws, combined with particular social factors, produced exceptionally high divorce rates in some of the western states. One reason for the liberal laws in these parts of the country was the fact that the western states entered the union at a time when divorce policies were being liberalized almost everywhere. The liberal divorce laws enacted in these states were their first divorce laws, and their legislators did not have to reverse or expand entrenched policies. The simple readiness of western legislators to legalize divorce is shown by their wasting no time in doing so. Ohio, for example, gained statehood in 1802 and legalized divorce in 1804; Illinois became a state in 1818 and introduced divorce the following year; Michigan legalized divorce in 1812, seven years after joining the union. The common readiness to enact divorce legislation should not obscure divergences in the terms of these laws, however, or the way individual western states liberalized their codes. When divorce was introduced into Ohio in 1804, four grounds were recognized (bigamy, adultery, extreme cruelty, and desertion for five years), and in 1822 two more were added (physical incompetence for intercourse and imprisonment for a crime). Further grounds were added in 1853: fraudulent contract, gross neglect of duty, habitual drunkenness, and cases where one spouse had been divorced in another state and had remarried in violation of that state's divorce law.

By midcentury, then, Ohio recognized ten grounds for divorce, but Indiana went even further. The territory's legislature began to dissolve marriages as early as 1807, and did so on 104 occasions between then and 1846. A general divorce law was passed in 1824, encompassing such grounds as inhuman treatment, adultery, and abandonment, but also including an omnibus clause permitting divorce "in all cases where the court in its discretion thinks it just and reasonable." In 1852 the law was reworked to include seven grounds (adultery, impotence, abandonment for one year, cruel treatment, habitual drunkenness, the husband's failure to provide for his wife, and conviction for an infamous crime), and the omnibus clause was rephrased to read "any other cause for which the court shall deem it proper that the divorce shall be granted." These provisions were liberal enough, but divorce in Indiana was made even easier by minimal residency requirements. The 1824 law demanded nothing more than residence in the county where the petition was filed, and although requirements of twelve and twenty-four months were put in place in 1831 and 1843, respectively, they were not enforced. The 1852 law seemed to reflect this reality by imposing no residency requirements whatsoever: A petitioner had to be a bona fide resident of the county where the divorce petition was filed, but the only evidence of residence that was demanded was the petitioner's affidavit. This permissive policy was the basis of Indiana's reputation as a divorce haven, and for the phenomenon of "Indiana divorces," which were analogous to later "Mexican divorces" and "Reno divorces."

Other western states went through similar stages of legal development, setting out specific grounds for divorce, increasing them, and then moving to omnibus clauses. Iowa, for example, passed its first state law on divorce in 1838, liberalized it in 1839, and again in 1842. In 1846 an omnibus clause was introduced to allow divorce "when it shall be made fully apparent to the satisfaction of the court, that the parties cannot live in peace and happiness together." Five years later, in 1851, the law was amended, and in 1855 provision was made for separations. In 1858, as a further act before the Civil War provided an intermission in this ongoing legislative drama, Iowa's legislators revived the 1851 act with a few modifications. Such a process ensured that the subject of divorce was constantly before the lawmakers and shows the sensitivity of divorce as an area of legislation.

There were significant variations among the western states' divorce laws, but their liberal tendency is clear. The inclusion of omnibus clauses was particularly important in that they gave the courts wide discretion to allow divorces in circumstances not covered by the specific grounds. A major exception in this respect was California, where the first divorce law, enacted in 1851, recognized only specific grounds: impotence, adultery, extreme cruelty, desertion or neglect for three years, habitual intemperance, fraud, and conviction for a felony. This law was influential, too, becoming the basis of early divorce legislation in Montana, Idaho, the Dakotas, and Nevada. California's legislators were also notable because, unlike their counterparts in other states, they did not fiddle ceaselessly with divorce legislation. The period of desertion or neglect in the 1851 law was reduced to two years in 1870 and then to one year in 1872, but the substance of the law remained intact. California's judges, however, expanded the definition of "cruelty" and thus liberalized the policy. An 1857 decision, for example, rejected the traditional notion that cruelty meant physical violence, to hold that "women's finer sensibilities deserved respect and that imprecation as to her sexual conduct constituted cruelty." Similarly, an 1863 judgment recognized mental cruelty and contributed to a redefinition of cruelty in the 1870 statute. These examples highlight the need to go beyond the formal terms of divorce legislation to understand trends in divorce policy.

Not only were the divorce laws of the western states liberal, but they generally required only short terms of residence in order to qualify a petitioner. Most set the residency requirement at a year, but Nebraska, Idaho, and Nevada demanded only six months, while in South Dakota it was only ninety days. Utah went further and required a petitioner to demonstrate only that he or she was "a resident or wishes to become one." This, together with an omnibus clause in Utah's 1852 divorce law gained the state instant notoriety among Americans concerned about the decline of marriage and the family. Alarm at events in Utah was increased by the practice of polygamy among Mormons who had settled there, a practice that was discontinued from 1890 after federal action against Mormons who married more than one woman.

It was not only liberal divorce policies that began to ring alarm bells in the minds of conservatives, but also a perception that the laws were being widely used, that a large number of divorces were being granted, and that many marriages were breaking down because of the easy availability of divorce. Unfortunately there are few reliable statistics on divorce until the last third of the nineteenth century because the states made little provision for the keeping and publication of such data. Tardiness in this respect is all the more surprising given the growing concern over the number of divorces after the Civil War. There are indications of the frequency of legislative divorces here and there before the war, however. The Ohio legislature had dissolved more than a hundred marriages by 1850, while the Kansas assembly granted one divorce in 1857, three in 1858, eight in 1859, and forty-three in 1860. (The large number in 1860 was a result of an 1859 decision to end legislative divorces at the end of 1860.)

Concern at the midcentury divorce rates in the Midwest was expressed by prominent social and political commentators. In 1852 and 1853 the *New York Tribune* published a series of articles on marriage and divorce by Henry James (father of the novelist) and Stephen Pearl Andrews, a former minister who had converted to an ideology of free love. Their advocacy of liberal divorce policies was opposed by the editor of the *Tribune,* Horace Greeley, who thought divorce justifiable only on the biblical ground, adultery. Greeley's prognostication of the effects of more liberal policies was pessimistic: It would result "in a general profligacy and corruption such as this country has never known, and few of our people can adequately imagine." In 1860, prompted by an attempt to liberalize New York's divorce law, Greeley returned to his attack on divorce. But unlike earlier opponents of divorce, who conjured up visions of the divorce-generated decadence of Rome or the sexual chaos of the French Revolution, Greeley was fortunate to have a closer point of reference: the (according to Greeley) "paradise of free-lovers" of Indiana, where men and women could "get un-married nearly at pleasure." Greeley attributed this state of affairs (so to speak) to the influence of Robert Dale Owen, a member of Indiana's legislature and son of the utopian reformer Robert Owen, whose policies on divorce are discussed in the next chapter.

A debate on divorce was carried on between the younger Owen and Greeley in the pages of the *Tribune.* Owen charged that the restrictive law of New York produced "elopements, adultery,... free love, and that most terrible of all social evils, prostitution." Marriage, he insisted, should be based on "all that is best and purest in the inner nature of man, love in the broadest acceptation of that much profaned word." It was not enough to say that a marriage *might* be dissolved when it was "defiled by evil passions"; in such cases "for the sake of virtue and for the good of mankind... [the marriage] *ought* to cease." Such arguments were countered by Greeley, who restated the doctrine of marital indissolubility and set out the social implications of allowing divorce. Not only was divorce harmful to children, but it encouraged hasty and ill-considered marriages. Moreover, divorce was bound to be abused: "To the libertine, the egoist, the selfish seeker of personal and present enjoyment at whatever cost to others, the Indissolubility of Marriage is an obstacle, a restraint, a terror; and God forbid that it should ever cease to be." If Indiana continued to pursue lax divorce policies, it would experience the same fate as Rome, "which under the sway of easy divorce, rotted away and perished, – blasted by the mildew of unchaste mothers and dissolute homes."

Table 6.1. *Divorces, separations, and annulments by year: United States, 1860–70*

Year	Number	Rate per 1,000 population	Rate per 1,000 existing marriages
1860	7,380	0.3	1.2
1861	6,540	0.2	1.1
1862	6,230	0.2	1.0
1863	6,760	0.2	1.1
1864	8,940	0.2	1.4
1865	10,090	0.3	1.6
1866	11,530	0.3	1.8
1867	9,937	0.3	1.5
1868	10,150	0.3	1.5
1869	10,939	0.3	1.6
1870	10,962	0.3	1.5

Note: The base population excludes slaves to 1865.
Source: Richard Wires, *The Divorce Issue and Reform in Nineteenth-Century Indiana* (Muncie, 1967), 7.

The debate on divorce was itself blasted from the pages of the *Tribune* and American popular consciousness by the outbreak of the Civil War in 1861. After the war, however, the concern about American divorce rates that was expressed in the 1850s was heightened by a rise in the number of divorces in the immediate postwar period. Statistics for this period are not wholly reliable, but it seems that divorces decreased somewhat between 1861 and 1865, while the war was in progress, but increased thereafter. Table 6.1 gives the combined numbers of divorces, separations, and annulments in the United States in the 1860s, and the image of decline during the war and increase after it is confirmed by the statistics on divorces in three northeastern states, shown in Table 6.2. The significant change was in the number of divorces in the wartime and postwar years. In the whole country there were 6,510 divorces, separations, and annulments a year from 1861 to 1865, but from 1865 to 1867 there were 10,519, an increase of 60%. In Massachusetts, Vermont, and Connecticut the increases were of the same order, ranging from 58 to 67%.

Although we should want much more detail on these divorces before putting forward precise explanations for the changes, divorces at other periods of military conflict suggest broad reasons. A decline in the number of divorce petitions during the war probably reflected the separation of wives and husbands while the latter were away on military

Table 6.2. *Divorces by year: Massachusetts, Vermont, and Connecticut, 1860-70*

Year	Massachusetts	Vermont	Connecticut
1860	243	95	282
1861	234	66	275
1862	196	94	257
1863	207	102	291
1864	270	98	426
1865	333	122	404
1866	392	155	488
1867	282	159	459
1868	339	167	478
1869	339	148	491
1870	379	164	408

Source: Nathan Allen, "Divorces in New England," *North American Review* 130 (1880), 549.

service. In the most banal sense, separation temporarily removed the sources of marital tension and unhappiness, and in fact the massive death toll of the Civil War (about two-thirds of a million people died as a result of it) must have terminated some marriages that would otherwise have been dissolved by divorce. But if separation of the spouses ameliorated some marriages for a short time, demobilization and the return to married life in 1864 and 1865 were accompanied by a rise in the number of divorces. No doubt some divorces were based on adultery that had taken place during separation, while others resulted from the difficulties of readjustment to marriage after a year or more of life apart.

That there might be quite reasonable explanations of an increase in divorcing after the war did not quell the alarm of social commentators, however, and they responded quickly to the image of spreading marital destruction in a time of national reconstruction. In 1867 the president of Yale University, Theodore Woolsey, following in the footsteps of his predecessor Timothy Dwight, published a series of articles on the history of divorce. Woolsey denounced what he saw as a widespread decay in morals, increasing vice, materialism, and "corruption in the family, as manifested by connubial unfaithfulness and divorce," and insisted that America's destiny "depends upon our ability to keep family life pure and simple." Woolsey was supported by others: A Connecticut pastor condemned divorce as leading to polygamy and bigamy, and the rector of Trinity College argued that divorce led to the breakdown of the family and ultimately to communism.

Significantly, such pressure brought results, at least in Connecticut, where it was concentrated. The state's legislature set up a committee to investigate the divorce rates, and in 1878 the omnibus clause of the 1849 divorce law (allowing divorce for misconduct that destroyed the happiness of the petitioner and defeated the purpose of marriage) was repealed. Two years later the procedure for getting a divorce was lengthened. In 1881, encouraged by these successes, Woolsey and Samuel Dike, a Congregationalist minister from Vermont, founded the New England Divorce Reform League, the first organization whose aim was specifically to oppose liberal divorce policies. The league soon had national dimensions, becoming the National Divorce Reform League in 1885, and the National League for the Protection of the Family in 1897. The creation of this organization in the United States was indicative of an unease about divorce and the future of the family that was expressed throughout Western society in the last decades of the nineteenth century. In this period, William O'Neill has written, divorce became "one of the first aspects of what we call the Revolution in Morals to become a matter of public controversy." Many issues were drawn into the vortex of the debate, prominent among them sexuality, venereal disease, prostitution, women's rights, and alcohol. What we might think of as a conservative response to the spread of apparently liberal social policies and permissive behavior (in respect of divorce and other matters) became a significant political force. Mass organizations, such as the purity leagues, temperance unions, and divorce reform leagues, were established to coordinate policy and activities, and to encourage state, provincial, and national governments to repeal liberal laws and adopt more restrictive social policies.

As far as the movement for divorce reform was concerned, we should begin by asking what the conservatives were reacting against. Were increasing marriage breakdown and divorce merely a perception or were they established facts? Initially the movement in America had access to few reliable statistics on divorce, although the number of divorces in New England (those shown in Table 6.2) had been published in 1880 to prove that "the evils of divorce" were spreading. The New England Divorce Reform League, set up the next year, successfully lobbied Congress for an official study of divorce, and in 1889 the Department of Labor published a report on marriage and divorce in the United States from 1867 to 1886. As faulty as its statistics were, this report confirmed what the conservatives feared: Divorces had increased dramatically in the period. In 1867 there had been 9,937, but in 1886 the number had grown to 25,535, an increase of 150%. Only about a third of the increase could be accounted for by population growth. Statistics were gathered more systematically and accurately from this time, and it was possible to demonstrate that the rate of increase in the number of divorces was anything but declining. Between 1880 and 1890 the number grew by 70%, between 1890 and 1900 by 67%.

The United States was not exceptional, for elsewhere in Western society divorces increased steadily up to the outbreak of World War I. In France, where divorce had been legalized again in 1884, the number of divorces rose from 4,227 in 1885 to 6,751 ten years later, and then to 14,261 by 1910, thus bearing out the worst fears of those who had opposed the divorce legislation. In other countries the absolute number of divorces was lower, but the rates of increase were sometimes even greater. Annual divorces in England and Wales increased more than fivefold between 1867 and 1910 (there were 119 and 588 divorce petitions in those years, respectively), and in Belgium divorces rose from 55 in 1860 to 393 in 1890 and then to 1,089 in 1910. Figure 6.1 gives the number of divorces in several countries between 1860 and 1910 and gives an idea of the general pace of increase as well as the differences in absolute numbers. The figure graphically shows the way divorces in the United States outstripped those in Europe by the turn of the century. To make the point more precisely, we can put it this way: In 1910 there were 83,045 divorces in the United States, compared to a combined total of 20,329 in England, Scotland, France (which alone contributed 14,261), Belgium, the Netherlands, Switzerland, Norway, Denmark, and Sweden. Not only that, but the United States had a smaller population than these European states (92 million compared to 108 million).

With the exception of the United States, the simple number of divorces around the turn of the century was not striking by modern standards. As a crude rate per thousand population, divorces in the United States grew from 0.3 in 1870 to 0.7 in 1900 and then to 0.9 on the eve of World War I. In no European country was the rate higher than 0.5 before the war: France's was 0.36, and Switzerland's was 0.41, and most were below 0.2 divorces per thousand population on an annual basis.

The thought that such rates might pale by the standards of a century later would not only have failed to mollify contemporary observers, but would have confirmed their belief that if prompt action were not taken to close the floodgates on divorce, Western civilization would be washed away in the deluge of depravity. American critics of divorce concentrated on the so-called divorce havens, the states with the most liberal policies, and conservatives in other countries focused, understandably, on the United States as an example of what divorce unchecked could lead to. Politicians in far-off New Zealand flayed

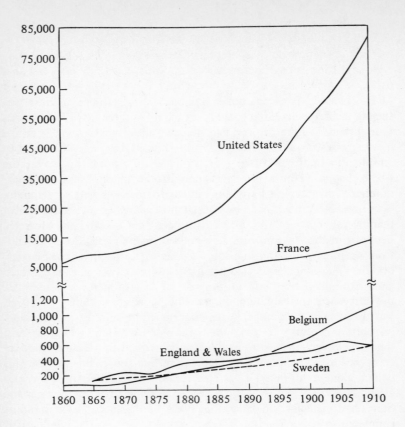

Figure 6.1

America for its "general carelessness with regard to the marriage tie," a trait one Member of Parliament attributed to the fact that in the United States "large numbers of families...live in hotels." Another described New England's divorce laws as permitting nothing less than "successive polygamy" and suggested that in New York and South Carolina "where marriages are almost indissoluble, the people are better in their social life and altogether of a better character."

The country most concerned with American divorce was Canada, where divorce law had lagged behind general Western trends. This fact heightened the distinction between Canada and its southern neighbor and was exploited by Canadians anxious to define a national identity and character distinct from those of the United States. Divorce was frequently cited by Canadian commentators, who contrasted the rarity of divorce in their own country with the excesses in some American states. Between 1867 and 1907 there were 431 divorces in Canada, and 1,274,341 in the United States, and even allowing for different populations, divorce was 230 times more frequent in the latter. Canadian observers either overlooked or made a virtue of the fact that divorce was available from the courts only in three maritime provinces, and was elsewhere available in Canada only by the expensive and time-consuming means of a special Act of Parliament. Rather, Canadians drew moral conclusions from the different divorce rates, seeing in the higher American rates evidence of moral inferiority. In 1880 the *Canadian Methodist Magazine* commented, "we are free from many of the social cancers which are empoisoning the national life of our neighbours. We have no polygamous Mormondom; no Ku-Klux terrorism; no Oneida communism; no Illinois divorce system; no cruel Indian massacres." In 1910 the chancellor of McGill University in Montreal drew the social implications of American divorce more clearly: It represented most of all the absence of social restraint in the United States, where "the same spirit which, carried to the extreme limit, is manifested in lynchings and murders finds a milder expression in the intolerance of control in the family."

Beyond the portrayal of America as a nation verging on perdition, there was a more general assault on the evil of divorce in the Western world. In the vanguard was organized religion, particularly the Roman Catholic church. In the Syllabus of Errors promulgated by Pope Pius IX in 1864, ten of the eighty articles were devoted to the family, and civil marriage and divorce were denounced as two of the errors of the modern age. Other churches, notably the Church of England and its affiliates throughout the British Empire, and American denominations such as the Reformed Church of America, also condemned divorce. Even those churches based on Lutheran and Calvinist principles, which accepted the permissibility of divorce in some circumstances, were opposed to the open-ended and discretionary approaches to divorce that had been adopted in some states of America, and that advocates of divorce liberalization were promoting in other countries.

One issue that particularly concerned the churches was the immediate and practical problem of remarriage. Many men and women quite clearly divorced in the face of their churches' doctrines, but then expected to be able to remarry in church. The churches had no control over divorce, of course, but they could decline to permit remarriages according to religious rites and force their divorced members to marry civilly. In general the churches adopted rigorous, even punitive, approaches: Those who divorced against God's law, as interpreted by each individual denomination, had to live with the consequences of their act. If, in the eyes of their church, they were still married to their first spouse, they could refrain from remarriage altogether or take their spiritual chances with a civil marriage. The Episcopal church in the United States acted on this issue as early as 1863, forbidding ministers to celebrate any marriage involving a divorced person, unless he or she had been the innocent party in a divorce for reason of adultery. By 1907 even this rule was restricted to prevent remarriage of an innocent spouse until a year after the divorce. Other major Protestant denominations in America, such as the Presbyterian, Methodist Episcopal, and Reformed churches, followed the lead of the Episcopalians in restricting the remarriage of divorced men and women. In 1884, for instance, the Methodist Episcopal church allowed its ministers to solemnize the marriages of divorced men and women only when they were the innocent parties in adultery suits or in the rare case of two divorced former spouses remarrying each other. In contrast, the Evangelical Lutheran church of America decided in 1907 that the innocent spouse in a divorce on legitimate grounds should be entitled to remarry in church after waiting at least a year. The church's General Synod adopted a relatively liberal view that legitimate grounds included not only adultery and desertion, the classic Lutheran doctrine, but also impotence, extreme cruelty, conspiracy against life, and habitual drunkenness.

In England the Anglican church wrestled with its remarriage policy with mixed results. A draft reform of canon law banning any remarriage after divorce was defeated in 1873, and in 1885 a committee of bishops advocated a more liberal stance, recommending that although divorced people should not remarry, the church should agree to solemnize a marriage involving an innocent partner, and might even agree to marry a guilty former spouse if he or she were repentant and if the bishop thought it "most consonant with the teaching of Holy Scripture and the mind and practice of the Primitive Church." In 1888 the Lambeth Conference, an international meeting of Anglican bishops, opposed the remarriage of the guilty in church, but proposed that clergy should not be instructed to deny remarriage to an innocent partner. The Anglican church, clearly, was divided on the issue of divorce, as it had been since its foundation. The variety of attitudes within the church was revealed by an 1895 survey of the way the thirty-four dioceses of the church in England dealt with granting marriage licenses to divorced people. Of the thirty-three dioceses that replied, eleven denied licenses to any divorced person, whether guilty or innocent, sixteen granted licenses to the innocent, and six had no fixed policy. Whether a divorced Anglican could remarry in church in England, it seemed, depended on where he or she lived.

Remarriage was an issue that was quite directly a concern of the churches, of course, but they also continued to play their traditional roles as general supervisors of public and private morality. The churches were prominent in the campaigns waged in most countries in favor of more restrictive divorce laws. In the United States twenty-five Protestant churches formed the Inter-Church Conference on Marriage and Divorce in 1903, and although it was unable to formulate a common policy on remarriage, it was more successful in pressing for uniform divorce laws throughout America. One of the targets that divorce conservatives had fixed their sights on was the liberal divorce policies of some western states, and a campaign for uniform state laws was begun as early as 1889 by the governor of New York. By 1901 a commission of states' representatives had agreed on a model divorce bill that recognized the grounds of adultery, extreme cruelty, habitual drunkenness, and desertion, but only two states actually proceeded to adopt laws on these lines. In 1903, however, the Inter-Church group combined with the National League for the Protection of the Family (the former New England Divorce Reform League) to lobby Congress, and in 1905 President Roosevelt called for the compilation of reliable marriage and divorce statistics that would aid the cause of divorce law reform. Roosevelt expressed the prevailing sense of anxiety: "There is a widespread conviction that the divorce laws are dangerously lax and indifferently administered in some of the States, resulting in a diminishing regard for the sanctity of the marriage relation."

One immediate result was a 1906 meeting in Washington of a National Congress on Uniform Divorce Laws, which had representation from forty-two states and territories. But although the delegates agreed on some points – that a federal divorce law was not feasible, for example – they could not agree on a single divorce code that would be acceptable to all states. At its first session the congress adopted a resolution that acceptable grounds for divorce included adultery, bigamy, conviction for some crimes, intolerable cruelty, desertion for two years, and habitual drunkenness. The delegates recommended that no state law should exceed these grounds, but that any state with more restrictive grounds might maintain its law unamended. In other words the notion of uniformity was interpreted not as meaning that laws ought to be uniform, but that the states with the most liberal policies ought to restrict divorce. That this was scarcely tenable was demonstrated in the congress's second session nine months later, when the same six grounds for divorce were listed, but it was resolved that "each state is at liberty to reduce or increase the same as its citizens may deem advisable." This was effectively an admission that uniform divorce legislation was impossible in the United States. On the positive side there was agreement on measures to reduce divorce migration, the temporary movement of individuals into jurisdictions with liberal divorce policies solely in order to divorce. A model act was adopted, specifying that if any inhabitant of one state went to another state to obtain a divorce on a ground not recognized by his or her own state of permanent residence, the divorce would have had no legal effect there. But even though this model statute was unanimously approved, only New Jersey, Delaware, and Wisconsin passed legislation based on it. For lack of satisfactory progress, the supporters of divorce law uniformity attempted to achieve their aim through an amendment to the Constitution that would have given the federal government jurisdiction over divorce. But although it was pursued for many years, this goal never attracted much support.

Just as the churches in the United States were at the front of opposition to liberal divorce policies, so they were elsewhere. In England a royal commission was set up in 1909 to examine the state of the country's divorce legislation, which was by then more restrictive than the laws in effect in many of the colonies. The opinion of the Anglican church, which at its most liberal supported the existing law with its sole ground (adultery) for divorce, was influential in blocking the liberalization of English divorce law, despite the recommendations of the royal commission. In the Australian colony of New South Wales, too, the Anglican church was instrumental in holding up the liberalization of the law. In 1887 the New South Wales legislature added desertion, drunkenness, assault, and long-term imprisonment to the existing law that recognized only adultery, but the colony's Anglican bishops petitioned Queen Victoria to withhold her approval. It was not until 1892 that assent was given and the reforms became law.

Overall, however, the conservatives' attempts to restrict divorce met with little success. A number of American states were persuaded to remove omnibus clauses from their divorce laws: Connecticut did so in 1878, and in the 1880s some others followed suit. In 1883 Maine abolished divorces in cases where the court judged it "reasonable and proper, conducive to domestic harmony, and consistent with the peace and morality of society," and restricted divorce to seven specific grounds. In addition, residency requirements were tightened, and a minimum delay of two years between divorce and remarriage was introduced. Other New England states (New Hampshire, Vermont, and Massachusetts) also restricted divorce in the 1880s under pressure from the New England Divorce Reform League. But the main targets, the "divorce havens" in the Midwest and West, were scarcely affected by the conservative pressure. Indeed, if it were true, as the opponents of the reaction argued, that it was not so much that the liberal divorce policies of these states attracted migrants, as that the restrictive policies of other states forced their citizens to migrate, then the limitation of divorce facilities in some of the eastern states can only have increased the incidence of migratory divorces.

Implicit in the arguments of the conservatives on the divorce issue was the centrality of legislation to marriage stability. Liberal divorce policies, they believed, not only allowed divorces to be obtained easily, but they encouraged men and women to treat marriage lightly, as something trivial that might be sloughed off on a whim or at the first sign of problems or conflict. They recognized that there was a fundamental issue of morality at stake, too, but they believed that legislation could contribute to a solution to it. Against the moral-legal view of marriage breakdown and divorce, there arose another that focused less on the legal act of divorce and more on the social aspects of marriage breakdown. Proponents of this view, the new social scientists of the late nineteenth century, sought to explain the divorce rate in social and economic terms. They stressed the difference between marriage breakdown and divorce, a distinction clearly expressed by Caroll Wright, the United States commissioner of labor who oversaw the first compilations of American divorce statistics. "Law does not create divorce," Wright declared; "divorce occurs when the husband and wife are estranged. Law steps in and defines the status of the divorced parties, but does not create it." Such an approach, which gave the law no active role in marriage breakdown, was wholly at odds with the conservative perspective.

Not only did social scientists shift attention from personal morality to environmental circumstances to explain marriage breakdown, but they also tended to support the more liberal divorce policies. George Eliot Howard, a University of Chicago professor whose major survey of marriage and divorce law was published in 1904, insisted that many marriages were bound to fail, given the characters of the spouses and their motives for marrying. "On the face of it," Howard asked, "is it not grotesque to call such unions holy or to demand that they shall be indissoluble?" As for the idea of preventing divorce in the interests of children, "are there not thousands of so-called 'homes' from whose corrupting and blighting shadow the sooner a child escapes the better for both it and society?" In conventional terms Howard and most of his contemporary social scientists were liberals. Divorce was the first major social issue to be confronted by the nascent social sciences, and no doubt the liberal perspectives to which their studies drove them contributed to the suspicion with which conservatives have viewed sociologists ever since.

There was one nagging question about the role of divorce law, however, and that was why the states with the most liberal policies had the highest rates of divorce. Was this not evidence, the social scientists' arguments notwithstanding, that liberal laws produced more divorce? Part of the answer, of course, depended to some extent on how many of these divorces could be attributed to migratory divorce. This was an issue not confined to the United States, for all over the Western world there were countries with permissive divorce laws, and countries with restrictive laws, not to mention countries (like Italy and Spain) where divorce was not permitted at all. Such variations became more important because of the vast movement of populations across the United States and around the world from the late nineteenth century. Not only was there a westward drift of population across North America, but millions of migrants left Europe for the new worlds of America and Australasia. And if the transport revolution, especially railroads and steamships, made travel for tourism and leisure accessible to the growing middle class, it also facilitated their more utilitarian journeys out of state or abroad where divorce might be obtained more easily and discreetly than in their places of residence.

The extent of migratory divorce in the nineteenth century is not known, but contemporaries believed that it was very widespread. Canadians were said to head in droves for the United States, despite uncertainty whether the divorces they obtained there would be recognized in Canada. An apparent influx of Ontario residents into upper New York State divorce courts was noted at the end of the century, and in 1905 one judge refused a divorce to a Canadian who had taken up residence in Niagara Falls (on the Canadian–U.S. border) a year earlier and who was still doing business in Toronto. The judge commented that "a noticeable percentage of the divorce cases before this department are brought by Canadians who establish a residence here mainly that they may sue for divorce."

There was more concern about divorce migration in the United States than elsewhere, mainly because of the ease of traveling and taking up residence in another state. The distinction of being the most popular divorce haven was shared by several midwestern and western divorce states at different times. In the 1850s Indiana had a reputation as the state most open to out-of-state petitioners, and one estimate was that two-thirds of divorce actions in Marion County in 1858 were filed by nonresidents. Not all Indiana's residents were delighted by this reputation, however, and the *Indiana Daily Journal* deplored the state's being "overrun by a flock of ill-used, and ill-using, petulant, libidinous, extravagant, ill-fitting husbands and wives as a sink is over-run with the foul water of the whole house." More rigorous residency requirements curbed this flock (or flood), and Indiana slipped in the divorce haven league: The state had America's highest divorce rate between 1867 and 1871, but by 1877–81 it had fallen to seventh place.

In the following decades other states gained notoriety as meccas for pilgrims in search of divorce. Illinois, Utah, and South Dakota each had its turn in the limelight, and in many places migratory divorce became a vigorous political issue. In the 1890s there was bitter conflict between Sioux Falls, South Dakota, clergymen who wanted to limit out-of-state divorce migrants, and the city's businessmen and hoteliers who benefited financially from the divorce traffic. In most cases, however, residency requirements were added to divorce laws so as to make them unavailable to transients. One state that held out longer than most was Nevada, where a minimal six-month period of residence was required. Cashing in on Nevada's reputation for easy divorce, one New York lawyer set up office in Reno and widely advertised the state's facilities and his own services. His advertisements in New York, Washington, and San Francisco newspapers read in part:

> *Divorce Laws of Nevada*
> Have You Domestic Trouble?
> Are You Seeking DIVORCE?
> Do You Want Quick and Reliable Service?
> Send for My Booklet
> Contains Complete Information

Only in 1913, when the Nevada legislature's assembly chamber was invaded by antidivorce campaigners, was a two-year residency requirement imposed in the state, but two years later pressure from business and lawyers, who were being deprived of divorce-related income, led to the restoration of the six-month rule. Nevada, in fact, has retained its status as a divorce haven throughout the twentieth century and is able to draw upon its reputation and tradition to attract out-of-state divorces.

Migratory divorces were considered offensive because they were a means of circumventing restrictive divorce policies. They also raised a number of serious legal and social questions, the most immediate being the recognition by one jurisdiction of divorces granted in another. In one notorious case an English peer, Earl Russell, divorced his wife in Nevada and promptly remarried, only to have the divorce declared null in England. Russell was tried for bigamy and imprisoned. The constant potential for such situations, with their far-reaching implications for those involved (and any children they might have), produced two responses. The first was to bring laws into greater harmony so as to eliminate the attraction of divorce migration. The failure of this enterprise in the United States has already been noted, but it was more successful elsewhere. In the first decade of the twentieth century there was extensive consultation and cooperation among Sweden, Norway, and Denmark (and later Finland and Iceland) on a broad range of legislation. One result was the adoption of generally uniform divorce laws after World War I.

The second response was the development of interjurisdictional conventions to establish the bases on which divorces in one jurisdiction would be recognized in another. Should a divorce granted in Indiana to a New York resident be recognized in New York? Should a divorce granted in France to a Spanish citizen be recognized in Spain? In the United States the issue was complicated by a section of the Constitution (Section I, Article IV) that bound each state to give "full faith and credit" to the public acts, records, and judicial proceedings of every other state. Some states skirted this provision by recognizing out-of-state divorces when granted to out-of-state residents but not when they were granted to their own residents. The main legal issue, then, was a question of domicile, and whether the courts of one state had jurisdiction over the marriages of men and women domiciled in another state.

Outside the United States the issue was less often one of domicile and more often one of nationality, as citizens of one country, where divorce was difficult or impossible, tried to have their marriages dissolved in a country with a more amenable divorce policy. International case law at the turn of the century became cluttered with Italians divorcing in France, Spanish couples seeking divorce elsewhere, and English men and women petitioning for divorce on the Continent. In many instances the courts refused to accept jurisdiction, even when the foreigner had taken out citizenship of the country where the divorce was sought. In 1897, for example, a French court declared that it had no competence to dissolve the marriage of two Italians, even though one of them had obtained French citizenship.

Confusion over international divorce laws led to an international convention signed in The Hague in 1902 by France, Germany, Austria-Hungary, Spain, Italy, Portugal, Switzerland, Sweden, Norway, Luxembourg, and Romania. The convention aimed to prevent any country's becoming a divorce haven for the citizens of others and specified that a divorce in one country obtained by citizens of another would be valid only if the laws of both countries recognized the ground on which the divorce had been granted. Thus a German could obtain a valid divorce in France for reason of adultery, because both German and French law allowed divorce for reason of adultery.

The need for an international convention testified to several important trends that had developed during the nineteenth century. One was development of migratory divorce on such a scale that a treaty was thought necessary to deal with it. A second was the persistent unevenness of divorce policies among states, provinces, and nations, as each jurisdiction constructed divorce laws and institutions in line with its traditions and political circumstances. Third, and perhaps most important, was the general trend toward liberal divorce policies that had been pursued across the Western world, though more successfully in some jurisdictions, as we have seen. Behind this convention lay an even more important dimension, however, and that was the rising incidence of divorce in the late nineteenth century. The statistics provided part of the background for a major debate, throughout the Western world, on the subject of marriage and the family and their importance in preserving a civilization that was widely represented as in decline.

Suggestions for further reading

Backhouse, Constance, " 'Pure Patriarchy': Nineteenth-Century Canadian Marriage," *McGill Law Journal* 13 (1986), 264–312.

Blake, Nelson, *The Road to Reno: A History of Divorce in the United States* (New York, 1962).

Chester, Robert (ed.), *Divorce in Europe* (Leiden, 1977).

Golder, Hilary, *Divorce in 19th-Century New South Wales* (Kensington, N.S.W., 1985).

Griswold, Robert L., "The Evolution of the Doctrine of Mental Cruelty in Victorian American Divorce, 1790–1900," *Journal of Social History* 19 (1986), 127–48.

Halem, Lynne Carol, *Divorce Reform: Changing Legal and Social Perspectives* (New York, 1980).

Horstman, Allen, *Victorian Divorce* (London, 1985).

Howard, George E., *A History of Matrimonial Institutions* (3 vols., Chicago, 1904).

Le Bras, Gabriel (ed.), *Divorce et séparation de corps dans le monde contemporain* (Paris, 1952).

McGregor, O. M., *Divorce in England* (London, 1957).

O'Neill, William L., *Divorce in the Progressive Era* (New York, 1963).

Phillips, Roderick, *Divorce in New Zealand: A Social History* (Auckland, 1981).

Wires, Richard, *The Divorce Issue and Reform in Nineteenth-Century Indiana* (Muncie, 1967).

7

Divorce as a social issue, 1850–1914

Divorce has never been discussed by social commentators as something that does not have broader implications. It has been condemned at times because it promoted social instability, weakened marriage and the family, and encouraged sexual license. Conversely, divorce liberalization has been defended in terms of individual rights, the promotion of harmonious marriages, and the encouragement of population growth. In general, in fact, attitudes toward divorce can be understood only in terms of prevailing social, economic, and demographic conditions, and the ways in which they are perceived.

This is seldom more evident than in the nineteenth century, when, as we have just seen, there was a wave of legislative and judicial activity related to divorce throughout Western society. This was also a century of rapid social and economic transformation. Industrialization intensified, urbanization accelerated, and the growth of the industrial working and middle classes heightened class consciousness. Population, which had begun to increase in the eighteenth century, continued to do so at accelerating rates in most Western countries, and there were unprecedented movements of population, particularly from Britain and Europe to the new worlds in North and South America, Australasia, and Africa, and westward across the North American continent.

It is true that there were many lines of continuity threaded through these changes. Many parts of Europe remained resistant to industrialization and urbanization, and popular traditions, customs, and attitudes often persisted in the face of change. Yet for all this, change was the order of the century, and the dramatic shifts in the social and economic structures of Western society highlighted new ideological alignments and social issues, many of which focused on marriage and divorce or dealt with them obliquely. Among the major political ideologies of the period were socialism, liberalism, and conservatism, and among the specific social issues that attracted attention from the middle of the century were women's rights and social purity, temperance, illicit sexuality, and the doctrines of femininity and domesticity.

One issue that was of concern to all social critics, no matter what their ideological position, was the place of the family in the social order. Progressives and conservatives alike recognized that marriage and the family were fundamental social institutions and that social change, or the maintenance of the prevailing social order, could not be achieved without taking the family into account. Some progressive thinkers saw the family as so fundamental that they believed social change would begin with the transformation of family relationships. Others saw it as less fundamental in this way, but nonetheless integral to social change. Conservatives sought to prevent social change by resisting any alteration of the family system, whereas the restoration of the "traditional" patriarchal family was on the agenda of many reactionaries who wanted to roll back the forces of industrial and city life and restore what they thought of as traditional social values. In short, marriage and the family lay at the heart of plans and descriptions of both social change and social conservatism, and in this context divorce became a common theme in the broader social and political debates of the nineteenth century.

Of particular interest are the social commentators and activists, such as Robert Owen, Charles Fourier, and Etienne Cabet, who are known collectively as the utopian socialists. Alarmed at the social and moral effects of industrialization, urbanization, and capitalism, many of the utopian socialists planned or set up model communities that would be models for the reform of society at large. Without exception they gave attention to marriage and the family in their contemporary society (what Owen called "the old immoral world") and in the regenerated society of the future ("the new moral world"). The family was generally considered problematic. It was undeniably the basic institution of society, but many utopians saw it as embodying the worst of social practices. Owen saw the family as even more socially divisive than classes: The family was a façade for much crime, vice, tyranny, and oppression – particularly of women – that produced widespread misery as well as a high incidence of insanity and suicide. Moreover (and this was a point echoed by other utopians), the loyalty demanded by family relationships tended to reinforce divisions within society at large and to work against a spirit of broader social cohesion and cooperation.

Owen did not advocate celibacy as a solution, however, but rather a radical transformation of attitudes, social practices, and legislation related to the family. For a start, marriage should be removed from the control of churches; this would eliminate the vices caused by unreasonable impediments to marriage and restrictions on divorce. In the society envisaged by Owen, people would not marry too early, and everything would be done to ensure that they were happy. Affection would be the sine qua non of marriage, and once it had disappeared, the marriage would be considered to have ended: It would be possible to divorce "when the esteem and affection cannot be retained for each other, and when the union promises to produce more misery than happiness."

Owen placed only two qualifications on the right to divorce: that women had equality and that the education and well-being of children were not compromised. However, divorce should not be undertaken lightly or hastily, would be allowed only after a suitable time, and when the couple had made three declarations of their mutual desire to separate (a procedure reminiscent of the divorce law of the French Revolution). Owen was confident, though, that divorces would be rare. He saw marriage breakdown as the result of a corrupt marriage system and believed that when couples married for the right reasons and when men and women were equal in rights and education, "it is most likely that marriages ... would be more permanent than they have ever yet been." In Owenite communities such as Nashoba (Tennessee) and Skaneateles (New York) these principles were practiced. In the latter, divorce was positively encouraged when the husband and wife no longer contributed to each other's happiness.

The utopian socialists varied in their approaches to marriage and divorce, however, and Owen's idea of a regenerated but still regulated system was at odds with the more libertarian approach of Charles Fourier. For Fourier, the family reinforced selfish sentiments. In a natural state men, women, and children tended to break away from the family group to join other social formations, such as peer groups. In the free society of the future that Fourier envisaged, social bonds would be looser and, because there would be no sexual exclusivity, marriage (and therefore divorce) would become anachronistic. Fourier believed, however, that as long as marriage existed divorce should be readily available.

Against Fourier and other libertarians who planned for the disappearance of orthodox family relationships stood some utopian socialists who upheld marriage and the family. Etienne Cabet, whose ideas inspired a number of communities in America, stressed the benefits of matrimony for women in particular, as long as marriage was purged of its prevailing vices, notably the tendency for marriages to be based on financial considerations. There was room in Cabet's scheme for divorce, despite his praises of marriage, and in his *Voyage in Icaria*, a fictional utopia, he allowed for divorce as long as the families of the couple concerned gave their approval. In the American communities based on Cabet's vision, marriage was encouraged and although divorce was permitted, men and women who divorced were exhorted to marry again as rapidly as possible.

But providing for divorce in their plans for society and in their communities did not commit the utopian socialists to the cause of divorce law reform in the nineteenth century. The divorce they advocated was divorce within an egalitarian social and matrimonial system, and they were less inclined to support legal reforms that merely tinkered with the worst abuses of the prevailing system. Unregenerated men, they argued, would divorce for the wrong reasons, and divorce would become even more a means of oppression. To this extent, and because their followings were limited, it is not clear what effect the utopians had on mainstream attitudes toward marriage and divorce. Because many of them abandoned notions such as the desirability of virginity until marriage and sexual exclusivity within marriage, the utopians were frequently branded as advocates of sexual promiscuity, adultery, and incest. Robert Owen's teachings touched off a vigorous debate in England in the 1830s and 1840s on the range of issues related to marriage and divorce, and Owenites complained that "the most licentious, vicious and brutalizing opinion" was ascribed to them. One critic charged that the Owenites were trying "to break up house, to tear asunder our household ties, and put to death the strongest and dearest affects of our hearts ... to throw our wives and children into one common stock."

Public debates on marriage and divorce, pitting socialists against their critics, attracted huge crowds: More than 5,000 tickets were sold for one 1840 match between Robert Owen and his arch-opponent John Brindley in Bristol. Although sex was more sensational, divorce commanded attention in its own right, and one result of their participation in the public debate was that the Owenites were drawn into the contemporary politics of marriage and divorce reform. They supported the English law of 1837 that allowed civil marriage and the licensing of any building for weddings, for under this legislation the Owenites could celebrate marriages according to their own rites. Despite accusations to the contrary, these were conventional marriages in intent, stressing mutual love and the ideal of indissolubility. An Owenite "social hymn" of marriage ran as follows:

> United by love then alone
> In goodness, in truth and in heart
> They both are so perfectly one
> Their bonds they never can part.
> Their union has love for its ground
> The love of a man and his bride;
> And hence in affection they're bound
> So close they can never divide.

On occasion, though, even Owenite love waned, and "divorces" took place even before divorce was legalized in England in 1857. In 1842, for example, three Cheltenham socialists contracted a "divorce" and a "remarriage," in which Amelia and James Vaughn agreed that they would separate and that Amelia would "marry" William Stanbury. This proceeding was more sedate than the wife sales that were taking place in England at the same time, but it had the same legal effect as they did: none.

The marriage and divorce doctrines of the utopians and their notions of the role of the family in social change were challenged within the socialist movement itself. Many of the utopians believed that the small-scale communities they formed would foment broader change and that reform of family relationships within them would necessarily lead to the reform of other relationships and institutions. This was the early view of Alfred Naquet, the prime mover of divorce law reform in France from the 1860s to the early 1900s. As a social revolutionary in the 1860s, Naquet thought that the transformation of society would begin with the family and spread to other socioeconomic relationships, but he later adopted the view that an economic revolution would come first and that "the freedom of the family, instead of being its origin, will be its result."

This formulation was more akin to that of the scientific socialists, who saw the family less as an agent of social and economic change and more as part of the superstructure of society that would be transformed as fundamental economic relationships underwent change. The classic formulations were those of Karl Marx and Friedrich Engels in *The Communist Manifesto* (1848) and Engels in *The Origin of the Family, Private Property and the State* (1884). These are discussed in the next chapter in the context of the 1917 Soviet divorce law, but we should note here that the nineteenth-century Marxists were less involved in the contemporary debate on marriage and sexual relations because they believed that to focus on them was to begin at the wrong end of the revolutionary process. After the socialist revolution, Marx and Engels argued, the characteristics of bourgeois marriage (the supremacy of men and indissolubility) that derived from bourgeois property relations would disappear. As Engels wrote: "Full freedom of marriage can therefore only be generally established [after] . . . the abolition of capitalist production and of the property relations created by it." This did not, of course, prevent socialists from writing on marriage and divorce, and many did so, particularly within the context of women's rights.

Besides the more radical progressive critiques of nineteenth-century society, the current of liberalism eddied around the questions of marriage and divorce. Liberalism, like other broad ideological tendencies, was varied and multifaceted, but its proponents shared a general concern for the achievement of individual happiness and a common aversion to external interference in matters of personal life. Such beliefs easily led liberals to support marriage and divorce policies that maximized individual freedom, and they approached these issues from the perspective of the individual, rather than with social implications uppermost in mind. This is not to say that they cared nothing for the consequences of marriage and divorce for the men and women involved, their children, or society, but that they stressed the need to provide the greatest degree of personal freedom within a system of minimal regulation and the recognition of individual responsibilities.

Two liberal perspectives on marriage and divorce were provided by John Stuart Mill and Harriet Taylor, each of whom wrote an essay on the topic in 1832. Both focused on women's status in marriage and society (a characteristic of much nineteenth-century writing on marriage and divorce), and both argued for the legalization of divorce, which was still (in England) a quarter of a century away as they wrote. Mill suggested, in good liberal terms, that marital status should be regulated not by law but by the individuals themselves. "Were divorce ever so free," he wrote, "it would be resorted to under the same sense of moral responsibility and under the same restraints from opinion, as any other of the acts of our lives." Social attitudes, Mill thought, would prevent men and women from changing partners too often or for trivial reasons, and he believed that couples would divorce only in two circumstances: when there was "such uncongeniality of disposition" as to make life together uncomfortable, and when one spouse conceived a "strong passion" for another person. For her part, however, Harriet Taylor foresaw the need for some limitations on divorce and proposed a long waiting period (a minimum of two years) before a divorce was finalized and the spouses could remarry.

Against the doctrines and policies adopted by the utopian socialists, Marxists, and liberals, most of whom sought a loosening of marriage ties, were ranged an equally heterogeneous group of conservatives and reactionaries. The reactionaries believed that historically marriage had been stronger, authoritarian, dominated by men, and more stable, and they adopted positions designed to resuscitate what they considered a more desirable marriage and family system.

Foremost among them was the Roman Catholic church, which was in the vanguard of campaigns to stop the legalization or liberalization of divorce. At several points in the second half of the nineteenth century the papacy intervened in the continuing debate on marriage and divorce. Perhaps the clearest affirmation of reactionary ideology was the Syllabus of Errors, an 1864 denunciation by Pope Pius IX of all contemporary tendencies in Western society and thought. In the Syllabus, which ended with a ringing affirmation that it was anathema to believe that the pope should accept "progress, liberalism and modern civilization," ten of the eighty articles were devoted to marriage and divorce.

Most reasserted the Catholic doctrine of marriage, and article 67 dealt specifically with divorce: "By natural law marriage is not dissoluble and [it is an error to assert that] in various cases divorce may be permitted by the secular power."

It is difficult to gauge the impact of the church's opposition in the nineteenth century. It might well have been critically important in Spain and Italy, and it might have delayed the reintroduction of divorce in France. In 1880, just before one of Alfred Naquet's divorce bills was to be debated, Pope Leo X issued his encyclical letter *Arcanum*, which reaffirmed Catholic doctrine of the indissolubility of marriage and condemned the almost universal enactment of laws that secularized marriage and facilitated divorce. Recalling that divorce had been legalized during the French Revolution (that "conflagration ... when society was wholly degraded by its abandoning of God"), Leo insisted that "divorces are in the highest degree hostile to the prosperity of families and States, springing as they do from the depraved morals of the people, and, as experience shows us, opening out a way to every kind of evil-doing in public as in private life."

The voices of the Catholic church could be heard across Western society, as bishops condemned divorce, priests denounced it in sermons, and the Catholic press campaigned against it. They were part of a chorus of reactionaries that included many secular intellectuals who sought the "recovery" of a family system that they believed had been lost, a family system characterized by well-defined family responsibilities, uxorial obedience, and marital indissolubility. The regeneration of the family along these lines was an integral part of their yearning for a time when there was a robust social harmony ensured by a clearly defined social hierarchy. A number of these thinkers were followers of the German sociologist Ferdinand Tönnies, who thought of the family as the purest form of *Gemeinschaft* (community) as distinct from *Gesellschaft* (conflict-ridden class society). In France similar notions were expressed by reactionary intellectuals, many of whom were associated with Action Française, the French fascist movement. One was Franz Funck-Brentano a historian who wrote many works on the Old Regime and the revolution and who emphasized the destructive effects of social and political turmoil. "The first work of the Revolution, its essential and fundamental work," he wrote, "was the destruction of the old French family." The continuing turmoil associated with the nineteenth century perpetuated the trend.

In France the debate on marriage and divorce became highly politicized in the final decades of the nineteenth century, partly because of the policies of secularization (including the legalization of divorce in 1884) pursued by the governments of the Third Republic. At this time of heightened antisemitism in France, some reactionaries insisted that divorce was part of a Jewish conspiracy to weaken French society; it helped that Alfred Naquet, the prime mover of divorce, had been born a Jew. One of the most prominent French antisemites, Edouard Drumont, suggested that Jews, whose laws had long accepted divorce, had persuaded the French judiciary that marriage was no more than "a simple encounter of a day or a night."

Although we have surveyed them only briefly here, it is clear that nineteenth-century social critics, whether they were utopian socialists, Marxists, liberals, or reactionaries, integrated marriage, divorce, and the family more generally into their social analyses. Some wanted to remove all institutional and legal constraints on marriage and divorce, some would abolish the family or would watch contentedly while it withered away, and still others would strengthen the family as a source of social and political authority and order. In all cases attitudes toward marriage and divorce must be understood within the broader social and political doctrines, many of which recognized the family as pivotal in promoting either social change or social stability.

Somewhere among these various critiques evolved the divorce policies described in the preceding chapter: the gradual liberalization of marriage and divorce, the progressive expansion of the grounds for divorce, together with attempts to minimize the use of divorce by keeping close statutory and judicial control over it. An obvious way of describing these policies in terms of the broad range of ideological positions on divorce would be as a middle-range, moderate course driven between the extremes, one that gradually and carefully removed the constraints on divorce but limited the pace and extent of change. They might be said to have accepted the need for reform while maintaining a commitment to the institution of marriage that had an existence over and above the will of the spouses. It is true that divorce law reform was achieved despite the opposition of conservatives in the strict sense, who wished to preserve the status quo. However, for the most part the legislators who reformed the divorce laws shared conservative ideals concerning the family, even though they differed from strict conservatives on the means to achieve their goal. The reforms in marriage and divorce law might be thought of as having been a more realistic and pragmatic approach to social conservatism.

This was one of the paradoxes presented by the liberalization of divorce laws: The reasons put forward to justify divorce law reform were essentially conservative and represented the aim of maintaining a system of values and behavior that was believed to be under threat. The main form of divorce law reform, as we have seen, was to add more and more grounds for divorce, and their effect was to highlight what was unacceptable within marriage. What was unacceptable should be understood, however, in terms of a conventional middle-class morality. Thus adultery contradicted the idea of sexual fidelity; desertion negated the duties of a spouse in any respect; wife beating ran counter to the ideal of harmony and of respect for women; and drunkenness was anathema to the ideal of moderation and sobriety in all matters. If we needed a picture of traits that made up the nineteenth-century middle-class ideal of marriage and family life, we would find it in the mirror image of the grounds for divorce, for divorce was designed to reinforce the conventional family, not to change it. One source of confusion over this is the common reference (in this book as elsewhere) to divorce law reform as "liberalization." It was indeed liberalized insofar as it made divorce more widely accessible than it had been early in the nineteenth century, but even by the beginning of the twentieth century divorce remained highly regulated: Divorce was confined by costs and other considerations to the middle and upper classes (see Chapter 9).

If divorce law liberalization was not intended to extend divorce to the lower classes, neither was it designed to emancipate women, despite the insistence of some historians that divorce reform reflected more sympathetic attitudes toward women's rights. The grounds recognized in the divorce laws were assumed to be male offenses for the most part, such that divorce was less a way of freeing women than of protecting them. To this extent the divorce laws were part of a complex of paternalistic legislation that sought to protect women from the most harmful implications of their inferior status without attempting to change their status significantly.

Another consideration that ought to make us think of divorce law reform in this period as essentially conservative is that it was carried out by men who were conservative on social matters. As unaccustomed and unwilling as we might be to accepting politicians' affirmations at face value, we ought to believe these men when they declared their intention to ensure the stability of the family and the permanence of marriages and their commitment to keep divorces to a minimum. Some reformers, like Alfred Naquet in France, might have had private radical political agendas, but most saw divorce only as an effective way of dealing with what they believed were mercifully rare cases of abuse and exploitation.

Finally, we should consider the way that divorce was drawn into a number of social, political, and moral issues during the nineteenth century. From the middle of the century drunkenness, habitual drunkenness, or drunkenness associated with other matrimonial offenses was made a ground for divorce in many American and Australian states, New Zealand, Germany, and Scandinavia, and elsewhere (such as Scotland and England) drunkenness was a made a ground for separation. This trend reflected a growing concern about the social effects of alcohol consumption, particularly as it was associated with other perceived social evils: Bars and saloons were not only places for drinking, but also for gambling and prostitution, and for dissipation of families' financial resources at the expense of wives and children. Alcohol, indeed, was seen as a fundamental cause of a wide range of social problems: It was used to seduce young women, it started women on careers of prostitution, and within marriage alcohol wrecked relationships and produced poverty and moral corruption.

The alcohol issue was taken up by the temperance movement, one of the most important elements in the wide-ranging movement for social and moral reform. By 1911 the Women's Christian Temperance Union in the United States had a quarter of a million members, making it the largest women's organization in the country, and far larger than any of the women's rights bodies. The concern about alcohol consumption and its social effects that underlay this movement also influenced the introduction of drunkenness into divorce laws as a matrimonial offense. It was made part of Maine's divorce law in 1838, and other American states such as Delaware and Virginia added it later in the century. In 1899 drunkenness was one of the grounds in the model divorce law proposed by the commission on uniform laws in the United States. In other places, drunkenness alone was not a ground for divorce, but it became one when associated with other offenses. In New Zealand and Australia in the 1890s drunkenness was made a ground when coupled when the husband's failure to support his family or the wife's failure to perform her domestic duties. Advocates of temperance and prohibition did not unanimously support divorce for reason of drunkenness, however, for the temperance movements attracted many women and men who were opposed to both alcohol and divorce for religious reasons. Even so, some temperance associations called for limited divorce reform, and they were influential enough to persuade some legislatures to include alcohol-related offenses within their divorce laws.

The very matrimonial duties that could be affected by drunkenness led to the articulation of new and the expansion of old grounds for divorce. The domestic ideology fostered by the ideal of the middle-class nineteenth-century family stressed the different spheres occupied by women and men. Married women were expected to concentrate their energy, attention, and labor on home and family, caring for their husbands and children and maintaining the household. Within and beyond these tasks women were appointed the guardians of morality, because prevailing ideology invested women with more virtue than men. Husbands, for their part, were expected to be active outside the home, working to support the family. Such a notion of separate spheres was not a description of how wives and husbands actually functioned, but it was a powerful ideological and moral prescription. Nothing could be more evident than that the consistent failure to practice the ideal should be a reason for terminating a marriage, and so it was that divorce codes began to express the principles bound up in the doctrine of separate spheres. As we have noted, Australasian divorce laws provided for the dissolution of marriage when either wife or husband failed to perform the general tasks expected of them: support and service, respectively. The trend is observable in American laws, as well. An 1883 Maine law recognized as a ground for divorce the "gross, cruel, and wanton neglect or refusal by the husband, being able, to provide for the wife." Kentucky law permitted a wife to divorce her husband if, because of habitual drunkenness, he wasted his estate "without any suitable provision for the maintenance of his wife and children." In many American states, however, the tendency was less toward statutory reform along these lines and more for the judiciary to extend the meaning of cruelty to include offenses such as extravagance, failure to support adequately, and negligence in caring for the household.

The essence of the doctrine of separate spheres was the difference between men and women, and although it was stoutly defended by many social reformers (who insisted that the relationship, although separate, was equal), other areas where law and practice had enshrined gender distinctions were vigorously assailed. The most important was the double standard of sexual morality that had traditionally given men more latitude in terms of sexual activity and initiative. In the nineteenth century there were attempts to breathe new life into this ancient belief by resorting to medical findings that purported to show that in terms of sexuality, men were highly motivated and active, and less modest, while women were naturally modest, had a low sex drive, and had an innate propensity toward chastity that men could only envy.

The social purity movement of the late nineteenth century had no time for this view, however, and saw in the double standard a cause of many of the most appalling vices: prostitution, seduction, adultery, illegitimacy, and the spread of venereal diseases. One speaker at the first American National Purity Congress in 1895 pointed out that "the only true way to deal with prostitution is, first, to diminish the demand upon which it is based by stamping vice with public reprobation in men as well as in women." She rejected the idea that prostitution protected family values by permitting men to satisfy themselves sexually without subjecting their wives to demands for frequent intercourse. In England and the British colonies, a different manifestation of the double standard was attacked: A campaign was begun against the Contagious Diseases Acts, regulations that required prostitutes (or women suspected of being prostitutes) to submit to examinations for venereal disease but that did not require their male clients to do likewise.

For our purposes the most important form of the double standard was the way men and women were treated differently in respect to adultery. The social purity campaigners argued strongly against laws that treated men who were guilty of illicit sexual activity more leniently than women guilty of the same offenses. The 1895 National Purity Congress was told by one speaker that "equality of moral obligation is the one idea which lies at the foundation of any true democracy." Another speaker called upon women to reject the double standard. Only the highest standards of sexual purity should be recognized in men and women, she said, and she called for the reform not only of private lives but also of public statutes.

Reform was far more rapid in legislation than in private lives, however, and one of the tendencies in divorce law reform was the removal of clauses that embodied the double standard. This kind of reform took place throughout the British colonies, which had earlier adopted the discriminatory principles of the 1857 English divorce law. In fact the colonies purged their divorce codes of this element of inequality well before the English Parliament did: Although its elimination was recommended by the 1909 royal commission on divorce, it was not until 1923 that women in England could divorce their husbands for reason of adultery, rather than having to prove aggravated adultery. The trend toward sexual equality was apparent elsewhere, too: The 1884 French divorce law omitted the qualification that a woman could divorce her husband for adultery only if he committed it in the family dwelling. In Germany the 1900 civil code reformed the 1875 divorce law provision that enabled a husband to divorce his adulterous wife, even if he too had been guilty of adultery, but permitted a wife to divorce her adulterous husband only if she were innocent of the offense.

It is clear that many of the reforms in divorce law and policy in the later nineteenth century reflected a concern at the status of women in the family. This being so, we might ask how divorce fitted into the program of the women's rights movement that developed from mid-century. The short answer is that there was no consensus on the issue. Despite the general agreement that women should have political and legal equality with men, the women's movement was deeply divided over many matters. Divorce was one of these matters, even though advocacy of liberal divorce policies is often associated with the campaign for women's rights, and despite the fact that the rise of divorce rates in the later part of the nineteenth century has often been attributed to the advance of women's rights.

However, many advocates of women's equality balked at liberalizing divorce laws for the very same reasons that it was opposed by men and women who were also against women's equality. They regarded marriage and the family as fundamental guarantors of social stability, and believed that making divorce more accessible would weaken the family and society together. Some women's rights supporters argued that once marriage law was equalized, the position of married women would improve and divorce would be unnecessary – at the very least, they insisted, it would not be a specifically women's issue. On the other hand, some supporters of women's equality saw divorce as a vital facility for women, enabling them to free themselves from oppressive marriages that no amount of legislation could reform. In the end the variety of attitudes toward divorce law reform reflected the heterogeneous composition of the women's rights movement: It was made up of women and men who shared the minimum goals of the political and legal equality of the sexes, but who differed radically on matters of broad social reform and on the role of women in it. The marriage and divorce questions drew these differences out and tended to accentuate the divergences within the women's rights movements.

The divergences emerged at the very earliest stages of the movement in the United States. At the first women's rights convention, in 1848 at Seneca Falls, New York, the 300 women and men present readily adopted resolutions calling for women to be granted the vote and full legal equality with men, but the consensus collapsed when the question of divorce was raised. Elizabeth Cady Stanton, who was to become a leader of the movement, introduced a draft resolution that divorce law should be liberalized, but it was opposed by others (including Antoinette Blackwell, another prominent campaigner for women's rights), who insisted that divorce was wrong in all circumstances. After vigorous discussion, the resolution was defeated.

From this point onward the American women's rights movement remained divided on the question of divorce. Prominent advocates of women's rights such as Stanton, Amelia Bloomer, and Susan B. Anthony insisted that liberal divorce policies were beneficial to women, but only Stanton pursued the issue assiduously and made it part of her feminist philosophy. The marriage question, she argued, "lies at the very foundation of all progress." At the 1852 Women's State Temperance Society conference, Stanton (who was the society's president) called for habitual drunkenness to be made a ground for divorce ("let no woman remain in the relation of wife with the confirmed drunkard"), and a letter from her to the 1856 women's rights convention shocked the audience by its radical proposals for divorce law reform. Marriage and divorce, she insisted at the 1860 convention, were private matters that should not be regulated by law, but if the state were to establish specific grounds for divorce, they should include drunkenness, insanity, desertion, cruel and brutal treatment, adultery, and simple incompatibility.

Such views continued to be rejected by the mainstream women's rights movement. Reformers such as Susan B. Anthony feared that too liberal a position on divorce would frighten away many potential supporters of the movement, and Lucy Stone lumped divorce, abortion, and infanticide together as subjects too sensitive to be discussed. Yet others were simply opposed to a policy of more liberal divorce, seeing in it a threat to the institutions of marriage and the family, and by extension to the social order. The dominant conservatism of the women's rights movement with regard to divorce reform is particularly revealing. As Carl Degler has pointed out, most American women did not rally to the cause of women's suffrage mainly because it was perceived as a threat to the family. Women's suffrage was predicated on the individuality of women and their right to assert their own self-interests, notions quite at variance with the role prescribed for women in the nineteenth century. The fear that the women's rights campaign would destroy the family inspired the movement (led by a woman) against women's suffrage from the 1890s. The great irony is that as far as divorce was concerned there was broad agreement between the women's suffragists and antisuffragists.

The fundamentally conservative objectives of many reforms in women's status extended to aspects of divorce law reform. As we have seen, one area of reform in many places was the removal of the double standard of sexual morality and the extension to women of the access men had to divorce. A case in point was New Zealand, which had legalized divorce in 1867 on English principles (adultery by the wife or aggravated adultery by the husband), and which in 1893 was the first country to give women the right to vote in national elections. The granting of women's suffrage reinforced arguments in favor of sexual equality in family law, and prominent women's organizations such as the Women's Christian Temperance Union and the National Council of Women campaigned for women to be given equal access to divorce. It was equalization and not liberalization that was sought, however; as a paper read to the 1898 conference of the National Council of Women warned, "the very free divorce laws in force in the United States of America did not lead to satisfactory results."

Despite the mixed attitudes to divorce of New Zealand women's rights advocates in the 1880s and 1890s, it was perceived as a feminist issue and attacked as such. Women who wanted equal access to divorce were portrayed, often by men who had voted in favor of women's suffrage, as corrupted and wishing to destroy the family. There was no necessary contradiction, however, between supporting women's suffrage and opposing equal access to divorce. In New Zealand as elsewhere at this time, women were given the vote not because they were considered equal to men, but because they were believed to be essentially different. It was expected that women, as repositories of domestic and moral virtues, would have a salutary effect on politics, especially on the frontiers of Western society. As one New Zealand conservative put it, "women's morality is the very safeguard of our social system," an assessment that seemed borne out by the involvement of so many women in movements for social purity and moral reform. The same belief that the participation of women improved the moral tone of politics was expressed in Wyoming, the first American state or territory to grant women the vote; in 1880 the National Woman Suffrage Association declared that "the vote of women [had] transformed Wyoming from barbarism to civilization."

From this perspective it is not difficult to understand why many conservatives and social commentators were appalled when confronted by women seeking equality in divorce laws, and thus apparently seeking the easier dissolution of the family unit they were assumed to be naturally predisposed to protect and strengthen. Any woman who supported divorce law reform, said one New Zealand politician, must be "corrupted in some way," and another pointed out that true women rejected divorce no matter what the circumstances: "It is one of the most beautiful points of women's character that she is frequently ready to forgive even such an offence as [adultery]."

Many women, whether or not they were active in women's rights or social reform movements, were as firmly wedded to marriage and the family as such politicians professed to be. In many respects the women's rights movements reflected the spectrum of ideological positions within society at large and, despite popular belief, were not solidly in the camp of those who would make divorce increasingly accessible. Although most of the examples cited here have been from the United States, the point is more widely applicable. In France, for example, the Conseil National des Femmes Françaises, a moderate feminist group, was far from unanimous in its support for the 1884 divorce law and was certainly opposed to making divorce any easier. There were, of course, exceptions, and the enactment of a liberal divorce law in Portugal can be attributed largely to the activity of the women's rights movement in the form of the Republican League of Portuguese Women. The league lobbied for the legalization of divorce from its foundation in 1909, and the revolution the next year brought quick results. Yet the fact that women in Portugal were denied the vote until 1945 is a further indication that divorce law reform could coexist with political conservatism.

In short, even though divorce law reform was advocated by proponents of radical social change, we should not think of the reforms that were enacted as having responded to any but essentially conservative objectives. As we have noted, individual reforms, such as making drunkenness a ground for divorce, reflected some of the most prominent social issues of the day. Few if any of the reforms satisfied the demands of progressives who wanted to equalize the status of wife and husband, for the grounds introduced into divorce laws everywhere were based on the principles that women were subordinate within marriage and that they needed not equality but simply protection from the worst physical and moral effects of their subordination. This is not to say that those who fought for social purity, temperance, and general moral improvement necessarily supported divorce even in the limited circumstances set down by law. Most campaigners in these movements, on the contrary, would probably have supported the tone and content of an 1895 letter to the American temperance newspaper, *Union Signal.* Concerning divorce the correspondent wrote:

I cannot think of anything more dangerous to home and to society. . . . Whatever breaks down the home, hurts the woman most, because she is most dependent upon home affections for her happiness. . . . There are no true friends of the real advancement of woman who would attempt to loosen the bond of marriage or to make it anything less than the life long union of one man and one woman.

A final but major area of divorce reform whose roots were firmly planted in the nineteenth century centered on insanity. The influence here was the eugenics movement, which intersected at vital points with the broader concerns with social purity and was a specific reaction to the perceived decline and degeneration of Western populations. Eugenics was based on pseudoscientific principles predicated on the belief that a wide range of physical, medical, and moral conditions, from insanity and syphilis to alcoholism to criminality, were biologically inherited. Eugenics theories purported to explain racial degeneration, and eugenicists put forward suggestions for policies and legislation they believed would increase and strengthen populations in general and discourage or prevent procreation by those with undesirable traits.

It is easy to understand that marriage became central to eugenics policies: Because almost all children were born within marriage, the prevention of marriage and reproduction by the physically, mentally, or morally defective would have the effect of reducing the proportion of such defectives within the population. Indeed, a long-term and effective policy of this sort would eventually purify any population of virtually all individuals with undesirable characteristics.

Eugenicists were, however, divided as to how marriage ought to be restricted. Some urged publicity and periods of delay before marriage, so that each party would have time to discover whether the other had a family history of, say, epilepsy, insanity, or tuberculosis. Others called for compulsion to be used to prevent marriages in certain cases. In France a campaign was mounted in the 1920s to make screening for contagious diseases mandatory before marriage. The French League for the Rights of Man, a liberal organization, supported premarital screening as a way of protecting the rights of newborn children to be free of defects that might be passed on by their parents.

Such proposals won a mixed reception from legislators. Although many legal codes prohibited marriage by the insane or feeble-minded (half the states of the United States had done so by the 1890s), the reasons were less eugenic than legal: Such persons were legally incapable of making a contract, including marriage. The first of the states to regulate marriage for the purpose of reproductive control was Connecticut, which in 1896 passed a law specifying that "no man or woman either of whom is epileptic, or imbecile or feeble-minded" could marry or have sexual intercourse while the woman was under forty-five years of age (and thus capable of conception). The minimum penalty was three years' imprisonment. Other states followed Connecticut's example: By 1905 they included Minnesota, Kansas, New Jersey, Ohio, Michigan, and Indiana, and by the mid-1930s forty-one American states prohibited marriage of the insane and feeble-minded, seventeen forbade marriage by epileptics, and four included "confirmed drunkards" among those to whom marriage was denied.

The eugenicist interest in marriage extended quite logically to divorce. It was one thing to try to persuade the defective and the unfit not to marry or to forbid them to do so, but no policy could guarantee that they would not, and no premarital screening could ensure that pathological characteristics would not emerge after marriage. In such cases, however, divorce could serve a eugenic purpose. One major work on eugenic theory argued that when a marriage proved to be a mistake from a eugenic point of view, "society should be ready to dissolve the union. Divorce is far preferable to mere separation, since the unoffending party should not be denied the privilege of remarriage, as the race in most cases needs his or her contribution to the next generation." Anticipating opposition to divorce in such circumstances, the authors argued that the time-honored grounds for divorce – among them adultery, cruelty, desertion, and nonsupport – were no more worthy of legal recognition than the "more purely dysgenic grounds of chronic inebriety, feeble-mindedness, epilepsy, insanity, or any serious inheritable physical, mental or moral defect." In such cases the mismating was the real evil, and it was the marriage, not its dissolution by divorce, that society ought to condemn.

Other eugenicists took a more cautious approach to divorce. Leonard Darwin, for example, argued that divorce could be either advantageous or disadvantageous from a eugenic point of view. On the one hand divorce was often used by a man who wanted to marry another woman who had "aroused sexual desires" in him. In this sense divorce increased the field for mating, and because divorced men tended to marry women younger than their first wives, divorce and remarriage could increase fertility. But as important as its size was, it was the quality of the population that most concerned Darwin, and in that respect he thought divorce could be problematic. Like tended to marry like, he thought, and it was probable that divorced people were below average in terms of what he called "civic worth." Although he conceded that this was "not a matter on which a decision can be given with perfect confidence," Darwin suggested that the inability to live in harmony with one's spouse indicated "some serious defect in character and qualities." He went on to point out that it was generally the less desirable partner who remarried and that because most divorces were obtained on the ground of adultery, remarriages would generally produce children with an inherited predisposition toward adultery. Such a tendency would undermine any precautions that might be taken to regulate sexual relations by regulating marriage. Darwin concluded that divorce should be very carefully controlled and that only one ground should be recognized, namely unbroken separation for seven years.

The effects of eugenicist principles on divorce legislation varied from place to place, but the most common form was the progressive inclusion of insanity among the grounds for divorce. It is true that insanity had been recognized as a ground for divorce as early as the seventeenth century in Sweden and in the 1792 French law, but only from the late nineteenth century were eugenic principles the reason for its inclusion. One of the first examples was a 1907 New Zealand law allowing divorce where one spouse had been confined to an asylum for ten of the twelve years preceding the divorce petition and where there was little hope for a recovery. A number of considerations lay behind this reform (one being that it was unfair to compel any man or woman to remain married to a permanently incapable partner), but the eugenic arguments were dominant. One Member of Parliament insisted that

We have got to guard this colony against the fertility of the unfit.... What is to become of the future peoples of this dominion if we allow either a man or a woman who has been certified to as a lunatic to come back and resume cohabitation, resulting in the breeding of a race which ... would be unfortunate in every sense of the word.

Taken to its logical conclusion this (and other eugenic principles) might have led to mandatory divorce, but the legislation did not go that far.

By making insanity a ground for divorce for eugenic reasons, New Zealand, then a socially progressive country, was well in the lead of other nations. The Scandinavian countries, also progressive in their social policies, followed. Insanity was already recognized in divorces by royal dispensation in Sweden, but such divorces were rare: Of the

4,735 divorces granted by all methods in Sweden between 1901 and 1910, only 132 (2.8%) were for reason of insanity. When the Swedish Law Commission was charged in 1910 with revising the country's family law, it noted the "increasingly strong demands ... for legislation which shall safeguard the future generations and improve the human race ... [legislation that would] prevent the marriage of those who are, from a eugenic point of view, unfit and also provide means for the dissolution of such marriages." The result was a 1915 marriage law that made insanity for three years, without hope of recovery, a ground for divorce. The same terms were enacted in Norway in 1918 and Denmark in 1922. Earlier, Switzerland had included insanity as a ground for divorce when it had lasted three years, was diagnosed as incurable, and rendered married life intolerable for the sane spouse. Elsewhere, however, the inclusion of insanity in divorce laws proceeded cautiously. The first Australian state adopted it in 1928, English divorce law did so in 1937, and insanity was made a ground for separation in Scotland in 1938. Most American states eventually adopted insanity as a ground, but in some cases imposed lengthy periods of proof: Alabama law required that the insanity have existed for twenty years before a divorce could be obtained.

As this chronology indicates, insanity was adopted as a ground for divorce only toward the end of the period under discussion, and it became widespread only in the 1920s and 1930s. It is important to note, though, that the eugenics arguments in favor of it originated in the late nineteenth century. It was, moreover, an essentially conservative movement. Despite the fact that parts of eugenics theory were adopted by radical racists like the Nazis, eugenicists were for the most part concerned with ensuring that Western populations remained physically, mentally, and morally healthy. They did not advocate changes in marriage and the family except those that would reinforce their most traditional characteristics. To this extent the inclusion of insanity in divorce codes, like the inclusion of drunkenness, failure to support, adultery, and desertion, was designed to consolidate and protect the conventional family, not to change it.

During the long nineteenth century, as this chapter has shown, social and political theorists and experimenters of all kinds put the Western family on the examination table, diagnosed its afflictions, and prescribed remedies. Some called for radical surgery, others for more cosmetic treatment. Hardly any declared the family to be in good health. The great debate over what became known as "the marriage question" drew in all manner of issues: free love, polygamy, fertility, the status of women, social purity, religion. As fascinating as it was, however, this debate proved unfruitful in practical terms. Indeed, in the short term the greatest impact of the marriage debate was found in the Soviet

Union in 1917, when the ideas of Western European socialists on marriage, divorce, women, and the family were translated into law (see Chapter 8). For the most part the real debate on marriage and the family (in the sense of the debate that resulted in law and policy) excluded the radical, the extreme reactionaries and social progressives, the libertarians, and the liberals. The debate that gave birth to late nineteenth- and early twentieth-century divorce law reform took place between two kinds of conservatives: those who believed that the conventional family was best protected by prohibiting divorce and those who thought the same aim was best achieved by allowing restrictive divorce. The divorce reformers were liberals only within this narrow spectrum, for they held to the primacy of marriage over the interests and wishes of the individual spouses. They rejected divorce by mutual consent or for reason of simple incompatibility, and divorce remained closely regulated in terms of procedure and access to it limited by costs. The outcry at the exceptions, notably the American divorce colonies, by men who were divorce law reformers in their own states, demonstrated their own relative conservatism. Divorce was to be no more than an escape valve, designed to release spouses, especially wives who needed the assistance and protection of the law, when the pressure of marital oppression reached intolerable levels.

Divorce law reform in this period involved many contradictions. There was the problem of reconciling equality of women and men before the law with conventional morality. There was the contradiction inherent between the belief that for the most part the behavior considered serious enough to warrant divorce (adultery, violence, drunkenness, desertion) was believed to be concentrated in the working classes, and the fact that the costs of divorce in this period placed it beyond the reach of working-class wives. Such contradictions, paradoxes, and tensions were, it seems, inherent in any conservative approach to divorce. Under the conflicting pressures to conserve and to modify, but with an eye constantly to social stability, legislators and judges in this period sanctioned divorce in ways they hoped would ensure that divorces were rare and marriage was fundamentally unaffected. When the number and rates of divorce began to rise throughout Western society in the last decades of the nineteenth century, they did so despite the divorce reforms, not because of them.

Suggestions for further reading

Degler, Carl, *At Odds: Women and the Family in America* (New York, 1980).
Gillis, John, *For Better, For Worse: British Marriages, 1600 to the Present* (New York, 1985).

Grossberg, Michael, *Governing the Hearth: Law and the Family in Nineteenth-Century America* (Chapel Hill, 1985).

Halem, Lynne Carol, *Divorce Reform: Changing Legal and Social Perspectives* (New York, 1980).

Muncy, Raymond Lee, *Sex and Marriage in Utopian Communities in Nineteenth-Century America* (Bloomington, 1973).

Paulson, Ross Evans, *Women's Suffrage and Prohibition: A Comparative Study of Equality and Social Control* (Glenview, Ill., 1973).

Phillips, Roderick, *Divorce in New Zealand: A Social History* (Auckland, 1981).

Pivar, David, *Purity Crusade: Sexual Morality and Social Control, 1868–1900* (Westport, Conn., 1973).

Taylor, Barbara, *Eve and the New Jerusalem: Socialism and Feminism in the Nineteenth Century* (London, 1983).

Thomas, Keith, "The Double Standard," *Journal of the History of Ideas* 20 (1959), 195–216.

8

The twentieth century and the rise of mass divorce

The half-century up to World War I was a vital transitional period in the history of divorce in Western society. In most countries, states, and colonies divorce was either legalized or liberalized, divorce rates began to rise appreciably, and divorce became a major social issue. These developments, which were discussed in the two preceding chapters, laid the foundations for the transformation of divorce that occurred in the following seventy-five years. From being difficult to obtain and effectively reserved for the better-off social groups, divorce became widely available to all social strata; the divorce rate underwent a steady if far from linear increase, with a sharp acceleration from the late 1960s; and attitudes toward divorce became increasingly tolerant, to the point of becoming positive. In sum, the twentieth century broke sharply with the earlier history of divorce, and divorce itself, once a marginal and deviant phenomenon, became central to social and family patterns in Western society. Like most revolutions, that experienced by divorce was not accomplished smoothly. Divorce policies, always sensitive to political change, became enmeshed in the political volatility Europe experienced between the two world wars, and these wars themselves, together with other social dislocations such as the economic depression of the 1930s, had their impact on marriage and divorce. This chapter focuses on the institutional aspects of divorce (law, policy, and rates) and plots their course through the upheavals of the twentieth century after the outbreak of World War I in 1914.

There were few changes to divorce laws during the war itself, but the conflict had important short- and longer-term implications that made it something of a watershed in the history of divorce. Throughout most of the Western world the number of divorces and the divorce rates rose dramatically in the immediate postwar period. In England, for example, the annual number of divorces averaged 701 between 1910 and 1913 and increased to 846 between 1914 and 1917, which were war years. But in 1918 there were 1,407 divorces, in 1919 that number almost doubled to 2,610, and in 1920 and 1921 there were 2,985 and 3,956, respectively. The annual average of 2,740 between

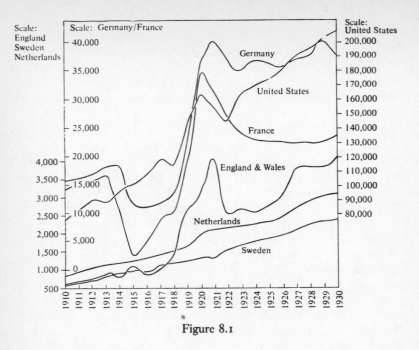

Figure 8.1

1918 and 1921 was four times higher than in the years immediately
preceding the war. In Germany the picture was similar. Divorces averaged 13,008 annually between 1910 and 1913, and although they
declined marginally during the war years (to 12,795), they shot up
after the war to an annual average of 33,592 between 1919 and 1922,
almost three times the prewar number. In the United States there was
also a big increase, albeit smaller than in England or Germany: There
were 111,340 divorces a year in the period 1914–18 (America joined
the war only in 1917), but 155,070 a year (a 40% increase) between
1919 and 1921. And not only did divorces increase in absolute numbers; so did divorce rates, however they are expressed. In England
there had never been more than three divorce petitions per 10,000
married women in a single year, but in 1919 there were eight, and in
1920, nine. In Germany the prewar rate of 27 divorces per 100,000
inhabitants more than doubled to 59 per 100,000 by 1920.

This general tendency for divorces to increase dramatically after
World War I is visible in most Western countries, and it is shown
graphically in Figure 8.1. The steep short-term increase is most
marked for France, England, the United States, and Germany. The
pattern in those countries not militarily involved in the war, however,

is quite different. Divorces in the Netherlands rose in a steady manner, with an accelerated but smooth increase in 1919 and 1920. Sweden, a neutral country spared the social and familial dislocation of war and postwar periods, was even less affected: Divorces rose at a constant rate during the period, and not only did not rise at the end of the war, but perversely dipped slightly from 1,325 in 1920 to 1,265 in 1921.

An increase in divorces is characteristic of many postwar periods. It has been noted after the American Civil War, and it also occurred, as we shall see, after World War II. Insofar as it is a general pattern, we can point to influences that wars appear to share that override place and period, influences on marriage generally and marriages in particular that seem to predispose them toward breakdown and their dissolution by divorce.

Four main circumstances appear to be involved in the weakening of marriages under wartime conditions. First, many marriages were contracted during the war after the couple had known each other for only a short time, certainly for a shorter time than the couple would normally (in peacetime) have waited before marrying. Wars accelerated courtship by imposing the expectation that the male partner might soon have to leave on active service, and this effect does not seem to have been neutralized by the possibility that the new bride might just as rapidly become a young widow. The early years of World War I in both England and the United States saw a brief marriage boom. In England there had been 288,000 marriages a year between 1912 and 1914, but in 1915 some 361,000 couples tied the knot, a 25% increase. (In the later war years, when the number of available marriageable men was reduced, marriages fell below prewar levels.) The effect of the war on the United States marriage rate can be calculated even more precisely. America declared war in April 1917, and from a monthly average of 74,000 marriages in the first three months of that year, the number rose to 112,000 in April, 93,000 in May, and 130,000 in June, giving a monthly average for the second quarter of 112,000, a 50% increase. (Some of this was the normal effect of the popularity of June as a marriage month.)

The link between increased war marriages and the postwar divorce rate is an assumption that many men and women married ill-advisedly and that their inherently fragile unions could not withstand the hardships of separation imposed by the war. This explanation, linking marriage boom to divorce bust, appeals to common sense and no doubt makes sense in relation to countries like England and the United States. But it does not help to explain the postwar increase in divorce in countries like France and Germany, where there was no rise in marriages during the war. In Germany, for example, the number of marriages declined from 513,000 in 1913 to 461,000 in 1914, then plunged to 278,000 in 1915. The fragility of wartime marriages, then, can have played a role in postwar divorce in only some countries.

There are three other broad explanations for the increased divorce rates in the wake of World War I. One is that the enforced separation of husbands and wives during the war weakened not only recent marriages, but also those of comparatively long standing. This factor should have been less significant in the United States, because there was only a year and a half between the departure of the first American troops for the European battlefields and the end of hostilities. It was potentially more important for French, German, British, and colonial divorce rates. Again, we can only speculate about the social, personal, and other factors at work here. One profitable area of investigation lies in the differing wartime experiences of a husband who was absent on military service and his wife who stayed at home. Their divergent experiences must have affected them in different ways such that they developed more individually, and less in tandem, than they would had they not been separated. It is possible, too, that women who entered paid employment during the war, as many married women did, gained a sense of independence that changed their attitudes toward their husbands.

A third category of explanations of the postwar divorce rate is wartime adultery. Quite simply, separation in time of war gave men and women the opportunities and perhaps the motivation — loneliness and the deprivation of sexual activity — to seek extramarital relationships. We can assume that men on active duty were sexually active in various ways. Apart from rape, which was no doubt frequent even if it cannot be put on a firm statistical basis, there were many casual sexual contacts between troops and local women, as well as prostitutes. The military authorities were well aware of this: Every British soldier received a personal printed letter from his commander-in-chief, Lord Kitchener, warning that "in this new experience you may find temptations . . . and while treating all women with courtesy, you should avoid any intimacy. Do your duty. Fear God. Honour the King." It was not so much God the military feared as venereal disease, as good an indicator as any of sexual activity among the troops. By 1917 a fifth of British fighting forces had venereal disease, and in that year the authorities capitulated to reality and issued condoms to their troops. For their part the French authorities provided official and medically inspected prostitutes for some forces as a way of containing the spread of the infection. We cannot, of course, know whether married soldiers were more, less, or equally likely as their unmarried comrades to be sexually active, but there is no reason to believe that adultery was not frequent.

It was the same for married women who remained at home during the war: Although it is probable that most were sexually faithful while their husbands were away, many were not. Some men returned home to children and pregnancies for which they could not possibly have been responsible. Some married women turned to prostitution, perhaps as a solution to financial hardship. What is important as far as divorce is concerned, however, is that a woman's adultery was more easily discovered and proved than that of her husband who had been away. Both, of course, risked betrayal by venereal disease, but women also risked pregnancy. Even without such misfortunes, married women at home lived under the surveillance of neighbors and community. Gossip about their wives must surely have reached the ears of demobilized soldiers, and some neighbors are known to have been thoughtful enough to send men on active service letters detailing their wives' sexual activities. In crude terms, then, an English wife's adultery at home was far more likely to be reported than, let us say, her husband's visits to a brothel in France or Egypt. Apart from the relative anonymity war can provide, there must also have been a tacit and mutually beneficial agreement that soldiers kept quiet about their comrades' activities of this sort.

Some effects of wartime infidelity were quite evident in England, where adultery was the sole ground for divorce. Up to 1915, women had filed more than 40% of divorce petitions (for reason of their husbands' aggravated adultery), but in the five years from 1916 to 1920, the proportion of women's petitions fell to between 20 and 33% on an annual basis. Only in 1921 did women's petitions rebound to the prewar proportions. The meaning of this is that in late wartime and immediate postwar years, more men than usual filed for divorce. In 1919 and 1920, in fact, 7,387 men divorced their adulterous wives, more than all the divorces in England in the war years combined.

The fourth category of explanation that can be invoked to explain the divorce boom after World War I is that it compensated for the decline in divorces during the war. Given the trends in divorce from the late nineteenth century to the outbreak of war, divorce numbers and rates ought to have increased steadily. In most countries engaged in the war, however, divorces and rates dipped, although the period of decline varied from country to country (three or four years in England, France, and Germany, compared with one year in the United States). The decline in divorces might well be explained in terms of a deferment of dissolution while the war, and the separation it entailed, effectively suspended the marriage conflict or reduced the urgency to divorce. There is no empirical way of verifying this explanation in terms of compensation, but, like the argument for the fragility of marriages after long separation, it is compelling and appealing to a commonsense understanding of the increase in divorces after World War I.

There are other dimensions to postwar divorce that also require explanation. Although it is easy enough to see why stresses and conflicts might have entered marriages as a result of the war, and why many marriages might have broken down, it is quite another question why the spouses were apparently so ready to turn to divorce. There were, after all, alternatives, such as living together unhappily, or simply separating informally. We must, in short, distinguish between marriage breakdown and divorce. There is no way of calculating the proportion of socially or emotionally dissolved marriages at any given time that do not end in divorce, but any explanation of the high postwar divorce rates that appeals to increased marriage breakdown due to the war rests on the assumption that the couples involved were predisposed to end their marriages legally and definitively. The assumption could be valid. It could well have been that the end of war and the onset of peace produced a sentiment that sought to shed or reject the past and look to the future. The question of one's marriage could well have been part and parcel of this sentiment. Put crudely, many men and women, having survived the trenches and the rigors and privations of the war at home, might have had little desire to participate in a peacetime marriage that meant stress or outright conflict. Looked at from this point of view, as part of a desire to start a new life after the war, divorce can be seen as part of the process of sloughing off the conflict-ridden past – as a sort of matrimonial demobilization.

A second important point about divorces in the immediate postwar period is that they ushered in a period in which the level of divorce was much higher than it had been before the war. As Figure 8.1 shows, after the phases of greatly increased divorce had passed, the number of divorces everywhere settled at levels significantly higher than before the war. Annual divorces in prewar Germany had been in the 15,000–20,000 range, but in the 1920s they averaged twice that, at between 35,000 and 40,000. Before the war there had never been more than 1,000 divorces in a single year in England, but in the 1920s they ranged from 2,500 to 4,000 a year. To some extent the increased use of divorce in the 1920s must have been spurred by the familiarity with divorce as a result of the postwar boom. Divorce must have lost some of its mystery and taboo qualities. A greater acceptance of divorce was revealed by a burst of legislating activity that increased the grounds and, in England particularly, gave women greater access to divorce.

Despite the economic and social problems of the postwar world, the 1920s have been characterized as "gay," "roaring," and "swinging." Broad changes in attitudes toward social and moral issues, together with increasing (though short-lived) prosperity later in the decade, had an impact on patterns of marriage and divorce. In most countries the crude marriage rate (the number of marriages each year in relation to population) increased between 1920 and 1930, and divorced men and women made up a growing proportion of grooms and brides. In the United States the proportion of divorced men and women among those married in the 1920s was twice that among those married before the war. The flood of divorces after the war cannot but have increased the exposure of ordinary people to divorce on a scale unthinkable ten years earlier. In *Only Yesterday*, his account of the 1920s in America, Frederick Lewis Allen wrote of the "decline in the amount of disgrace accompanying divorce," and commented that, in the cities at least, divorced men and women were socially accepted without question. Indeed, he went on,

there was often about the divorced person just enough of an air of unconventionality, just enough of a touch of scarlet, to be considered rather dashing and desirable. Many young women probably felt as did the young New York girl who said, toward the end of the decade, that she was thinking of marrying Henry, although she didn't care very much for him, because even if they didn't get along she could get a divorce and "it would be much more exciting to be a divorcee than to be an old maid."

Changes in attitudes alone cannot explain the higher levels of divorce in the 1920s. Divorce behavior, which is examined more closely in the next chapter, was part of a broader set of changes in social political life. For example, the status of women rose somewhat with the extension of women's suffrage during or after the war. Before World War I women had been granted the vote only in New Zealand (1893), Australia (1902), Finland (1907), Norway (1913), and in eleven of the western states of the United States. From the war's end women's suffrage was granted in the United States nationally, Britain, Sweden, Germany, and in many other Western countries. The interwar period (1918–39) also witnessed an extension of social welfare and related programs, shifts in the composition of the labor force that had implications for separation and divorce, and changing expectations of marriage. The rest of this chapter will focus on legal reform, divorce policy liberalization, and the effects of political change on them.

It was in the interwar period that English divorce law, substantially unchanged since 1857, was liberalized. In 1912 a royal commission on divorce had recommended removing those parts of the law that discriminated against women and expanding the grounds for divorce, but the government of the day had declined to take action. There were further attempts, in 1913 and 1921, to have the commission's recommendations implemented, but it was not until 1923 that reforms were made. Even then the change was important, but limited: Women were given equal access to divorce for reason of simple adultery (rather than having to prove their husbands guilty of aggravated adultery).

Even this modest reform – it left adultery as the sole ground for divorce – was bitterly opposed on all sides. Politicians who wanted a more substantial liberalization of divorce law were afraid that such piecemeal changes would delay general divorce reform. Others argued in favor of the double standard, claiming that a woman's adultery was indeed much more serious than a man's and that the law ought to recognize the fact. Praising the superior virtue of women, the basis of the double standard, Sir Henry Craik exclaimed in the House of Commons that

chastity in women is a star that has guided human nature since the world began, and that points to far higher and teaches us of the other sex things which we could not otherwise know. We bow in humble reverence to that high star of chastity, and we celebrate it in song and poetry.

But, Sir Henry added, "I do not think that any mere man would thank us for enshrining him in such a halo." Such views were finally out of step with majority opinion. Major Entwhistle, the sponsor of the 1923 equalizing bill (it was not a government bill) called sexual inequality an "anachronism and an indefensible anomaly." He pointed out that from the married women's property acts of the 1870s onward, there had been a succession of laws in favor of women (including the right to vote in 1919) and that the time had arrived for the principle to be applied to divorce.

The 1923 act had immediate consequences for divorce in England, as the number of petitions filed by women rose so that for the first time women sought a majority of the divorces. Between 1923 and 1939 women's petitions accounted for between 50 and 60%. And because the 1923 law did not affect men's access to divorce, but simply improved women's, the increased petitioning by women pushed up the number of divorces and the divorce rate. Divorces had risen appreciably in England after World War I, but the application of the 1923 act ensured that the postwar surge ebbed only temporarily, as Figure 8.1 shows. By 1927 there were as many divorces in England as there had been in 1921, the peak year of the postwar divorce boom, and the number and rate steadily increased until the outbreak of World War II. From the pre–World War I base, the petitioning rate had risen three- or fourfold in the 1920s and four- or fivefold in the 1930s. Part of the increase can be attributed to a general trend that is independent of specific legal changes, but one study estimates that the 1923 act alone was responsible for between a fifth and a quarter of the increase in the divorce rate.

Liberalization of divorce policy in England proved to be a painfully slow process. After the 1923 legislation there was some improvement in the Poor Persons' Procedure in 1926, but it was not until 1937 – eighty years after the divorce law had been passed – that a general revision of the law took place. This reform extended the grounds for divorce in England beyond adultery for the first time, to include three years' desertion, cruelty, and prolonged and incurable insanity. Women were also enabled to divorce husbands guilty of rape, sodomy, or bestiality. With the exception of insanity, these had been the grounds recommended by the royal commission on divorce a quarter of a century earlier, and cruelty and desertion were not entirely new to English divorce law, because they were recognized as circumstances that might "aggravate" adultery so as to justify a woman's divorce before the 1923 law came into effect. Nonetheless, the 1937 divorce law did extend the grounds for divorce, although it also incorporated a new restriction, designed to prevent hasty divorces, that is, a stipulation that, except in cases of extreme hardship, no petition for divorce could be filed during the first three years of marriage.

The liberalization of divorce in 1937 was accomplished with relative ease, although it was fought by the perennial opponents of divorce, such as the Roman Catholic and Anglican churches. One of the arguments invoked to justify reform was that allowing only the one ground for divorce encouraged spouses wishing to terminate their marriages to commit either adultery or perjury. One Member of Parliament described a "well-known" way of circumventing the existing law: "The thing can be done by the wife writing a letter to the husband asking him to come back, and then the husband writes a letter refusing and sends the wife the address of some hotel where she can obtain evidence sufficient to obtain a divorce." Above all, however, there was a sense that divorce law reform in England was well overdue, a sentiment expressed by one Member of Parliament who described the existing law as being "like some architectural monstrosity that stands upon a hill and offends the eye of all beholders year after year, and yet, because it is so familiar, if anybody tries to pull it down, there arises a great outcry." Such outcry as there was at divorce law reform in 1937 was ineffective, however, and the liberalized legislation, itself an indicator of changing attitudes, went into effect in 1938.

It was ironic that the passage of this law was accepted so easily, however, for soon after it had been read in Parliament a second time, in November 1936, Britain was faced with a constitutional crisis that centered on divorce. The issue involved King Edward VIII, who had succeeded to the throne in January 1936, and who was romantically involved with an American woman, Wallis Simpson. The prospect of a marriage between the two was complicated by her being an American and a commoner, but it was made critical by the fact that she was divorced – and not only divorced, but divorced twice, the most recent having taken place in October 1936. In early December of that year the British prime minister, Stanley Baldwin, discussed the matter with the king and pointed out that a marriage would not receive "the approbation of the country." Baldwin rejected the king's suggestion that he be allowed a morganatic marriage (such that his wife would not be queen), and Edward was faced with a choice of giving up Mrs. Simpson to remain king or giving up the throne to marry her. Edward decided in favor of love, abdicated, and left for France, where he and Wallis Simpson were married in June 1937.

This abdication crisis brought into focus a number of issues related to divorce. It served, first, as a reminder that although divorce was becoming more acceptable for ordinary people, it was unthinkable that a king of England should marry a woman who had two previous husbands still living. There was also the question of the Church of England's response when required to celebrate a royal wedding involving a twice-divorced woman, and there would inevitably have been questions about the legitimacy of succession (although the fact that Wallis Simpson was forty-two made this issue unlikely). Apart from British public opinion – represented by the prime minister as being hostile to divorce – there was fear that if Edward married Mrs. Simpson the British Empire would be weakened. Canadian sentiment was said to be particularly against the marriage; it was reported to the British government that "Canada is the most puritanical part of the Empire, and cherishes very much the Victorian standards in private life.... Canadian pride has been deeply wounded by the tattle in the American press, which she feels an intolerable impertinence." Clearly, Canadians were embarrassed by American press coverage of the relationship between Edward and Mrs. Simpson, which seemed to suggest that the royal family, the epitome of imperial virtue and British respectability, was enmeshed in the type of scandal that Canadians had long enjoyed portraying as peculiar to America.

In fact the American connection was important to the whole issue. The term "American divorcee," which aptly described Mrs. Simpson, was loaded with connotations for non-Americans, suggesting a woman of loose morals. It made no difference that Mrs. Simpson had been the petitioner, and thus the innocent party, in her two divorces. The point had frequently been made in the English debate on divorce, which was going on just as the royal scandal became public, that many divorces involved collusion between the spouses and that many husbands, faced with an adulterous wife, were wont to do the honorable thing and let their wives divorce them. For these various reasons, all related to divorce, Mrs. Simpson was unacceptable to Parliament, to the representatives of the British Empire, to the English establishment, to the press, and probably to the English people, too, even though there was a wave of sympathy toward a man who gave up a crown for the woman he loved. But that was not enough. Divorce was still too scandalous to be permitted to stain the royal family. As one Member of Parliament observed, "I could have wished that the king had been able to live here married, happy, and king, but he has wished otherwise. A thousand years hence, perhaps, we shall be liberal enough to allow such a thing, but it is too early now."

It was not too early to allow greater freedom of divorce to the English people at large, however, and when the 1937 law reform took effect in 1938 there was evidence that the liberalization of divorce was welcome. Divorce petitions, which had numbered 5,903 in 1937, almost doubled to 10,233 in 1938. Because of the backlog in the courts, the actual number of divorces rose more gradually, but still progressed from 5,044 in 1937 to 7,621 in 1938 and then to 8,248 in 1939. The number of divorces in 1938–9 was 60% higher than in 1936–7, but it is difficult to calculate the longer-term results of the 1937 law because of the disruptive effects of World War II, which broke out in September 1939. The English divorces of 1938–9 bore two characteristics, however. First, they dissolved marriages of relatively long standing: More than 68% ended marriages that were ten or more years old, compared to 53% and 55% in 1936 and 1937, respectively. Many of the additional divorces evidently dissolved marriages that had ended de facto years earlier (particularly those based on desertion, of course). Second, the additional divorces in 1938 and 1939 were accounted for by men and women using the new grounds (especially desertion); the number of divorces for reason of adultery scarcely altered between 1936–7 and 1938–9. This was one example of changes in divorce law clearly affecting the number, rate, and type of divorces.

It was not only England where practical effects resulted from changes in divorce laws and policies during the interwar period. In Scotland the substance of sixteenth-century divorce law had scarcely been changed for almost four hundred years, although some procedural changes had been made in the nineteenth and twentieth centuries, and there were reforms in the law regarding separations. For example, drunkenness was made a ground for separation in Scotland in 1903. It was not until 1938, however, that its divorce law was expanded to include (in addition to adultery and desertion) cruelty and habitual drunkenness.

An even more cautious approach was evident in Canada. A bill to create a uniform divorce law for the whole country except for Quebec was defeated in 1920. In 1925 a modest reform based on the English 1923 law gave women equal access to divorce wherever it was available in Canada. Finally, in 1930 there was a breakthrough (in Canadian terms) when Parliament granted the citizens of Ontario, the country's most populous province, the right to sue for divorce from provincial courts, rather than by means of individual Act of Parliament. The sole ground remained adultery, however.

By contrast New Zealand, another British colony at the beginning of the interwar period, pushed ahead with ever more liberal divorce policies. In 1919 a statute reduced the period of desertion in the divorce law from five to three years, when the defendant was a person "of enemy origin" – doubtless a response to a specific case, but one that ignored the fact that the war was over. In 1920 a further reform made divorce for insanity easier to obtain, gave the courts discretionary powers to grant a divorce where a couple had been legally separated at least three years, and added as a new ground for divorce the conviction of either spouse for wounding the other, or his or her child.

As usual, the United States presented a rather more complicated picture of state divorce legislation, but a continuing trend of liberalization is evident. The reasons were mixed, however. In the late 1920s a veritable divorce trade war broke out among states such as Nevada, Idaho, and Arkansas, each vying to attract out-of-state petitioners. In 1927 Nevada reduced its residency requirement from six to three months, and in 1931, when the other two states seemed about to match it, the requirement was lowered again, to six weeks. The aim was not to gain the distinction of having America's most lax divorce policies, but to attract the millions of dollars that were spent by divorce migrants on legal fees, court costs, travel, accommodation, and subsistence. The effects of changing the residency requirements were palpable: There were 1,021 divorces in Nevada in 1926, but in 1927 (after the requirement was reduced) they almost doubled to 1,953 and in 1928 rose again to 2,595. Between 1930 and 1931, when the six-week residency rule was introduced, the number of divorces again doubled, rising from 2,609 to 5,260. By 1940 Nevada accounted for only one in fifty of the divorces in the United States, but on a population basis its rate was by far the highest in the country: at 49 divorces per thousand resident population, it far outranked Florida, which had the second highest at 5.8 per thousand.

In the interwar period Americans were inveterate divorce migrants. Some of the divorce migration resulted from very restrictive divorce policies in states such as New York, where adultery was the only ground and where perjury in the divorce courts was said to be the norm. Were it simply a matter of going to a divorce-friendly jurisdiction, New Yorkers had no reason to look further afield than the nearest American divorce haven, yet thousands of Americans traveled to France in the 1920s to divorce. Apart from the undoubted gastronomic and cultural advantages that Paris had over Reno and Miami, the wealthy found in France a publicity-free divorce facility, for the 1884 French divorce law forbade the reporting of divorce cases in the press. Moreover there were no effective residence requirements to satisfy, and lawyers in Paris advertised "*divorces rapides*" for foreigners. Travel and other costs restricted French divorce to the wealthiest Americans, of course, but it is estimated that in 1926, some 300 American couples had their marriages dissolved in Paris. It is significant that the number fell (to 100 by 1928) after American newspapers, which were not subject to the press restrictions, began to publish the names of Americans who divorced in Paris.

Americans sought equally exotic divorces in the Virgin Islands, Cuba, and especially in Mexico, where divorce was legalized in 1917. As in the United States, Mexican law varied from state to state, and some quickly recognized the fiscal and economic benefits that the American divorce trade might bring. In 1918 Yucatan state set minimal residency requirements in the hope of attracting American divorce petitioners, and other states followed suit. In Morelos state, there was no residency requirement at all, and divorces could be granted within twenty-four hours. The most popular Mexican state for American divorce migrants, however, was Chihuahua, which shares a border with Texas. There residency for the purpose of divorce was established by registration on arrival, and divorce was available for reason of incompatibility. Between the world wars the popularity of Mexican divorces grew, and it is estimated that in the period 1926–40 at least 13,500 American marriages were dissolved there. Matrimonial transients from the north no doubt injected useful funds into local economies and government coffers. In Sonora state there was a state tax of between 100 and 500 pesos ($50 to $250 at 1925 rates of exchange), and the Mexican government imposed an additional levy of 25%.

The extent of migratory divorce in the interwar period was impressive, but it is important to keep it in perspective. The 13,500 American marriages dissolved in Mexico pale against the more than three million divorces granted in the United States between 1926 and 1940. Other nationalities migrated in search of divorce too, but it was the Americans who got the attention. That was a result of widespread perceptions that American marriages were fragile and morals low, and in turn the publicity given to American divorce migration reinforced the negative image of American marriage. The opposition to King Edward VIII's marriage to Wallis Simpson must be understood in this context, for Mrs. Simpson came to be viewed as representative of a breed of women of questionable morals and a weak commitment to marriage.

Beyond the difficult issue of migratory divorce and the pattern of divorce policy liberalization between the world wars, divorce was also given explicit political dimensions in the period. We have already noted the links between political ideology and divorce in other contexts, such as the English and French revolutions, and in general terms during the nineteenth century attitudes toward divorce correlated with conservative and liberal orientations. The interwar period, which is now under discussion, witnessed another set of links. It was marked by a polarization of political ideologies in continental Europe and was characterized by the coming to power of fascist regimes in Italy, Germany, and Spain, and by semifascist administrations in Portugal and in France after 1940. Standing against these regimes were the movements of the left, often inspired by the example of the Soviet Union. In each case the regimes and ideologies of the right and the left articulated ideologies of marriage and adopted specific divorce policies.

Although not part of the Western world, the Soviet state that was formed as a result of the 1917 revolution had a far-reaching and immediate impact on social and political thought in Western Europe, where political movements and parties were inspired by the Soviet model. The short-lived "Red Republic" in Bavaria in 1918–19 was an attempt to emulate the October Revolution in Russia, and Communist parties were established everywhere. Many Western intellectuals traveled to the Soviet Union after the revolution, and although many were disillusioned by what they saw, one of the innovations that they found encouraging was a family policy that was radically different from that of any Western country.

Abortion was not only legal, but available at no cost in public hospitals. There were no limitations on the dissemination of birth control information, and contraceptives were freely available. Marriage was secularized, and women were given complete equality with men in all aspects of law. This new Soviet family policy represented a rejection of traditional concepts of the family, and was based on the writings of Karl Marx and Friedrich Engels, who had pointed to the bourgeois family as integral to bourgeois society, and had predicted that it would disappear as part of the fundamental transformation of society. In the *Communist Manifesto* they had written that "the bourgeois family will vanish as a matter of course when its complement vanishes, and both will vanish with the vanishing of capital." Communism, wrote Engels, would "transform the relation between the sexes into a purely private matter which concerns only the persons involved."

It was this principle that was quickly translated into law by the new Soviet government in 1917 and 1918. The aim was to reduce the legal barriers to freedom within the family so as to allow the forces of historical change to do the work that would lead to the disappearance of the bourgeois family. Divorce was a keystone of the new code of family law because it removed the restrictions imposed by marital indissolubility. Engels had recognized the need for divorce, writing that partnerships of men and women should last only as long as there was love – something that "varies very much in duration from one individual to another, especially among men." Closer to the Bolshevik revolution – a year before it, in fact – Lenin had envisaged the necessity of divorce: "One cannot be a democrat and a socialist without demanding full freedom of divorce, for the absence of such freedom is an additional burden on the oppressed sex, woman." (Lenin added that "the recognition of the *right* of women to leave their husbands is not an *invitation* to all wives to do so!")

The first Soviet divorce law was decreed in principle in November 1917, then promulgated in detail in 1918. Under it, divorces could be obtained by the mutual desire of the spouses or at the request of either. There was no question of fault. The minimal procedure required the petition to be made orally or in writing to the local court, and the defendant spouse, if there were one and if his or her address were known, would be summoned to appear. Because the law required no evidence of fault, however, there was no defense, and although there was provision for an appeal, it is not clear what grounds might be invoked. The local court was to decide matters related to the custody, upbringing, and maintenance of any children. According to one commentator, judges tended to grant custody to the parent with the greatest "proletarian sympathies."

Divorce in the early years of the Soviet state was thus easy, speedy, and inexpensive. It was actually easier to divorce than to marry, for divorce required the consent of only one person, marriage of two. Precise statistics on the use of divorce are difficult to obtain, but there were ten for every twenty-two marriages in the urban population of the European USSR in the 1920s, and ten divorces for every thirteen marriages in Moscow. A survey of students in Odessa in the 1920s indicated that 11% of males and 16% of females had been married and divorced.

By the later 1920s and 1930s there was increasing official concern at the ease of divorce and at abuses of the law. It was alleged that peasant men, needing help during the harvest, would marry before the harvest and divorce after it, using their temporary wives as unpaid labor. Women criticized the law, arguing that it was women who suffered most when men married, divorced, and remarried in rapid succession. By the mid-1930s the government responded to these concerns and introduced restrictions on divorce, including financial sanctions that cut deeply into the divorce rate. At the same time (1935–6) other parts of the libertarian family policies of the early Soviet period were abandoned, partly to boost population growth.

The eventual rejection of the early family laws was unforeseen, of course, and they were praised not only by Soviet leaders but by many Western observers who found the policy fascinating and exciting. A British journalist wrote from the Soviet Union in 1924 that the new marriage code reflected "intelligent Russian opinion." The English philosopher Bertrand Russell, who visited the Soviet Union in 1929, was greatly disillusioned by most of what he saw but wrote favorably about marriage and the family. Attacking the bases of traditional Western marriage, Russell wrote that "there is no country in the world and there has been no age in the world's history where sexual ethics and sexual institutions [including marriage] have been determined by rational considerations, with the exception of Soviet Russia." Other commentators, as we might expect, were appalled by the Soviet policies. One wrote that the communists aimed to destroy marriage and the family and that the new laws left both resting "on little else than the unstable element of sexual affinity and satisfaction." Divorce, he went on, was so easy to obtain that "men and women so minded stand in line before the proper officers as compunctionless as those in bread queues."

Ironically, such criticisms of Soviet divorce policy were expressed at the very time when divorce rates in America and Europe were rising after World War I. Continuing Western criticisms of Soviet family policy were made against the background of continuing high divorce rates and a spread of anxiety about marriage and morals. Perhaps it was this conjunction that reinforced conservative alarm, a fear that the Soviet experience represented the future of the West if socialist ideologies were to prevail there too. Certainly, many Western socialists found Soviet policy an attractive model. The socialist Independent Labour Party in England praised Soviet divorce as having "worked on the side of freedom" and "purified the relation of women and men." Writing of divorce, George Bernard Shaw urged "the good example of Russia" on his readers.

Despite some qualms about the abuses of the first Soviet law in practice, it generally found favor across the liberal and socialist spectrum in Europe and America. It responded to liberal and socialist hostility to the oppressive character of bourgeois marriage and complemented the socialist feminist critiques of Western family institutions and practices.

To this extent, family policy was one issue (a relatively minor one, it is true) that distinguished the left from the right in the interwar period. Whereas the left stressed individualism within marriage and the family, the right tended to adopt a corporative approach, emphasizing the integrity and coherence of the family and elevating the interests of the group above those of the individual members. A well-ordered family life, they often insisted, was the foundation of a well-ordered society and polity. To this extent right-wing family policies tended to oppose divorce outright or to regulate it closely. The dichotomy between the left and the right was expressed in the divorce policies adopted by regimes of both kinds between the world wars.

Divorce was a contentious social and political issue in Spain during the turbulent 1930s. The republican government that came to power in 1931 pursued left-liberal policies that included extensive secularization as a means of reducing the power of the Roman Catholic church in sensitive areas of law and education. The 1931 constitution gave the state jurisdiction over the family, declared that marriage was founded on the equality of rights of both spouses, and specified that marriage might be dissolved "for mutual discord or at the request of either of the spouses, with evidence of just causes in each instance." This statement of broad principle was soon followed by specific divorce legislation, which was approved in early 1932 after a heated debate in the Cortes.

The lines of the political division over divorce were to become all too familiar later in the 1930s, during the Spanish civil war. The nationalist bloc of monarchist and Catholic deputies, most from rural areas, opposed divorce, whereas liberals, republicans, and socialists supported it. Opponents of divorce insisted that it was contrary to Catholic doctrine and the religious traditions of Spain, and that the legalization of divorce would be catastrophic. One Basque deputy cited statistics purporting to prove that the crime rate among divorced and widowed Germans was twice the average. Divorce, he argued, led to increased crime, juvenile delinquency, and suicide, and would result in an additional 4,500 deaths a year in Spain. Supporters of divorce ignored such dire predictions and held to the arguments that divorce was a basic right, but one that Spaniards need not resort to if it was repugnant to their religious views.

Objections to the 1932 law were based not only on the principle of divorce, however, but also on the fact that the law was very liberal. In its final form Spain's divorce law was Europe's most liberal code, allowing divorce by mutual consent (provided the spouses were of the age of majority and had been married at least two years) and on thirteen specific grounds: adultery by either spouse; bigamy; an attempt by the husband to corrupt his wife, or by either spouse to corrupt their son's morals or to prostitute their daughters; the disappearance of either spouse; desertion for one year; absence for two years; either spouse's attempt to murder the other or their children or ill-treatment or insults; a violation of conjugal obligations or immoral behavior that made life in common impossible; contagious and serious sexual diseases; serious illnesses that made fulfillment of the conjugal duties impossible; loss of liberty (imprisonment for more than ten years); de facto voluntary separation for three years; and incurable mental illness.

The 1932 law also retained separations, which gave devout Catholics an alternative to divorce. Separations could be obtained by mutual consent for any of the grounds recognized for divorce and also where a marriage was disturbed by a difference in behavior, mentality, or religion. This last category allowed separation essentially for incompatibility, and, because separations could be converted to divorce after three years, it further extended the grounds for divorce, albeit indirectly.

The only reliable statistics on divorce in Spain under the liberal 1932 code relate to the relatively stable period from March 1932 to December 1933. During these twenty-two months there were 7,059 petitions for divorce and 832 for separation, of which 4,920 (62%) were granted. Most of the divorces were in the country's two largest cities, Madrid and Barcelona. On an annual basis that would have given Spain 2,382 divorces, which translated into one of the lowest divorce rates in contemporary Europe. Interestingly, because divorce was often claimed by its supporters to be beneficial to women, most unilateral divorce petitions (56%) were filed by wives. When it came to separations, women were even more preponderant as petitioners, seeking some 81%.

The divorce trends in Spain after 1933 are unclear. It has been suggested that the number of divorces increased in republican-dominated regions of the country, particularly as divorce procedures were simplified when the legal system broke down during the civil war (1936–9). Hugh Thomas writes in his history of the war that "marriages were celebrated with the greatest ease at [republican] militia headquarters, and the partners shortly afterwards with equal facility forgot them." The republican government later validated any marriage involving a militiaman that had been celebrated before a war committee or an officer, and in 1937 the government also instituted a form of "marriage by usage." This meant that a man and a woman were considered legally married if they lived together for ten months or if the woman became pregnant. This decree was later repealed because it led to a large number of bigamous marriages when married men or women took up long-term cohabitation without first divorcing.

The fascist government of Francisco Franco that took power in Spain in 1938 had close links with the Roman Catholic church and would almost certainly have abolished divorce even if it had been legalized in a very restrictive form. But faced with what appeared to be matrimonial anarchy in the former republican zone of Spain, Franco's regime moved quickly to restore order on Catholic principles. Legislation of March 1938 suppressed civil marriage, suspended the divorce law, and reactivated the 1889 code as an interim measure. In September 1939 the 1932 divorce legislation was repealed with the express purpose of restoring to Spanish laws "the traditional value, which is the Catholic one." Divorces that had been decreed were declared void, with the implication that any remarriage following divorce was also void. This resolution thus placed in jeopardy the validity of many marriages (and the legitimacy of children), but this was seen as a short-term problem that was preferable to maintaining divorce or recognizing republican divorces. Spaniards were thenceforth protected from the dangers of divorce throughout Franco's rule, and even well after his death in 1975, for divorce was not legalized again until 1981.

Although Catholic influence was important in the suppression of divorce by the fascist regime in Spain, it had less impact in Portugal under Oliveira Salazar, who ruled as a semifascist dictator from 1932 to 1974. Despite embracing a conservative ideology of marriage and the family, Salazar did not repeal the liberal divorce law that had been introduced after the 1910 revolution. There were some attempts to abolish divorce in 1935 and 1936, but the most serious inroads into it were made as a result of a concordat signed between Portugal and the Vatican in 1940. The agreement effectively deprived the predominantly Catholic Portuguese of divorce by requiring couples, at the time of their marriage, to renounce the right to divorce. A further limitation was placed on divorce in 1942 when a law qualified a wife's right to divorce for reason of adultery. She could do so only when there was clear evidence that the adultery implied that conjugal love had disappeared from the marriage. An adulterous husband could thus defend himself against divorce by arguing that he loved his wife.

Despite evident misgivings about divorce, it was reaffirmed in the Portuguese civil code of 1944. It was available by mutual consent, unilaterally, and by conversion of a judicial separation after a specified period. An explanation of the retention of divorce by Salazar's socially conservative regime might well have been the popularity of divorce. Between 1930 and 1946, divorces in Portugal averaged 868 a year, which produced a relatively high rate.

The retention but restriction of an existing divorce law by the right-wing regime in Portugal was reminiscent of the situation in Vichy France under the administration of Marshal Pétain (1940–4). Under the slogan *"Travail, Famille, Patrie"* ("Work, Family, Motherland") the regime, which came to power following the German invasion and French surrender, adopted policies designed to strengthen the family in traditional conservative ways. Fertility was encouraged and abortion prohibited. The existing divorce law, which had been liberalized during the 1920s and 1930s, and under which there had been 26,300 divorces in 1938, was reformed so as to make divorce more difficult. Adultery and imprisonment were retained as grounds, but women were permitted to divorce for reason of ill-treatment only when the violence constituted "a serious or continual violation of the obligations of marriage and rendered the maintenance of married life intolerable." Moreover, marriages could not be dissolved in their first three years, and there was an increase in the delay that had to be observed before a separation could be converted to divorce. The aim of these reforms was to reduce the number of divorces, which was seen as a threat to social stability and the birthrate. An apologist of Pétain's regime argued that the reforms would "restore the great French family that constitutes the nation." How could one establish a family, he asked rhetorically, "when on each marriage registration there appeared, superimposed, a registration of divorce"?

The effect of the Vichy divorce law reforms is difficult to gauge. The number of divorces had already fallen to 21,188 in 1939, but it then plummeted to 11,070 in 1940. If anything, in fact, the number of divorces recovered somewhat, ranging between 14,000 and 18,000 a year in the Vichy period, a number that was still lower than the annual number up to 1938. After the liberation, however, divorces increased slightly (to just over 20,000 in 1945) before rising rapidly (to almost 52,000 in 1946) as France participated in the general postwar divorce boom. In the general confusion of influences during the war, however, it is all but impossible to isolate the particular effects of the Vichy legislation, although its intent was clear enough.

Like other fascist or semifascist regimes, Mussolini's in Italy had to face the issue of developing a divorce policy. Divorce, as we have noted, was not available in Italy despite a number of attempts to legalize it in the late nineteenth century. After World War I, Italy was granted territories (Alto Adige, Venezia Giulia, Trentino, and the city of Fiume) that had been part of the Austrian Empire, and where non-Catholics were permitted to divorce. The Italian policy prohibiting divorce was imposed there in 1924 (Fiume) and 1928 (the other territories). Fascist policy favored standardizing law throughout Italy, in any case, but a more important factor in the suppression of divorce was Mussolini's aim to attract the support of the Catholic church to his regime, which governed Italy from 1922. Divorce played a minor role in the fascists' religious policy between the wars.

The spector of divorce had haunted the Catholic church since the creation of the unified Italian state in 1870, and the Vatican had staunchly opposed any divorce bills introduced into parliament. There was awareness that the principle of marital indissolubility coexisted somewhat uneasily with civil marriage, which had been introduced in the 1865 civil code, and it seemed only a matter of time, particularly in view of developments in France and elsewhere, before divorce was legalized in Italy. Mussolini, a socialist in his earlier days, did not advocate divorce, but at the Socialist party's 1910 conference he moved a resolution calling for socialists, under threat of expulsion from the party, to avoid religious marriage. In 1916, even though he had by then left the Socialist party, Mussolini married in a civil ceremony.

He modified his position, however, when he was on the verge of gaining power and needed the support of the Catholic church. Throughout the 1920s Mussolini supported reforms to family laws that would be palatable to the Vatican. In his very first speech in the Chamber of Deputies in June 1921 Mussolini declared: "Fundamentally I am not in favor of divorce because I believe that problems of an emotional nature cannot be solved with judicial formulas." He suggested, however, that a decision should be made either to abolish divorce in the previous Austrian territories or to extend it to all Italians. The fascists soon opted for the suppression of divorce throughout Italy, however. By 1923, when the fascists were in power and negotiating for a concordat with the Vatican, the minister of justice declared that the Fascist party shared the Italian people's "profound and general repugnance to the institution of divorce." The following year divorce was banned in Fiume, and in 1928, the year before a concordat was signed, it was suppressed in the other territories Italy had acquired from Austria after the war.

The fascists' desire to rally the Roman Catholic church to its cause led to a general shift in Italian matrimonial policy and law. It was heralded by Mussolini himself going through a religious marriage ceremony with the woman he had married civilly in 1916 and culminated in the matrimonial provisions of the 1929 concordat between the fascist state and the Vatican. The concordat reversed the principle of giving full legal recognition only to civil marriage and specified that "the Italian state, willing to restore to the institution of marriage, foundation of the family, a dignity consonant with the Catholic traditions of its people, recognizes civil effects in the sacrament of marriage ruled by the canon law." In a confusing move, parliament allowed Italians to choose between civil and religious marriage but transferred jurisdiction over all matrimonial issues from the civil to the ecclesiastical courts. This alone ruled out the possibility of legalizing divorce.

In some respects the Italian fascists' approach to divorce resembled that adopted later by Franco's regime in Spain: Both opposed divorce outright for fundamentally religious reasons. Both differed radically from the policies adopted in Nazi Germany, however, for there marriage and divorce policy were designed to achieve demographic and racial goals. In *Mein Kampf* Adolf Hitler was quite unequivocal as to the purpose of marriage: "Marriage is not an end in itself, but it must serve the greater end, which is that of increasing and maintaining the human species and the race. This is its only meaning and purpose." Such a belief might well be construed as a reformulation of the traditional Christian doctrine that the purpose of marriage was procreation. This doctrine was secularized by pronatalists in the eighteenth and nineteenth centuries, and from Hitler's pen it appeared in *völkisch* religious and racial terms: "A folk-State should in the first place raise matrimony from the level of being a constant scandal to the race. The State consecrates it as an institution which is called upon to produce creatures made in the likeness of the Lord and not create monsters that are a mixture of man and ape." By regulating marriage and preventing nonmarital fertility, the Nazis sought to produce successive and progressively larger and purer generations of "Aryans."

It is scarcely surprising that the Nazis turned quickly to reform marriage laws. Marriage laws passed in 1935 as part of the infamous Nuremberg Laws forbade marriage and sexual intercourse between specified racially defined categories of people. Marriages and intercourse between Jews and Aryans were specifically prohibited. Later in 1935 a Marriage Health Law prohibited the marriage of any person suffering from a mental or physical disease that might adversely affect his or her partner or any children they might have. Men and women who wanted to marry had to be certified fit (as defined by the law) before they could legally be married.

Purifying the race was one thing, increasing it another. In 1933 a system of loans was introduced to encourage young Germans, of approved race and health, to marry. The loans were made in the form of vouchers that could be exchanged for furniture and other household goods. A portion of the loan was forgiven for each child born, so there was a distinct financial advantage to having several children early in marriage. The loans certainly contributed to a rise in the German marriage rate: In 1932 (before the loan scheme) there were 517,000 marriages, but in 1933 there were 639,000, in 1934 there were 740,000. From 1935 to 1939 marriages averaged 660,000 a year, far higher than the preloan rate. It is true, of course, that marriage rates rose in many parts of the Western world as the effects of the Great Depression ebbed in the early- to mid-1930s, but no country achieved a growth in the marriage rate comparable to that of Nazi Germany. The exception was Austria, where marriages leapt after Anschluss (incorporation into the German Reich) in March 1938. In 1937 there had been 46,000 marriages in Austria, but in 1938 there were 89,000, and in 1939 there were 117,000. In both Germany and Austria there were also significant increases in fertility, partly a result of the large numbers of marriages, and partly also of Nazi pronatalist policies that closed birth control centers, banned the advertising of contraceptives, and restricted abortion.

It was in this campaign to promote the Aryan population that divorce was given a role to play. The National Socialist government inherited the divorce provisions of the 1900 civil code, but as early as 1934 (the year after Hitler became chancellor) there were plans to bring divorce into line with the regime's marriage policies. However, a new divorce law was not promulgated until 1938, when Austria, where divorce was prohibited to Catholics, was incorporated into Germany. This new law was conventional in appearance but bore the unmistakable stamp of the Nazi preoccupation with population growth and racial purity. Refusal to have children was a ground for divorce, quite logically in light of the doctrine that the purpose of marriage was procreation. In fact some divorces were granted for this reason even before the 1938 divorce law was enacted. The law also permitted divorce if either spouse used an illegal means to prevent a birth, a ground evidently aimed at abortion. Marriage could also be dissolved when one spouse was suffering from premature infertility or from a mental or physical disorder. This included short-term emotional disturbances, mental illness, and diseases that were either contagious or repugnant to the other spouse. Again, the clear rationale underlying these grounds was the restriction of marriage and fertility to the mentally and physically fit so as to ensure a robust and healthy "Aryan" population. A further ground, this one retained from the 1900 divorce code, was adultery. But even this might be construed in terms of National Socialist ideology, for adultery – sexual activity outside marriage – made nonsense of the care Nazi law took to ensure that marriage (and therefore sexual intercourse and fertility) took place only between approved couples.

Apart from these grounds for divorce, all based on notions of fault or unfitness for marriage, the National Socialist law provided for no-fault divorce. Divorces were allowed where a couple had lived apart for three years and where there was no hope that married life would be resumed. No fault had to be attributed, and although the 1938 law provided for refusal of a divorce if it were proved that the separation took place primarily because of the petitioner's behavior, this defense was abolished in 1939. No-fault divorce of this kind in other Western countries rested on notions of the happiness and well-being of the couple, but in Germany the justification was again demographic: Couples who lived apart did not reproduce, but if the spouses were allowed to divorce, they could remarry and become fully reproductive members of the Reich. Approval of the principle was expressed by the Nazi newspaper *Völkischer Beobachter*, which commented that such marriages were unprofitable and "deprive the partners of any opportunity to make full use of their energies for the benefit of the community."

Clearly, the dominant interest served by the 1938 German divorce law was the state, and there was far less concern for the particular marital circumstances of individuals. The official SS newspaper *Schwarze Korps* commented:

The value of this new law consists in the fact that the liberal thesis which looked upon marriage as a private contract has been done away with, whereas the interests of the national community have been given due prominence. Useless and barren marriages, and those whose continuation is morally unjustified, are to be dissolved.

To this extent the National Socialist divorce law represented a radical departure from Western legal tradition. It is notable that of the basic grounds for divorce recognized almost everywhere by this time, the 1938 law included only adultery. The breeding projects undertaken by the Nazis to produce a perfect Aryan race indicate no great fastidiousness about confining sexuality to marriage, and the overriding concern that sexuality should be regulated by the state and not left to the whims of individuals, suggest that adultery in Nazi law was an offense against the state, not against an individual marriage or spouse as it was in conventional divorce legislation.

Yet for all that divorce was intended to serve the state rather than the happiness of individuals, it is likely that most who used the law did so for personal reasons. It is surely probable that adultery was viewed by ordinary men and women in quite traditional ways, as infidelity rather than an act that threatened the Reich with a child whose parentage was not approved in advance. It is equally probable that the other grounds were also invoked for quite selfish and personal reasons, rather than out of an overwhelming desire to sacrifice, for example, a happy but infertile marriage for the chance to breed workers for Hitler. Yet there were explicitly political divorces as well, some apparently based on ad hoc criteria established by Nazi judges. One court agreed to a man's petition based on his wife's insistence on patronizing Jewish stores: "If the wife of a National Socialist, especially of a National Socialist official, makes purchases at Jewish stores and shops, in spite of the explicit veto of her husband, he cannot be blamed for growing cold in his matrimonial feelings," the court held. In another case a woman was granted a divorce because her husband kept "incessantly sneering at her being a member of the Union of National Socialist Women," and expressed indignation when his son gave the Nazi salute "Heil Hitler." The German supreme court later ruled that "disparagement of the Führer by a wife entitles the husband to claim a divorce."

Whether motivated by personal or political considerations, however, Germans rallied to the new divorce law. Between 1930 and 1938 divorces in Germany had averaged 46,243 a year, but in 1939 they rose to 61,848, more than 12,000 the number in 1938. This might have been viewed with satisfaction by the government, but the Vatican protested that the divorce law, like the rest of Nazi marriage policy, was repugnant to Catholic doctrine. The 1933 concordat between the Vatican and the Nazi state had accepted the long-standing church demand for a revision of German marriage law, but this was clearly not what the church had in mind. The Nazi code not only gave total control of marriage to the state, but it was also a rejection of the fundamental Western traditions of both ecclesiastical and secular marriage law.

A survey of the interwar period suggests, then, that there was no simple correlation between political ideology and marriage and divorce policies. It might generally be true that there is a predisposition on the part of conservatives to prefer restrictive divorce policies, and of liberals to opt for more permissive policies. But in concrete historical terms, family policy in this period was the product not only of ideology, but also of specific social, economic, and cultural conditions. The libertarian family policies adopted by the Soviet Union in 1917 proved to be socially and demographically so disastrous that they were abandoned within two decades. As for the fascist states, Franco's Spain was inherently conservative in social policies and adhered to the family doctrines of the Roman Catholic church; Mussolini's regime was ideologically flexible but pursued a family ideology that was in tune with Italian tradition and Catholic doctrine; and in Hitler's Germany family policy marched to the beat of Nazi demographic and racial goals. Although we can dismiss easy generalizations about the relationships between political ideology and family policy, the integral role of family policy within broader sociopolitical aims is clear in all these examples.

Apart from the influences of variations in divorce law and policy on the rate and patterns of divorce, the more general economic climate also played a discernible role at specific times. It is generally accepted that divorces tend to increase in times of prosperity, and there is an impression that the economic depression from 1929 also depressed divorce rates. However, outside the United States the effects of the depression on divorce were negligible (see Figures 8.1 and 8.2). Both England and Germany were severely affected by the economic crisis and experienced a decline in divorces in 1929, but in both countries the rates recovered quickly enough and increased during the first half of the 1930s. No Western country was affected as much as the United States, where the divorce rate peaked in 1929 but then declined for four years, until the number of divorces in 1932 and 1933 was 20% lower than the 1929 level. The decline in the American divorce rate meant that there was a deficit of between 100,000 and 150,000 in the number of divorces that would have taken place had predepression trends not been interrupted.

There are several explanations for the decline of divorces during the depression, but it is difficult to understand why they should have had such great effect in the United States and not elsewhere. The most immediate result of unemployment and financial hardship should have been to relegate divorce to a low priority in terms of expenditures. Second, although financial difficulties must have placed scarcely tolerable pressures on many marriages, they were counteracted by other pressures. Welfare assistance was given more readily to families than to individuals, and men with families were given priority in employment on relief projects. Some commentators have suggested, moreover, that the common adversity drew American couples together – even if temporarily, for the divorce rate rose steadily after the worst of the depression was over. A further influence on the divorce rate in the United States must have been the decline in women's employment (married women whose husbands were in paid employment were often fired or denied employment); two-thirds of American divorces were sought by women, and the loss of financial independence can only have deterred them from divorcing. In the end it is impossible to generalize about the effects of the depression on divorce, for they varied widely. Only in the United States did the divorce rates accompany the indices of industrial performance as they fell from 1929 onward, but it is difficult to isolate the factors that applied in this one case that were not involved elsewhere.

The mid- to late-1930s was a period of relative stability in divorce rates, but new divorce legislation in such countries as England, Germany, Austria, and (a little later) France produced short-term shifts, as Figure 8.2 shows. It was World War II (1939–45), however, that much more dramatically affected divorces: In the last year of the war and the two or three immediate postwar years, divorce rates reached levels that were not only unprecedented but would also not be equaled again for another twenty years. In looking at postwar divorce in countries where there had been legal changes just before or during the war, however, we must bear in mind the effects of laws as well as of the military conflict. The case of Germany is particularly complex because there are no statistics on divorces there between 1941 and 1946 and because after the war West and East Germany adopted different divorce codes when they replaced the Nazi divorce law of 1938.

Yet despite the influence of nonmilitary factors, the rapid and dramatic increase in divorces throughout most of the Western world between 1945 and 1948 was mostly an effect of World War II. Evidence of this lies in the general exemption of nonbelligerent countries from the postwar divorce boom. Sweden, Portugal, and Switzerland, for example, all registered increases in divorces in 1946, but they were nothing like the massive peaks shown for countries such as the United

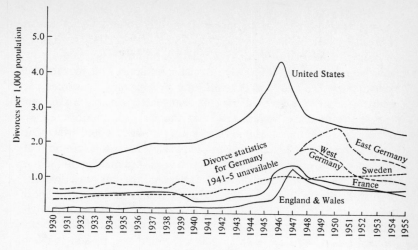

Figure 8.2

States, England, and France. It is likely that the same kinds of influences and conditions that resulted in the higher divorce rates at the end of World War I (discussed earlier in this chapter) were operative again at the end of World War II. Immediate postwar divorces were due to wartime adultery, the effects of long-term separation during the war (and the difficulties of readjustment to married life), and the apparently inherent weakness of marriages contracted, many in haste and the passion of crisis, just before or during the war.

Certainly, many of the divorces arose from adultery. In England, adultery had been the ground alleged in 56% of the divorces granted in 1940, but it rose to 71% of divorces in 1947, when divorces peaked. At the same time the percentage of divorces obtained by men increased (as it had done after World War I): Women had consistently filed 50–60% of divorces between 1923 and 1939, but their proportion fell to the 40–50% range between 1940 and 1945, then declined to 37 and 39% in 1946 and 1947, respectively. This was a pattern replicated in many countries and indicated the tendency of men to divorce their wives because of wartime adultery. As pointed out earlier, it was easier to detect and prove women's than men's adultery under wartime conditions.

The increased divorce rate after the war was also fueled by the instability of wartime marriages. In the United States in 1946 alone, one in every twenty-eight (almost 4%) of marriages celebrated in the preceding four years was dissolved by divorce. In England, too, marriages celebrated between 1940 and 1945 had a higher and more rapid dissolution rate: Four to five times as many marriages were dissolved within five years than was the case with those contracted just before or just after the war.

These characteristics of postwar divorce are not always as obvious, and in some countries there were peculiar influences on the divorce rate. In New Zealand, for example, the proportion of divorces for reason of adultery increased by 50% between 1942 and 1946, but most of the increase in divorces after the war was contributed by divorces based on the refusal of one spouse to obey a court order that he or she resume cohabitation with the other. This was a ground that frequently involved collusion and was used to avoid making public the embarrassing details of married life, such as adultery. Other divorces in New Zealand (and elsewhere) dissolved the marriages of local women to foreign soldiers who had been stationed there. Although many war brides and grooms of this kind were reunited after the war, many were not, and in 1947 special legislation was passed in New Zealand to facilitate divorce in such circumstances. Many women, it was pointed out in parliament, had married "sailors belonging to the [United States] Fleet, and when the Fleet sailed away that was the last the girls heard of their husbands."

In short, World War II had dramatic short-term effects on the divorce rates of the countries involved. In absolute figures there were more than 3 million divorces in the United States between 1942 and 1948, compared to about 1.75 million in the preceding seven-year period. At their peak, in 1946, the 628,760 American divorces dissolved, in a single year, 1 in every 55 existing marriages in the United States. If they had been distributed evenly across the land, there would have been scarcely a street without a divorce that year. In England the figures were less spectacular but still impressive and without precedent: In 1947 petitions were filed for the dissolution of 1 in every 150 marriages. The war, then, had a ravaging effect on marriage in Western society, for in addition to those unions terminated by divorce, hundreds of thousands of others were dissolved by the deaths of men and women on active service, and by the deaths of civilians as a result of military actions and the Holocaust.

The postwar divorce boom dissipated as rapidly as it had swelled, and the immediate aftermath was reminiscent of the period after World War I. Just as they had done in the 1920s, so in the 1950s divorce rates stabilized at rates higher than those that had prevailed before the war (Figure 8.3). In some countries this can be accounted for in terms of the natural trend of increase. In the United States, for example, the crude divorce rate ranged between 2.1 and 2.5 annually in the early 1950s, a rate not much higher than the rates of 1.8 and 1.9 of the late 1930s. In England, however, the divorce rate in the 1950s was four

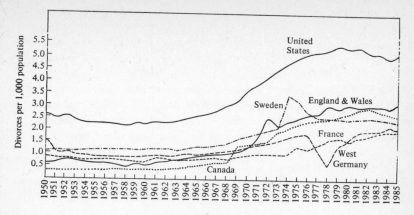

Figure 8.3

or five times that of the mid-1930s, but in this case we must take into account legal changes such as the 1937 divorce law and a legal assistance act of 1949 that facilitated access to divorce. When divorces in England stabilized in the 1950s, they did so in the range of 25,000–30,000 a year, a massive increase compared to the 3,000 or 4,000 divorces a year that had been usual in the mid-1930s.

Patterns of divorce in other countries were also influenced by legal change. In Germany and Austria the 1938 divorce law was purged of its racist and eugenic elements; divorce on the ground of infertility was removed, for example. In Austria, the maintenance of the denazified divorce law represented a major liberalization of pre-Anschluss divorce policy. Before 1938 Austria's Catholics – the great majority of the population – were denied divorce, and the extension of divorce to them in 1938 accounted for the rapid increase in divorces: There had been some 700 divorces a year in Austria before 1938, but there were more than 8,000 in 1939 and never fewer than 6,000 a year during the war. They peaked at 14,162 in 1948, and in the 1950s settled at between 8,000 and 9,000 a year. As in England, so in Austria, legal change must be considered the most important single influence on divorce rates during and after the war.

Apart from individual cases where the war marked a transition in the level of divorce, the most striking characteristic of the 1950s was the stability of divorce rates. In virtually all the countries of the Western world with which we are concerned, divorce rates remained relatively stationary for a ten-year period starting around 1950. This was a stark contrast to the preceding decades of volatility superimposed on a clear line of increase. Such a near universal stability of divorce rates (it can be extended beyond the examples shown in Figure 8.3) was unprecedented since rates had begun to rise appreciably in the 1870s and 1880s, and several explanations are possible. One must be the relative rarity of legal changes in this period, for with few exceptions, legislators took a respite from their continual tinkering with divorce legislation. Other reasons, related to marriage stability and breakdown (as distinct from divorce) are discussed in the next chapter. We might simply note at this point that they include a phase of conservatism in social attitudes, a higher estimation of marriage and family among those married in the postwar period, economic prosperity, and a possibility that the stabilization of divorce rates was a statistical effect resulting from the postwar divorce boom. Whatever the effects, though, the stabilization of divorce rates did not last, and in the 1960s they entered another period of growth.

The 1960s was a decade of change in many aspects of social life in the Western world, and many of the changes affected the family. Because of the postwar baby boom a higher proportion of the population than before was in the youthful age groups, and many of them seemed bent on challenging authority, conventions, and norms of all kinds. The civil rights movement in the United States, antiwar movements everywhere, pressures for educational reform, and later the women's movement, were signs of changing attitudes among the young. What is too often overlooked, however, is that the questioning of authority and tradition was shared by governments and churches, as well, even if it took quite different forms. Within the Roman Catholic church, the Vatican II reforms represented the victory of progressive forces. For their part governments in Western countries relaxed censorship, extended sex and birth control education, adopted legal and penal reforms, and promoted awareness of the extent and roots of poverty and inequality. We should not overstate these trends, which were taken much further in some countries than in others, but there is no doubt that the 1960s were quite different from the 1950s in these respects.

More liberal attitudes toward authority were reflected in family law reform, and in no part of it was this more true than in terms of divorce law. What began in the 1960s was a reevaluation of marriage in the light of more liberal attitudes, and its translation into legislation and social policy, such that between 1960 and the mid-1980s divorce policies in almost all countries of the West were completely or substantially revised. In some places legislators once again began to tinker with divorce law, fine-tuning it in response to judicial and public criticism, and to particular cases where existing law seemed to produce inequities or hardship. In Belgium, for example, legislation on divorce was passed in 1962, 1967, 1969, 1972, 1974 (two acts), and 1975. The amendments repealed various limitations, such as the need for parental consent to divorce, and a section retained from the Code Napoléon that forbade the divorce of a woman over the age of forty-five.

The most important divorce law reforms passed from the early 1960s, though, concerned the grounds for divorce. Earlier divorce law liberalization, during the nineteenth and most of the twentieth centuries, had tended to be little more than the steady accumulation of specific grounds, usually specific matrimonial offenses or circumstances that justified divorce. To the grounds recognized in the sixteenth century – adultery and desertion – were added others such as ill-treatment, drunkenness, insanity, and absence. Divorce laws accommodated more and more couples by adding more and more grounds, and the judiciary added to this process by broadening definitions of what constituted cruelty and discord.

This process of liberalizing divorce by the simple addition of grounds and expansion of definitions stopped in the 1960s. In part there was a recognition that legislation was becoming impossibly unwieldy and that the determination of grounds would fall increasingly to the discretion of the courts. It was also clear that many couples who wanted to divorce did not qualify under the specific grounds. The solution to the perceived problems was the adoption of no-fault divorce that allowed for the dissolution of marriages in circumstances where no fault, responsibility, or offense need be attributed to either spouse. The concept, which by the early 1980s underlay divorce laws in most jurisdictions, revolutionized divorce policies in Western society and marked a distinct break in the history of divorce.

No-fault divorce was not a new concept, however. It had been included in the 1792 French law, which provided for divorce for reason of incompatibility of temperament or by mutual consent. Neither kind of divorce required proof that either spouse was to blame for the breakdown of the marriage. The omnibus clauses adopted in numerous American state divorce laws, allowing divorce where the circumstances of the marriage frustrated the purposes of marriage, also fell, in some senses, into the no-fault category, although it was generally understood that one of the spouses was more responsible than the other for creating the circumstances. We might even think of such grounds as insanity, impotence, and unavoidable absence as no-fault grounds, although they, too, tended to highlight the actions or condition of one spouse as precipitating the divorce.

The no-fault divorce laws adopted from the 1960s, however, attributed blame to neither party. They simply recognized that a marriage had broken down in such a way that it was, depending on the wording of individual codes, "irremediable," "irreconcilable," or "irretrievable." The laws did not require information on the reasons for the breakdown of the marriage, but simply evidence of it. The evidence required by most of these laws was that the couple had lived apart for a minimum specified period of time. By leading independent lives for two, three, or five years (depending on the law), the spouses were deemed to have shown that their marriage had no practical meaning. That being so, the divorce was no more than the translation of a social fact into legal status.

We should not assume, however, that all no-fault divorce laws of this kind are necessarily permissive, for although they remove the restrictions imposed by specific grounds, they can impose long periods of de facto separation as qualifying periods for divorce. One of the most restrictive in this respect was the 1974 Belgian law that required spouses to have lived apart for ten years to demonstrate that their marriages had broken down. The English law of 1969 required five years de facto separation when a divorce petition was contested but only two years when both spouses agreed to have the marriage dissolved. Many laws set the minimum period at two years, whereas others, such as the 1986 Canadian law, require only one year's separation. It is to be expected that future divorce liberalization in many places will take the form of the progressive diminution of the period of de facto separation needed to demonstrate the irremediable breakdown of marriage.

One important effect of the introduction of no-fault divorce was to shift the responsibility for defining marriage breakdown. Historically the churches and the state established the criteria for acceptable behavior in marriage by limiting the grounds on which a separation or divorce might be obtained. Thus, in some codes, adultery needed not be tolerated, but violence had to be. As the specific grounds accumulated, the limits of tolerance imposed by the state on married men and women fell, but the adoption of no-fault divorce transferred to the spouses themselves the definition of acceptable marital behavior and conditions. Under no-fault laws, a couple could separate for any reason whatsoever: violence, adultery, financial irresponsibility, sexual incompatibility, jealousy, a forgotten anniversary, or any other reason. As long as they lived apart for the required period, either spouse could then have the marriage dissolved. To this extent no-fault divorce overthrew the centuries-old principle that divorce should be closely regulated.

The adoption of no-fault divorce by legislators throughout Western society was not only the result of a long debate about the character and functions of marriage, but was also a response to specific practical issues in the 1960s. The growing influence of a social scientific approach to understanding social behavior had shifted attention from individual responsibility to broader socioeconomic conditions. Part of this trend was the replacement of the moralistic and retributive principles that had underlain dominant theological and secular conceptions of marriage and divorce by views that stressed the social, economic, and environmental conditions. Age at marriage, family background, socioeconomic status, religious and other factors were linked to the incidence of divorce. Behavior such as adultery, cruelty, and desertion were increasingly seen not as causes of marriage breakdown but as symptoms. To this extent the notion of fault became increasingly inappropriate to an explanation of the breakdown of individual marriages. Even some quite traditional fault-based divorce laws had recognized the difficulty of attributing all responsibility to one spouse and none to the other. Adultery by one spouse might be mitigated if the other spouse had venereal disease or refused sexual intercourse. Nonetheless the principle of primary fault was retained in such laws, and the novelty of no-fault legislation was to have abandoned the principle entirely.

One of the most startling shifts in attitude took place within the Church of England, which had historically opposed the dissolubility of marriage. In 1966, however, a church commission recommended that divorce should be allowed when a marriage had broken down. This was a breakthrough, and this report, together with that of a law commission that reported the same year, laid the basis for English no-fault divorce legislation that was passed in 1969. In turn the English divorce law reform influenced legislators elsewhere. It is not that legislators blindly emulated others, but there was everywhere a keen awareness of the state of international divorce legislation.

The reform of divorce laws not only reflected a shift of attitudes, but also responded to changes in marriage and divorce behavior in the 1960s. After the stabilization of divorce rates in the 1950s, divorces began to rise steadily throughout Western society. In figures rounded to the nearest thousand, divorces in England and Wales rose from 25,000 in 1960 to 34,000 in 1964 and then to 45,000 in 1968, the year before no-fault divorce was introduced. In short, the number of divorces almost doubled in eight years, as did the divorce rate, moving from 0.52 divorces per thousand population in 1960 to 0.92 in 1968. As Figure 8.1 shows, it was not only England and Wales, but also the United States and other countries that broke out of the divorce doldrums around 1960.

It is significant that these initial increases in divorce were not produced by changes in legislation. Although legal reform might have been responsible for an acceleration in the divorce rates later, an underlying trend of increase was in place when the laws were reformed. This is not to say that legislators were complacent about rising divorce rates and wished to encourage them to rise further. The governor of California described divorce at this time as a "festering problem," and established a committee to investigate it so as to suggest ways of reducing it. The result was a compromise law, passed in 1969, between no-fault principles and the maintenance of judicial control and discretion. Divorce would be granted in cases of incurable insanity and where there were "irreconcilable differences . . . which have caused the breakdown of marriage." Evidence of the difference was to be assessed by the courts, which could delay proceedings for thirty days if there seemed to be hope of reconciliation.

It is indicative of the pervasiveness of divorce reform in the 1960s that it should also have taken place on the other side of the United States from California, in New York State. Unlike California, however, New York had not had a liberal divorce law before this phase of reform. The sole ground for divorce remained that recognized in 1787 – adultery – and the only significant change in almost two centuries had been an 1879 act allowing the adulterous spouse to remarry. The New York law had fallen into disrepute, however. Collusion and perjury were perceived as widespread, the typical case involving a prearranged "discovery" of the husband in an act of adultery. The judiciary demanded less and less rigorous proof of adultery, until evidence of a spouse in bed with an accomplice, even if both were fully clothed, was deemed sufficient. Pressure to reform the New York law came to a head in the early 1960s when the state's governor, Nelson Rockefeller, obtained a divorce in Nevada (and showed that the wealthy could evade the law), and when the state court of appeal ordered that divorces obtained in Mexico should be recognized in the state.

When New York's divorce law was reformed in 1967, it too combined fault and no-fault principles. Adultery was maintained as a ground, as were other matrimonial offenses such as "deviate sexual intercourse," but divorce was also permitted when a couple had lived apart for two years (this period was reduced to one year in 1972), following a separation decree. Fault was retained in the grounds for separation, however, and other obstacles (costs and a compulsory conciliation conference) were introduced in order to prevent hasty divorces. Despite these restrictions, the number of divorces in New York rose quickly, trebling from 7,136 in 1967 to 21,184 in 1969.

California and New York were only examples of the way divorce law was reformed in the 1960s and 1970s. Most U.S. states had introduced no-fault provisions by the late 1970s, and by the mid-1980s the principle of no-fault lay at the center of divorce law in almost every state. Thirty-six states specified irretrievable breakdown of marriage as justifying divorce, another six allowed divorce when a couple had lived apart for a specified period, and still others recognized mutual consent, incompatibility, or judicial separation. Many states mixed fault and no-fault divorces, but only one recognized fault divorce alone: South Dakota, the state excoriated in the nineteenth century for its lax divorce policies, clung to the grounds of adultery, alcoholism, desertion, conviction of a felony, and extreme cruelty. Variations among the American states' divorce laws persisted, but the liberalization of laws in almost all reduced the incidence of migratory divorces in the 1970s. Apart from the convenience of combining a vacation, gambling, and sun-tanning with a divorce, there were fewer and fewer reasons to travel out of state to places like Nevada to terminate one's marriage.

The trend toward legislative uniformity was perhaps more marked in Europe than in the United States. Although some European countries retained fault grounds while introducing no-fault provisions, the clear trend was toward the elimination of fault-based divorce. In 1960, fault was recognized in all thirteen European countries with established divorce laws, no-fault (marriage breakdown) in seven of them, and divorce by mutual consent in six. By 1981 fault grounds had been retained in eight, and no-fault divorce extended to twelve, as had mutual consent divorce. (Switzerland alone retained only fault-based divorce.) This trend, of extending no-fault provisions, was echoed in all major divorce laws outside Europe, such as those in Australia (1975), New Zealand (1980), and Canada (1986).

One country, Sweden, broke with the European tendency toward uniformity by adopting a divorce law so permissive that even the other Nordic countries were reluctant to emulate it. In 1973 Swedish law recognized the right to divorce at the request of either or both spouses, without any qualifying period of separation. Only when the couple had children under the age of sixteen would a divorce not be granted immediately, and even then the delay was only six months. The Swedish case notwithstanding, a trend in divorce legislation was evident from the early 1960s to the early 1980s. This period constituted a third generation of divorce legislation in Western society, following the first generation of the Protestant Reformation, and the second of the nineteenth century. Unlike the first two phases, however, the third abandoned moralistic and fault-based precepts, and to this extent it was an integral part of the changing attitudes toward the individual's relationship to society that were current in the Western world from the 1960s.

It was a sign of the strength of the divorce reform movement after 1960 that it was taken up in parts of Europe where the Roman Catholic church had historically been especially influential in shaping family law: Italy, Portugal, Spain, and the Republic of Ireland. Of these four countries, only Portugal had provision for divorce before 1970, and even there divorce was forbidden to those who married according to

Roman Catholic rites. By 1981, however, divorce was generally available in Italy, Portugal, and Spain, leaving Ireland the distinction of being the only European state without divorce legislation.

The first of these three south European countries to change was Italy, where the legalization of divorce had been successfully resisted throughout the post-Napoleonic nineteenth century and most of the twentieth. Attempts to pass very restrictive divorce laws (known as *piccolo divorzio*, or little divorce) in the 1950s had failed, and public opinion was anything but favorable to divorce; a 1955 survey showed that 34% of Italians supported the legalization of divorce but that 56% opposed it, and four years later the proportion opposed had increased to 61%. Public opposition to divorce was represented in the Italian parliament by the dominant conservative Christian Democratic party, but in 1962 the party was forced to form a coalition with the Socialist party. The Socialist party had long advocated the legalization of divorce, and although a Socialist-supported bill failed in 1965, another was introduced after the 1968 elections. This bill set off a major debate, inside and outside parliament, in which divorce was supported by the Socialists, Communists, and liberals, and opposed by the Christian Democrats and other parties of the right. Outside parliament, the battle for divorce was led by the Italian Divorce League, whereas the Catholic church marshaled forces against divorce. Despite opinion polls showing a clear majority against divorce, the Justice Committee of the Chamber of Deputies passed the bill by a large majority, as did, in turn, the chamber itself and the senate (which amended the bill in a more restrictive direction). On December 1, 1970, the president of the republic signed the bill into law, and it went into effect a week later.

Italy's first divorce law reflected the compromises that had been necessary to incorporate legal and social traditions, political realities, and contemporary trends in European matrimonial law. There were several specific grounds for divorce, including a prison sentence of more than fifteen years, certain crimes of violence, failure to support the family, and failure to consummate the marriage. The second category of divorce was conversion of a judicial or formalized separation. Separations could be obtained only on specific grounds such as adultery (the husband's adultery had to be shown to have been a "serious injury to the wife"), desertion, cruelty, long-term imprisonment, or the husband's failure to establish a home appropriate to his means. Under the 1970 divorce law, a separation on the basis of any of these grounds could be converted to divorce after a fixed waiting period: after five years if both spouses agreed, after six years if it was contested but if the divorce petitioner was the spouse who had sought the separation, and after seven years if it was contested and if the divorce petitioner was the spouse whose action had been the ground for the separation. Essentially, then, fault lay at the heart of the 1970 divorce law. If Italy did not participate fully in the European trend toward no-fault divorce in 1970, it was at least an achievement to have legalized divorce at all.

But the achievement was thrown into question almost immediately. The Christian Democrats and their antidivorce allies, convinced that public opinion was opposed to divorce, were able to force the Socialists and their allies to put the divorce law to a national referendum. However, there was a delay of three years between the coming into force of the divorce law at the end of 1970 and the referendum, which was held in May 1974. In the intervening period divorces took place, but they were far fewer than the antidivorce forces had predicted. There were 17,134 divorces in 1971, 32,627 in 1972, but only 18,172 in 1973. These were remarkably low numbers, and they seemed to reduce public fears about the effect of divorce on Italian society. In the end only 41% of those who voted in the referendum supported the repeal of the law.

This show of support for the divorce law encouraged Italy's legislators to go even further. The year after the referendum the no-fault principle was entrenched in the law when the specific grounds for separation were replaced by a general clause allowing a separation in cases where married life appeared to be intolerable or where it would have harmful effects on children. Even so, no-fault divorce remained a two-stage process and divorce Italian-style was one of the most restrictive in Europe. This did not prevent the legalization of divorce in Italy giving impetus to divorce reform in Portugal and Spain, two countries with overwhelmingly Catholic populations. In both countries (as in Italy), a critical factor was political: the overthrow of Salazar's regime in Portugal and the death of Franco in Spain.

As we have seen, divorce had been legalized in Portugal in 1910, but restricted to non-Catholics under the concordat of 1940. In 1966 even these divorces were restricted, when mutual consent divorce was abolished, and only divorces based on fault retained. Portugal thus ran counter to the European legal trend in the 1960s. The overthrow of Salazar's government in 1974 brought a new direction to Portugal's family policy, however. Within a year of the revolution the critical article of the concordat was modified, and by 1977 the country's divorce law had been completely overhauled. The new law recognized three kinds of divorce: mutual consent, a variety of fault and no-fault grounds (the latter including de facto separation for six years), and conversion of a judicial separation after a delay of two years. This law gave Portugal a more liberal divorce policy than Italy, and it was reflected in the divorce rate: The Italian rate fell between 0.21 and 0.26 per thousand population from 1976 to 1985, while in Portugal the rate ranged from 0.50 to 0.88.

Spain followed suit shortly after, in 1981. Divorce, easily available under the republic in the early 1930s, had been abolished by General Franco's regime, but with Franco's death in 1975 and the liberalization of social and political policies there was growing pressure for the legalization of divorce. The divorce debate recalled the vicious conflicts of the 1930s. Prodivorce meetings were bombed, and in early 1981 the daughter of Pablo Picasso cited the lack of a divorce law as one reason she would not allow the return to Spain of her father's famous painting *Guernica*, which evoked fascist violence. By the end of 1981, however, divorce had been legalized, but in a way that incorporated the no-fault principle less ambiguously than in Portugal or Italy. The Spanish law allowed divorce a year after a separation based on mutual consent, two years after a separation on other grounds (including adultery, desertion, drug addiction, and violence), after five years de facto separation, or when one spouse was convicted of attempting to murder the other or one or more of the other's relatives.

With the legalization of divorce in Spain, only the Republic of Ireland remained divorceless among the major European states. (There is no divorce in the Vatican State, Andorra, and San Marino.) Divorce was prohibited by the Irish constitution of 1937, which stated that "no law shall be enacted providing for the grant of a dissolution of marriage," and the constitution also forbade the recognition in Ireland of any foreign divorce decree. In the absence of divorce, separations were permitted, but they were so expensive and procedurally demanding that they averaged only 33 a year between 1968 and 1977. Thousands of couples sought to circumvent the ban on divorce by having their marriages annulled by the Catholic church (there was a backlog of 1,300 applications by 1977), while thousands of deserted wives applied for maintenance and welfare benefits.

From the 1960s Ireland's family laws and policies came under increasing criticism from women's rights and divorce reform groups, but no government was prepared to take up such a sensitive issue in a country where the Catholic church was so influential. In 1979 Pope John Paul II, visiting Ireland, had added his voice to the resistance to divorce by praising Ireland's devotion to the "sanctity and indissolubility of the marriage bond." In 1986, however, the prime minister, Gareth FitzGerald, called a referendum on a proposal to amend the constitution to permit a divorce law to be enacted. The debate was reminiscent of the Italian referendum a dozen years earlier, with opponents of divorce predicting widespread marriage breakdown, social disintegration, and the breakup of farms, abandoned families, and ruined women. Their point was made graphically by one woman who led the antidivorce campaign: "A woman voting for divorce is like a turkey voting for Christmas." Against this campaign, in which the

Catholic church played a prominent role, lined up a heterogeneous coalition of liberal politicians, women's groups, and civil liberties organizations. But if the 1986 referendum campaign echoed 1974 in Italy, it did so only until the votes were counted: The proposal (which was only to allow the introduction of a divorce bill) was defeated by the healthy margin of 66 to 34%.

The passage of a divorce law in Ireland would have completed the extension of divorce law throughout Europe and would have been an appropriate way to end a narrative history of divorce in the Western world. As it is, Ireland must stand as a symbol of the continuity of the opposition of the Roman Catholic church to divorce, and a reminder of the changes that have taken place in marriage law in the rest of Western society during the past five centuries.

Suggestions for further reading

Alberdi, Ines, *Historia y sociologia del divorcio en España* (Madrid, 1979).

Blake, Nelson, *The Road to Reno: A History of Divorce in the United States* (New York, 1962).

Camp, Wesley D., *Marriage and the Family in France since the Revolution* (New York, 1961).

Chester, Robert (ed.), *Divorce in Europe* (Leiden, 1977).

Commaille, Jacques, et al., *Le divorce en Europe occidentale. La loi et le nombre* (Paris, 1983).

Degler, Carl, *At Odds: Women and the Family in America* (New York, 1980).

Fitzpatrick, David, "Divorce and Separation in Modern Irish History," *Past and Present* 114 (1987), 172–96.

Geiger, H. Kent, *The Family in Soviet Russia* (Cambridge, Mass., 1968).

Halem, Lynne Carol, *Divorce Reform: Changing Legal and Social Perspectives* (New York, 1980.)

Jacob, Herbert, *Silent Revolution: The Transformation of Divorce Law in the United States* (Chicago, 1988).

Jacobson, Paul H., and Pauline F. Jacobson, *American Marriage and Divorce* (New York, 1959).

McGregor, O. M., *Divorce in England* (London, 1957).

Phillips, Roderick, *Divorce in New Zealand: A Social History* (Auckland, 1981).

Rowntree, Griselda, and Norman H. Carrier, "The Resort to Divorce in England and Wales, 1858–1957," *Population Studies* 11 (1957), 188–233.

9

Explaining the rise of divorce, 1870s–1990s

The steady rise of divorce rates throughout Western society from the end of the nineteenth century, and their acceleration since the 1960s, have provoked much serious research, analysis, and comment, as well as a lot of silly and superficial speculation. Various hypotheses and explanations of the divorce phenomenon have been put forward, and attempts have been made to define the correlates and causes of changes in the extent of divorce. In the late nineteenth century the spectacular increase in divorce rates in the United States was widely attributed to deficiencies in the morality and "character" of Americans, and such explanations were extended to other nationalities when their divorce rates also rose. Opponents of divorce in France, for example, insisted that the cool, rational temperament of Belgians had kept divorce in check there, but they feared the consequences of giving the temperamental and passionate French access to it.

As scientific analyses of divorce – or analyses couched in the language of the social sciences – emerged, divorce was discussed and explained in social and social psychological terms. Divorce, like suicide and criminality, was seen as a sign of social pathology, and there was increasing interest in the effects on marriage and the family of all manner of social and economic change: industrialization, urbanization, the decline of religious observance, changes in morality, and the liberalization of marriage and divorce laws. The association of women and divorce (most divorces were sought by women) was given particular attention, and the divorce rate was often explained in terms of women's emancipation generally and of the expansion of women's employment in particular.

More recently, research on the causes of divorce has swelled in tandem with divorce itself. Since the 1960s thousands of popular and scholarly books, articles in mass circulation magazines and academic journals, radio and television documentaries, together with government, university, and private research reports have focused on divorce, its causes, and its consequences. Findings have referred to global and continental trends, to samples of national and state populations, and

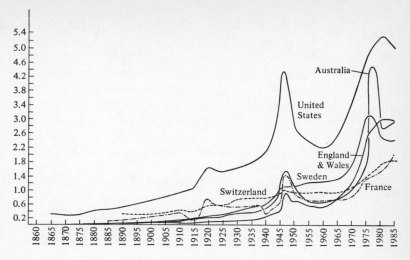

Figure 9.1

to interviews of relatively small groups of divorced women and men. A multiplicity of factors, correlates, and causes has been summoned up to explain divorce and its characteristics. Some factors, such as the employment of women and changes in divorce law, are still popular. Others that are given emphasis include the ages of spouses at marriage, changing expectations of marriage, the life experience of divorced couples, changed attitudes toward divorce, and the feedback effects of an increasing divorce rate.

Ironically, though, despite the wealth of plausible explanations that has been offered, we seem almost as poor in our understanding of divorce as earlier generations were. The earlier, monocausal (and often implicitly moral) explanations have given way to far more complex analyses in which the range of factors invoked and their relationships have become quite unmanageable. There is, of course, no virtue in ignoring the complexities, but it is useful to try to cut through much of the confusion generated by the multiplicity of specific studies so as to understand the broad issues that have influenced divorce rates in modern Western society.

This chapter focuses on divorce during the past hundred or so years, a period during which there was a generally similar pattern in most countries: Divorce rates rose steadily to the 1960s, with marked fluctuations following each of the world wars, accelerated from the 1960s to the 1980s, and then either stabilized or continued to rise. Actual divorce rates varied enormously from country to country, as Figure 9.1 shows, and national divorce rates conceal significant regional, state, and provincial variations. There have been, moreover, differences in the timing of changes in the divorce rates that were associated with divorce law reform. Nonetheless, the common shape of changes in divorce rates throughout the Western world, whether in North America, Europe, or Australasia, makes it a compelling and fascinating subject for investigation. To some extent the rise of divorce, like earlier rises of illegitimacy and declines in mortality, seems to have been a phenomenon that has overridden variations in economies, social structures, cultural climate, and demography, even if these variables have had their impact on the distinctly national and regional differences in the timing and nuances of change.

For the purpose of this discussion, the recent history of divorce will be divided into three periods according to the phases of growth discernible in Figure 9.1. The first was a phase of takeoff during the late nineteenth century and up to World War I. Divorce rates were not high by recent standards, but sustained growth had begun, and the rates were becoming worth measuring. The second phase, from the end of World War I to about 1960, was one of overall increase marked by fluctuations associated with the world wars. The third and most recent phase, starting in the 1960s, was a period of rapid increase in divorce rates.

Phase 1: Up to World War I

Although there is no direct evidence of changes in the extent of marriage breakdown over time, we must conclude that it increased steadily from the end of the eighteenth century and that the rate of increase accelerated from the second half of the nineteenth. Indirect and oblique evidence lies in the decline of the constraints that had locked husbands and wives into marriage, and in rising expectations of marriage: The two go hand in hand, as explained in Chapter 5, and as further analyzed here. Even though there is no explicit documentary evidence of the considerable increase in marriage breakdown, skeptics should bear in mind that in many Western countries the likelihood of recent marriages ending in divorce (i.e., not counting other forms of separation) lies between 30% and 50%. No historian has ventured to suggest that marriage breakdown before the twentieth century ever approached such levels. The increase in marriage breakdown during the past two hundred years must be accepted, even if its precise magnitude, causes, and timing are subject to debate.

One of the most important factors in this increase has been the decline of the economic constraints that in earlier times bound husband and wife together until one of them died. The traditional family or conjugal economy was the foremost expression of this relationship of mutual dependence and, as we saw in Chapter 5, it declined in the face of broad economic changes. From the late nineteenth century, the process continued until the traditional form of the family economy, in which the spouses had tightly knit and complementary work roles, all but disappeared. A new form did emerge with the evolution of housewifery as a full-time occupation for most married women during the second half of the nineteenth century. A decreasing proportion of married women worked in paid employment outside (and inside) the home, and they devoted themselves to what became known as the "woman's sphere": care of the household, the preparation of meals, and responsibility for caring for children. In providing these services, even though they were unpaid and deprived of social status, women performed tasks that complemented their husbands' work outside the home. Even in the working class, married men were relieved of the need to spend the time and energy that domestic matters demanded, could leave for work reasonably refreshed, and could return home to the haven that the family offered from the demands of work. The complementarity of wives' and husbands' tasks created the reciprocal obligations enshrined in many nineteenth-century laws: the duty of the husband to maintain and provide for his family and the duty of the wife to perform her domestic tasks. So important were these respective gender-specific obligations considered that, as we have seen, failure to perform them was a ground for separation or divorce in many places.

Yet this new form of the family economy, with the wife an unpaid houseworker and the husband gainfully employed away from home, was not simply a variant of the traditional family economy. With his work independent of the home, the husband had more freedom of initiative. And although the housewife was in many ways bound to her marriage by dependence on her husband's income, the social and economic context had, by the later nineteenth century, changed so as to increase the potential for her independence, too. The labor market had expanded and changed so that it was increasingly possible, even if far from easy, for women to obtain work in the service and manufacturing sectors. At the end of the nineteenth century women quickly dominated growth areas of employment such as teaching, nursing, clerical work, retail sales, and especially domestic service. It is undoubtedly right, as Carl Degler has suggested, that the widening of employment opportunities for women around the turn of the century was "a necessary but not sufficient condition to explain the increase in divorces." It is not that the availability of work caused marriages to break down, but for the first time in the history of Western society women were able, in large numbers, to survive economically outside marriage, and they were thereby enabled, in large numbers, to leave their husbands or file for separations or divorces.

Certainly, most divorce petitions in many jurisdictions were filed by women. In the United States more than two-thirds of all divorces between the 1880s and World War I were granted to women, and within this period the proportion of women's divorces generally increased. In France, women obtained between 55 and 65% of divorces each year between 1885 and 1914, while in New South Wales (Australia), more than two-thirds of divorces in the 1890s were granted to women. Where women's petitions were a minority, it was usually because divorce laws discriminated against women. In England, for example, women had to prove their husbands guilty of aggravated adultery; that even with these restrictions they sought an impressive 40–45% of divorces from the 1860s onward is evidence of the demand for divorce by women.

When formal discrimination against women was removed from divorce laws, petitions by women quickly rose to form a majority. After the equalization of English divorce law in 1923, women's petitions rose from the previous 40–45% to 50–60%. Another example was New Zealand, where discrimination against women had been integral to divorce until 1898. There the proportion of divorces sought by women increased steadily during the nineteenth century (from 19% in 1868–78, to 30% in 1879–88, and to 39% in 1889–98), but when the divorce law was reformed the effect was immediate: Women sought 52% of the divorces granted in 1899, and 63% of those the following year, and thereafter the majority of divorces in most years were obtained by women.

Statistics like these indicate the ability of these women at least to survive outside marriage. It is safe to assume that most women would stay married if the alternative were an impoverished existence. Even many of the divorces obtained by men might be read as indicative of improvements in women's conditions and changes in their attitudes. Carl Degler notes that more than 80% of the grounds cited by husbands in American divorces in the 1870s indicated that their wives refused "to live up to the ideal of a submissive subordinate." Desertion and adultery were the main grounds, behavior that certainly did not fit the image of the Victorian wife. The same conclusion might be drawn from other countries, where women were divorced for similar offenses as well as for cruelty, drunkenness, and failure to perform domestic duties. Such women need not have been particularly assertive, however, and the preponderance of women's divorce petitions is a far better sign than women's matrimonial offenses of the increasing autonomy of women.

There is, however, a paradox in citing expanding employment opportunities as a factor in women's turning in increasing numbers to divorce, for as the divorce rates climbed during the nineteenth century, the proportion of married women in the paid labor force fell. In the United States, for example, less than 4% of white married women worked outside the home by 1900, and even though the rate rose in the early twentieth century, it was only about 7% by 1920 and 12% by 1940. Elsewhere the situation was similar. The apparent contradiction between such small labor participation rates and rising women's divorce rates can be resolved in various ways. It could simply have been that divorces were drawn from this expanding population of "working wives," no matter how small its numbers. It could have been that women entered the labor force after divorcing, and were thus not counted as married women in work outside the home.

Local studies, such as Robert Griswold's of divorce in nineteenth-century California, suggest that divorcing women had a much higher employment rate than the national average, although even then only a minority of them are known with certainty to have been employed. The underregistration of women's occupations, so familiar to historians of women's work, adds to the difficulty of determining the precise relationship of employment opportunities and divorce. Elaine Tyler May's study of divorces in Los Angeles and New Jersey is less ambiguous, however. In the 1880s some 33% of wives in divorce cases were employed, compared to only 23% of all women, married or single, in the city. May concludes – and this is surely the least that can be said – that "financial independence might have made it easier for a woman to go through with a divorce."

Work was arguably the most important single resource required by women who wanted to divorce, but there were other dimensions to economic independence, and they too were improved. The last three or four decades of the nineteenth century saw legislation enacted in many countries to give married women the right to own and control their own property and income, rather than have them owned or administered by their husbands. Before the passage of these married women's property acts, married women in many countries did not have the right to keep and spend their own wages, and as for property, it had simply to be abandoned if a woman left her husband. Provisions giving women rights to property and income were integral to divorce laws in some cases, but whatever their form, they made divorce a more viable alternative to marriage for many women.

England and France are merely examples of this kind of legal innovation. In England, women first received guarantees of property rights under the 1857 divorce law, but thereafter (by laws of 1870, 1874, and 1882) these rights were extended more generally to married women who did not divorce. In France the situation was rather different because marriage contracts commonly protected the property women brought to marriage, but even then a wife's right to manage her property was limited, and there was no guarantee that she could control her income. However, a series of laws from 1881 to 1907 gradually extended the financial autonomy of married women: In 1881 they were permitted to have their own savings accounts in banks, in 1893 they were granted absolute control of their property, and in 1907 they were given complete control of their wages and other income. In the United States between 1869 and 1887, thirty-three states and the District of Columbia gave married women control over their property and earnings. In short, the trend toward giving women economic independence in law (which we must always distinguish from independence in reality) was general throughout Western society and was an integral part of the improvement in women's legal status in the late nineteenth century.

Greater potential for economic independence and improvements in their legal status must have contributed to creating the material conditions in which an increasing number of women could divorce or separate, but they did not cause divorce. An important variable in this respect seems to have been a rise in expectations of marriage. As suggested in Chapter 5, rising expectations of marriage imply a lower tolerance of unsatisfactory behavior or conditions in marriage and result from the interaction of social attitudes, individual perceptions, and the material conditions of marriage. If this is so, we should expect the improved potential for women's independence in the late nineteenth century to have led women to be less tolerant of unsatisfactory or oppressive conditions and to be more prepared to consider separation or divorce as an alternative to marriage.

There is ample evidence of rising expectations of marriage from the late nineteenth century. Some writers have pointed to the increase in divorces itself as evidence that husbands and wives were increasingly demanding of marriage, but this produces a circular line of reasoning. Divorce law reforms, however, are very good indicators of rising expectations, because the grounds recognized as justifying divorce and separation indicate the kinds of behavior that husbands and wives are not expected to tolerate. When the grounds are extended, the range of conditions that is considered tolerable contracts, and correspondingly higher expectations of marriage are officially approved. To this extent the liberalization of divorce laws from the later nineteenth century and the legalization of divorce where it had not been available, together with the pressure to liberalize them even further, are indicative of rising expectations of marriage. Although wives and husbands in many places in the eighteenth century and earlier might have had to tolerate (in the eyes of the law) everything but adultery and desertion, by the end of the nineteenth century laws widely declared intolerable such behavior as drunkenness, physical and mental cruelty, insanity, the husband's failure to provide for his family, and the wife's failure to carry out her domestic duties.

Rising expectations of marriage were expressed not only by the accretion of such grounds for divorce, but also by the reinterpretation of specific grounds to include an ever-widening range of circumstances. The notion of matrimonial cruelty was extended first by the courts, and only much later by statute law, beyond simple physical violence to include mental and emotional cruelty as well. Judges in various parts of the United States accepted as grounds for divorce "grievous mental suffering" (an 1883 Kentucky decision), a husband's neglect and insensitivity to his wife during her eight pregnancies (Kentucky, 1894), and a wife's telling obscene stories in the presence of friends and neighbors (North Dakota, 1907). A similar process took place elsewhere. In France, for instance, article 231 of the 1884 divorce law, allowing divorce for ill-treatment or cruelty, was extended by the courts to include other than physical assault. Robert Griswold's comment on the American judiciary's expansion of the definition of cruelty probably holds true generally:

The increasingly affectionate, expressive and psychologically demanding nature of marital relations in the nineteenth century virtually guaranteed that definitions of unacceptable matrimonial behavior would expand. Mid-to-late-nineteenth-century couples would not tolerate behavior that earlier generations had endured, for when a spouse expected love and mutual respect and instead received insults and gratuitous slights, divorce became a logical option.

It might be argued that the views of a handful of males (the judges) were not representative of social attitudes generally. But we must recognize that the restrictive definitions of cruelty were rolled back not at the whim or initiative of the judiciary, but under pressure from the husbands and wives who sued for divorce and insisted that they should not have to put up with conditions they considered intolerable. To this extent, the judges (and later the legislators) responded to changing attitudes among the clients of the divorce courts. They probably constituted the leading edge of changing attitudes toward marriage, and insofar as they often failed at first to convince the cautious and conservative judges to agree to new definitions of cruelty and of what was tolerable in marriage, the court decisions probably represented a middle range of attitudes. If there are such things as general social attitudes toward marriage, perhaps these decisions were the expression of them.

Expectations of marriage rose not only in emotional terms, but also in material terms in this period. As a mass market for consumer goods developed, expectations of the material standards of life increased. Married men came under greater pressure to provide not only the necessities of life but also the outward signs of financial and social success, signs that varied from class to class. By 1920, financial disputes were significant in many American divorces: in 33% of divorces in New Jersey and 28% of those in Los Angeles. And just as the definition of cruelty was expanded so was the definition of "provide" and "support" to include the material elements of a lifestyle that was considered appropriate. In one divorce case the wife condemned her husband for working for $12 a week when he had had the chance of getting a job at $21 a week, which would have given his family a higher standard of living.

Rising expectations of marriage, the decline of the traditional family economy, and employment and other economic opportunities for women contributed to increasing marriage breakdown and divorce in the three or four decades before World War I. They impinged upon women more than men, for they gave women unprecedented opportunities outside marriage and allowed their expectations of marriage to rise to a similar level as men's. For centuries men had had expectations of marriage and their wives that were higher than their wives' expectations of marriage and their husbands. The tendency of men to beat their wives and to desert their families were eloquent statements of dissatisfaction. Violence and desertion, as much as we might deplore them, were responses to unfulfilled expectations. Women, locked much more firmly into marriage, had kept relatively low expectations and are found far less frequently than men initiating violence and desertion. With the change in economic and other conditions that permitted greater autonomy, women's expectations rose, and this was manifested in their dominating the divorce lists.

Men, it seems, persisted in their traditional behavior by deserting rather than divorcing when their marriages became intolerable. This was evidence that men continued to have greater autonomy and that they acted as freer agents than their wives, abandoning their homes and families with far less compunction than their wives would do. This highlights an important association between women and divorce. In traditional society, and even in the twentieth century, men tended to react to marriage breakdown by informal means, by violence and desertion. Women, possessed of less social and domestic power, turned to an external agency, the law, for assistance. It is not surprising, in this light, to find women as the majority of petitioners for divorce, separation, and other matrimonial remedies throughout Western society.

To some extent this conclusion blurs the important distinction between marriage breakdown and divorce. Factors like rising expectations might explain an increasing incidence of marriage breakdown, but not of divorce, for it was possible for husbands and wives to separate informally or to desert. Divorce, however, offered advantages that informal measures lacked. It allowed for a distribution of property, alimony, arrangements for the custody of children, and the possibility of remarriage. Divorce thus offered solutions to the more pressing problems that faced men and women (but especially women) when they contemplated leaving their marriages: How would they survive independently, what resources would they have, and what would happen to their children?

Maintenance or alimony were particularly important for women, whether or not they were in paid employment. So it was that the financial provisions of the 1857 English divorce law made divorce that much more feasible, because they allowed for a man to be compelled to pay maintenance for his ex-wife. The amount was determined by his ability to pay, by her resources, and by the behavior of the parties during marriage. At first there was reluctance to "reward" an adulterous woman with maintenance, but by the early twentieth century it was recognized that no woman, whatever her behavior, should be left destitute. As for property, the English law specified that after separation or divorce a woman was to have the same property rights as a single woman: She could own and dispose of property freely, bequeath it, and sue and enter into contracts.

Similar provisions were integral to divorce legislation elsewhere. Divorce laws in the British colonies followed the English model. Those in the United States varied, but generally allowed for the discretionary award of alimony and permitted divorced women to own and control property and income. Curiously, though, alimony was rarely sought. It was requested in only 13% of American divorces between 1887 and 1906 and granted in 70% of those cases, so that awards were made in about 10% of all divorces. By 1916 the proportion of divorces with alimony awards was still only 15%. Even when we take into account divorces based on desertion and other circumstances where a husband could not be ordered to pay alimony, these rates are low, and they buttress the impression that women who sought divorces had their own incomes or other resources. Robert Griswold's study of California divorces found that three-quarters of the women involved earned enough to support themselves partly or completely.

In addition to alimony, the nineteenth-century divorce laws made provision for the custody of children, and in this respect there were developments that would have made divorce increasingly acceptable to women in particular. In most Western codes until the nineteenth century the father was deemed to have primary rights over his children. English common law, for example, regarded children as virtually the property of their father. During the nineteenth century there were reforms such as the 1839 Infant Custody Act, which allowed the courts to give mothers custody of children up to the age of seven, but it was not until the 1857 divorce act that women were given anything like equal consideration for custody of their children. In 1873 women's rights to custody were extended even further, and later, in the twentieth century, it became a principle that custody of children in cases of divorce should be vested in the mother unless there were compelling reasons otherwise. Beginning in the second half of the nineteenth century, then, the principles of child custody law in England were transformed.

In America, too, the progressive reform of divorce law was associated with the decline of the notion that the father had a natural right to custody of the children. The main criterion for the allocation became "the best interests of the child," and those in turn were generally determined by the behavior of the spouses within marriage, so that custody was generally vested in the petitioner. As we have seen, some two-thirds of divorces in the United States in the late nineteenth century were sought by women, so it is not surprising that women most often won custody of their children. This tendency was magnified by a clear preference on the part of judges to place children in the care of their mothers; child care was, in their eyes, an important role women played within their special "sphere." An example of the transition to maternal custody was nineteenth-century California, where 91% of women, but only 37% of men, who sought custody were granted it. Throughout Western society, in fact, in places like New South Wales and Canada, law and practice followed the same trend.

Developments in areas of family law such as the custody of children reflected changes in ideas about the family. The principles of property and ownership that underlay paternal prerogatives in custody issues gradually made way for an emphasis on education and guardianship, which placed children firmly within women's sphere of influence. Not only were divorce laws important media through which the legal relationship between mother and child was reformed in the nineteenth century, but the custody provisions made divorce a more attractive option than other, informal means of ending an intolerable marriage.

Provisions for child custody and for property ownership were also included in laws regulating judicial separations, but divorce offered two advantages that no other legal remedy could match. The first was the psychological and emotional satisfaction of a complete severance of legal bonds with the former spouse. The second, derived from the first, was the ability to remarry. During the nineteenth century divorce laws shed most of the residual restrictions on remarriage by the guilty spouse, so that all divorced people could marry again. How often they did so in the period before World War I is not clear, however. Divorce

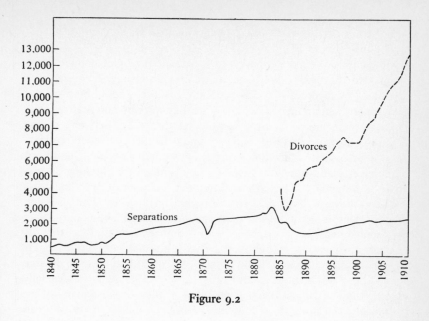

Figure 9.2

was still scandalous, and remarriage (unless it was to another divorced person) cannot have been easy. The option of marrying again must, nonetheless, have been one of the attractions of divorce.

That divorce was considered a more satisfactory response to marriage breakdown is demonstrated by its increased popularity compared to the declining use of alternative legal actions. As a general rule, judicial separations decreased as divorces increased, and the obvious conclusion to draw is that couples who might have filed for separations increasingly turned instead to divorce. France is a good example of this tendency. As Figure 9.2 shows, separations increased steadily from the 1830s, but peaked in 1883 and fell in 1884, the year that divorce was legalized again in France. Thereafter the number of divorces rose steadily, while the number of separations stablilized and the rate fell against population. The gap between the divorce rate and the judicial separation rate grew wider and wider.

There was a similar pattern in England and Wales where, in addition to judicial separation, other forms of matrimonial relief were available. The most common was a maintenance order, an order issued by a magistrate to compel a husband to support his wife if they lived apart because of the husband's behavior. Divorce gradually became the most popular legal action among the alternatives available in English law. While divorces accounted for only 10% of all matrimonial actions before 1920, they accounted for 24% by the early 1920s and 55% by the early 1950s. One side effect was a decline in the use of separations and other legal measures that simply did not offer the advantages brought by divorce.

The implications and consequences of divorce were in many respects similar to those of widowhood in traditional society. Marriage was dissolved by divorce, as it was by death; resources could be provided by property settlements and alimony as they were by inheritance; children were secured by custody as they might be by survivor's rights; and both divorced and widowed men and women were free to remarry. As we have seen, widowhood cast many women (and their children) into poverty and hardship, and it could scarcely be thought of as a state to be envied. The crucial difference between divorce and widowhood, however, was that a woman chose to divorce after weighing the costs and benefits of her marriage against those she could expect when divorced. But the analogy with widowhood reminds us that although divorce was undoubtedly the most attractive option, it was far from an easily chosen option. Up to World War I and beyond, divorce everywhere was expensive and procedurally difficult, it was socially stigmatized, and most married people – women in particular – were in no financial position to contemplate life outside marriage. Women in paid employment were poorly paid, and men's incomes would rarely run to supporting two separate households.

The costs of divorce were an immediate deterrent to the poorer social strata in all countries and states. In early twentieth-century England a straightforward divorce cost about a hundred pounds, well beyond the means of manual workers. In New South Wales, divorces could cost hundreds of pounds (depending on their complexity and the number of witnesses called), and it was the same in many other places, whether in New Zealand, the United States, Europe, or Canada: Costs alone explain why cheaper alternatives such as separations and maintenance orders were more often used in this first phase of the modern divorce history of the Western world.

How did the social profile of divorced men and women reflect the expense of divorce and other considerations such as the ability to forge an independent livelihood after divorce? Surprisingly, despite the evidence that the divorce laws discriminated against ordinary people, the divorce lists in some areas spanned the social spectrum. In some nineteenth-century California divorces studied by Robert Griswold, a high percentage (14%) of the couples were farmers, while cases in which the husband was in skilled or unskilled trades or was a manual laborer accounted collectively for 52% of divorces. Couples in the middle and upper classes accounted for 17%, and overall the social composition of the divorced population was roughly the same as the population at large. This suggests not only that expectations of marriage were rising throughout society, but also that there were no obvious social or economic barriers to divorce.

Most case studies, however, point to an overrepresentation of the better-off in divorce proceedings. May's study of divorces in Los Angeles in the 1880s showed an imbalance in favor of couples from the higher social strata. The same was true of Canada, where the costly parliamentary divorces tilted divorce toward the wealthier sections of society. In New South Wales, large landholders and managers were overrepresented, and in both nineteenth-century Nova Scotia and New Zealand, middle-class couples predominated. More than half (59%) of the couples divorced in England in 1871 came from the highest strata of gentry, professionals, and managers, whereas only a fifth (22%) came from the working class. Farmers, shopkeepers, and clerical and retail workers made up a quarter.

Given what we know of costs, the general underrepresentation of couples from the lower social groups is hardly unexpected. They were far from entirely absent, however, and although we do not know for sure how so many women and men of apparently very modest incomes were able to afford to divorce, several cases suggest that it must often have been made possible only by patient saving over a period of years. In one English case reported shortly before World War I, a woman had saved for twenty years for her divorce. A New Zealand woman, explaining why she had waited until 1894 to divorce her husband for an act of adultery she had discovered in 1885, wrote that "I would have applied for this Decree of dissolution of marriage before this only that I was destitute of the necessary money." Australian women borrowed and saved for divorces, and in Nova Scotia one man saved for nineteen years until he could afford to dissolve his marriage. In such cases the costs involved had a delaying rather than an absolutely deterrent effect. These cases also demonstrate the determination and high priority some women and men gave to getting a divorce.

Another inhibition was the stigma attached to divorce before World War I. If there was an increasing recognition that divorce was necessary, and even desirable, in some situations, it was still regarded as an evil and as a sign of weakness or failure on the part of both spouses, not only the partner guilty of a matrimonial offense. Women who divorced in the most compelling circumstances might still find themselves treated as social pariahs, as if they had caused their husbands' behavior. A submission to the 1909 royal commission on divorce in England noted that "public opinion generally condemns a divorced woman without regard to circumstances...the 'disgrace' is dreaded and we are told that 'it would go against you at the works' and can be a hindrance in looking for employment." Moreover the stigma attached not only to the spouses but also to their children and wider kin.

In the absence of opinion polls, we have only impressionistic evidence about attitudes toward divorce and the divorced. The treatment of divorce in literature might reflect prevailing social attitudes, but there is no way of determining it. Divorce was certainly a literary theme, however. Thomas Hardy highlighted the hardships of restrictive divorce laws in *Jude the Obscure* (1896), and Arnold Bennett stressed the social stigma ("this disgraceful renown") attached to divorce in *Whom God Hath Joined* (1906). A study of divorce in American novels between 1850 and World War I concluded that divorce was portrayed negatively and was generally condemned as a moral and social evil.

Despite these attitudes – if they were the prevailing attitudes – divorce rates began to rise slowly in the forty or fifty years up to World War I. The reasons that have been suggested here are that economic changes and increasing expectations of marriage led to a greater incidence of marriage breakdown and created a wider constituency on which divorce might draw. At the same time, divorce and its attributes – property settlements, custody of children, the ability to remarry – became increasing attractive. All these factors, it is suggested, were especially important for women, whose status in marriage made them more likely than their husbands to want to divorce. Against these developments that favored divorce, others militated against it. Divorce was expensive, stigmatized, and couples from the lower socioeconomic groups found access to it difficult. One way of understanding the overall effect of these characteristics of divorce in the decades before World War I is in terms of a balance of forces – social, economic, legal, and attitudinal – for and against divorce. Whereas the balance had tilted against marriage breakdown and divorce until the nineteenth century, it shifted first in favor of marriage breakdown and then later, toward the end of the century, toward divorce. In this first phase, however, the deterrents to divorce were still heavy counterweights, so that although divorce rates began to rise, they did not do so rapidly or dramatically.

Phase 2: 1918 to the 1960s

The second phase of the modern rise of divorce, a long period between World War I and about 1960, saw the rates of divorce increase more quickly, and divorce, a marginal phenomenon before 1914, become established as an integral part of the social and demographic system in Western societies. The world war itself and its aftermath were partly responsible for the changes that differentiated this phase. As we have seen, there was a sudden surge in divorces after the war, and it is likely that the presence of unprecedented numbers of divorced men and women had the effect of undermining hostile attitudes toward divorce. Before the war it is likely that most citizens in many countries had never knowingly come into contact with a divorced person. After the war not only were the divorced more prevalent in society at large, but a much greater proportion of families included a divorced person. Attitudes toward divorce changed slowly, but the changes were part of a cultural climate that was increasingly receptive to divorce.

There was also a decrease in the real costs of divorce in many places, either because greater prosperity lowered the costs relative to income or because legal aid schemes were established. In England in 1914, for example, there was an increase in the maximum personal income allowed for divorces under the "poor persons" procedures, and more than half the divorces sought by men in the immediate postwar period were assisted financially in this way. Indeed, throughout the 1920s and 1930s, between 30% and 40% of English divorces were obtained with financial aid. When the legal aid scheme was liberalized in 1949, the proportion of assisted divorces rose to more than 50% overall, and more than two-thirds of divorces were sought by women.

The wider affordability of divorce was manifested in changes in the social composition of those who divorced. Before World War I, as we have noted, the wealthier social strata were overrepresented in divorces almost everywhere, but between the wars the proportion of working-class marriages increased significantly. May's study of Los Angeles divorces in 1890 and 1920 showed that in the space of thirty years divorce changed from being dominated by the upper and middle class to being more or less proportionally distributed throughout society. The same trend is observable elsewhere. In New Zealand divorce evolved from being disproportionately upper and middle class to disproportionately lower middle and working class by 1926. In England the timing of change is less observable because of the difficulty of obtaining data, but the change took place. Between two sample years, 1871 and 1951, manual workers increased their representation in divorces from 22 to 69%, farmers and shopkeepers declined from 16 to 8%, while the higher social groups (gentry, professionals, and managers) plummeted from 54 to 16%. In the course of eighty years, then, the social character of divorce in England was transformed, not least because of the reduction of the costs involved.

The shift in the class character of divorce evident in most places during this phase is essential for an understanding of the steady rise of divorce between World War I and 1960. Whether what might be called the "democratization of divorce" was a result of changing attitudes, divorce law liberalization, rising expectations of marriage, or cheaper and more accessible divorce, the transformation of the class composition of divorcing couples was necessary for a sustained increase in divorce rates. Had divorce retained the elite social bias it possessed in the late nineteenth century, its potential for growth would have been severely restricted.

An important aspect of the social extension of divorce was the employment, or potential for the employment, of women. During the twentieth century there has been a general association between divorced and employed women, although it is not always clear whether employed women divorced or divorced women obtained employment. In either case, if actual or potential employment is a factor in decisions to divorce, there must be a labor market for women, and in this respect conditions in the twentieth century have favored divorce, for the proportion of women in the labor force outside the home has increased throughout Western society. In the United States, for example, labor force participation rates for all women doubled from 18 to 36% between 1890 and 1960. In the same period the proportion of married women in paid employment rose much faster, from 5 to 30%. In England, women accounted for 27% of the labor force in 1927, and 42% in 1966. Throughout the Western world the trend was the same, and although women remained concentrated in specific and low-paid areas of employment, the sheer fact or possibility of an independent income bore directly on divorce: Either it was a precondition for a woman who wanted to divorce or it was a resource to which a divorced woman could turn.

In addition to these economic developments, there were changes in divorce laws and policies. There is no need to recapitulate the developments described in the preceding chapter, except to note the broad trends: the expansion of the grounds for divorce to include more and more matrimonial offenses or to add mutual consent or various forms of incompatibility.

There is no doubt, moreover, that social attitudes toward divorce changed in a more positive direction between World War I and 1960. Again, it is often impossible to gauge opinion at any given time, and thus to plot precisely the timing and direction of change, but there are indicators upon which we can draw. One is the very pace and persistence of divorce law reform in this period. Divorce laws were liberalized and expanded, the notion of fault was undermined in many codes, divorce was made more accessible, and there is evidence of public pressure for even more liberal divorce laws. It might have been that proponents of liberal divorce were better organized or had more effective access to the mass media, but it is plausible to argue for a general shift in attitudes.

Public opinion surveys in the United States indicate a change in attitudes between 1936 and 1966. In 1936, 23% of people questioned thought that divorce should be easier to obtain, while 77% thought it should be more difficult or kept as it was. By 1945 (during the postwar divorce boom), 9% wanted more liberal laws, 31% thought the laws were "about right," and 35% wanted the laws made more strict. (The other 25% were undecided.) This might have reflected an opinion that because divorces were so common in 1945, there was no need to relax the laws. Twenty years later, in 1966, a survey showed that 12% of respondents wanted more liberal laws, 18% though they were satisfactory, 34% wanted more restrictive laws, and a full 35% were undecided. This indicates only a marginal shift in favor of liberal divorce legislation between 1945 and 1966, but it is important to remember that the divorce laws with which Americans were satisfied or believed too restrictive in 1966 were considerably more liberal than those in place in 1945. To this extent the liberalization of divorce laws seems broadly to have paralleled the movement of public opinion. On a more impressionistic level, a study of the treatment of divorce in American novels concluded that while divorce was portrayed as a social evil before World War I, in the interwar period novelists took the less moralistic position that divorce was a matter of personal decision that was of little concern to society, especially when no children were involved.

Shifts in public attitudes to divorce, and the decline of its scandalous connotations, must be counted with broad social and economic changes in any explanation of increasing divorce rates between 1918 and 1960. A further factor must have been the increase in divorce itself, for although it may be debated whether divorce produces marriage breakdown, it seems probable that divorce can encourage divorce. There is no explicit or unambiguous evidence on this point, but it is surely reasonable to suppose that as divorce became more extensive, notions that divorced men and women were morally depraved were undermined. The increased divorce rate thus had an effect on the normative context of divorce and thus contributed to its own increase by reducing the deterrent of social stigma. There is, however, no way of measuring this hypothetical feedback effect of the rising divorce rate.

Another way of thinking of this is to consider the emulative factor in the decision to divorce, as men and women followed the example of others in turning to the divorce courts. There are examples of this in the eighteenth century when divorces clustered at specific limited periods in individual neighborhoods in urban France, and there is a striking case of emulation in eighteenth-century Massachusetts. At a broader social level of analysis, it is difficult to identify emulation precisely. If, however, there is a tendency for divorce rates to increase because of some internal dynamic of this sort, we should expect the divorce booms that followed each world war to give boosts to the divorce rates that followed in turn. This might well have been the case after World War I, for divorce rates in the 1920s were significantly higher than a continuation of prewar rates of increase should have produced. But the surge of divorces after World War II did not have this effect, for after divorces peaked around 1946 and 1947, divorce rates either stabilized or even declined a little during the 1950s. Certainly, they were lower than we should have expected had prewar divorce trends been sustained. This was true of the United States, where divorce rates did not begin to rise consistently until 1962, and also of England, France, Switzerland, Sweden and Australia, as Figure 9.1 shows.

The reasons for the failure of divorce rates to continue their rise during the 1950s are unclear. One area of explanation advanced for the United States is a change in attitudes that favored marriage, the family, home, and children. Some analysts have interpreted these values as a reaction against the preceding two decades of economic hardship and war, and they portray Americans, exhausted by the 1930s and 1940s, as retreating to their suburban homes and adopting a domestic version of isolationism. There is no doubt that social attitudes were generally conservative and family centered during the 1950s, but it is not clear how this relates to divorce. To propose attitudinal change as the reason for a decline in the use of divorce places a great burden on a single factor.

Two other areas of explanation, also related to attitudes, seem more promising. One is that the marriages that would have been dissolved by divorce during the 1950s, but were not, were those of men and women who had grown up during the 1930s and 1940s, and that these people were so affected by their experiences of economic deprivation and social dislocation, that they had particularly strong attachments to home and family when they married. An additional factor was that, having grown up in times of hardship, they married in times of prosperity, when their expectations could be not only realized but exceeded, at least in material terms. This explanation would explain not only a change of marriage breakdown and divorce rates in terms of the fulfillment of expectations, but also contributes to an understanding of other contemporary demographic trends: earlier marriage and the rise in fertility that is called the "baby boom."

Such explanations of stabilized divorce rates might well apply to the United States, but they seem much less applicable to Europe. While America enjoyed relative prosperity in the 1950s, much of Europe suffered the economic and social aftermath of the war well into that decade. Yet there, too, divorce rates failed to sustain their trends of increase. Even in England, where changes to the legal assistance rules made divorce more accessible from late 1950, divorces increased in 1951 but then quickly receded and then declined until the early 1960s. Faced with a trend that was pervasive throughout the Western world, regardless of the economic and social conditions of individual countries, it is tempting to apply the more general explanation suggested for the United States, that in the 1950s conditions favored marital stability and that the experiences of the 1930s and 1940s produced a cultural reaction, one of whose manifestations was a higher level of marital satisfaction.

Phase 3: Divorce since 1960

The most recent phase of divorce, from the 1960s onward, has been characterized by a rapid and dramatic increase in divorce rates in every country, as Figure 9.1 shows. Even without the stagnation or slight decline of rates in the 1950s, the increases that began in the early 1960s represented marked accelerations over earlier trends. In the United States, for example, the annual changes in the divorce rate (the percentage increase or decrease in one year in relation to the preceding year), showed a decline from 1947 to 1958, a steady increase of 4 or 5% from 1959, and then increases of 9–12% in the period 1968–72. After 1973 the rate of increase slowed and even fell slightly in some years in the early 1980s.

Elsewhere divorce rates accelerated in an unprecedented manner in the 1960s. The rate in England doubled between 1960 and 1970, then more than doubled again in the 1970s. In France the timing of change was later, but the divorce rate more than doubled between 1970 and the early 1980s. In other places the increases were smaller but still dramatic. West Germany's divorce rate almost doubled in the fifteen years from 1968 to 1983, for instance. Even taking into account the differences in the magnitude and precise timing of change, we can conclude that during the 1960s divorce in the Western world entered a new phase of growth. It was not a return to "normal" trends after the stable or declining rates of the 1950s and cannot be explained as such. In short, we must seek a particular set of explanations for this period of growth.

As we have already seen in the previous chapter, divorce law reforms had little or nothing to do with setting off the increase in divorce rates. Almost everywhere, divorce rates had begun to rise before legal reforms – notably the widespread adoption of no-fault divorce – were introduced. If anything, the divorce law reforms were a response to the rising incidence of divorce rather than causes of it. This is not to say that the reforms did not reinforce existing trends; as Figure 9.1 shows, in countries as diverse as Sweden, Australia, and England, legal reforms gave a short-term boost to divorce rates, and it is possible that it carried through to the longer term.

Legal changes apart, various explanations of the increased divorce rates have been advanced. They range from the breakdown of family life because of the increasing employment of married women, to more liberal divorce policies, to changed individual attitudes toward divorce, to shifts in sexual morality, to the women's movement. There is also the redistributive hypothesis, the notion that the rising divorce rate reflects the legal dissolution of a greater proportion of broken marriages than before. By and large, the explanations of the greater use of divorce from the 1960s echo the explanations offered for increases at other periods: easier access to divorce, women's employment, and changing social attitudes. There was, in fact, an impressive conjunction of these factors in the 1960s and 1970s. Not only that, but where we are able to measure them, it appears that there was a marked increase in their intensity.

We have noted the historical association between divorce and the employment of women, the greater likelihood of women's seeking divorce when employment opportunities for women were good. What is often overlooked is that women's employment might equally encourage men to divorce by reducing a former wife's level of financial dependence. Without suggesting that divorces can be undertaken lightly when a wife is (or has the potential of being) employed, it does nonetheless mean that divorce can be contemplated more readily. It is therefore important that rates of employment of married women have increased dramatically since the 1950s. If we consider married women with children below school age, we find that in the United States 19% were in the labor force in 1959, 29% in 1969, and 43% in 1979. In 1980, 50.2% of all married women in America, with a husband present, were employed. In Canada in 1981, more than half of all married women with a child under the age of three were in the work force, and the rate for those with older children was 63%. In Sweden the employment rate of married women was already high (46%) in the late 1960s, but it rose to 57% within a decade. The examples can be multiplied, as can the association between employment and separation. In the United States in 1980, as we have noted, 50% of married women with a husband present were employed, but the rate rose to 59% for married women with no husband present (i.e., deserted or separated women), and 75% for divorced women.

The broader reasons for the increased employment of women need not concern us here. What is important is that actual employment or the possibility of employment are critical preconditions for separation and dissolution of marriage at the initiative of women. Some research has demonstrated that women perceived the lack of financial support as the main barrier to divorce. In one American study, for example, 36% of women cited finances as a deterrent to their deciding to divorce, whereas only 10% of men did so. To this extent the changing employment patterns in favor of women's employment from the early 1960s can only have militated in favor of an increased divorce rate, despite persistent limitations on the range of occupations available to women and relatively low salaries.

Married women often entered employment in this period, it is suggested, not because they wanted a career or sought personal fulfillment in work, but because they had to, either through sheer financial necessity or because two incomes were needed for a couple to realize their material expectations. Expectation of an improved material standard of living was one facet of the general expectations of living that had been rising from the middle of the nineteenth century. It is possible that the very financial pressure that led to the wife's employment might have been active in predisposing a couple toward marriage breakdown.

From the 1960s expectations of marriage not only rose further, but their emphasis shifted toward the affective aspects of the conjugal relationship. Recent decades have seen unprecedented emphasis on the importance of emotional compatibility within marriage and the desirability of deriving emotional and personal fulfillment from marriage. Indeed, with the decline of the birthrate in Western society in this period, and other changes in the family life cycle, the conjugal relationship has come to dominate the family. Easier access to contraceptives and abortions has enabled many couples to have no children at all. Those who do have children have fewer (the ideal family size having fallen), and children are present within the family for a smaller proportion of the potential duration of marriage. With longer life expectancies, parents can expect to have thirty or more years of married life after their children have left home.

The increasing emphasis on the emotional aspects of marriage has placed intense demands on that part of the relationship that is arguably the most fragile and volatile. Evidence lies in the outpouring, during the 1960s, 1970s, and 1980s, of books and articles advising husbands and wives how to relate to each other, how to communicate, how to fulfill themselves within marriage, how to understand each other's needs, and how to improve their sexual relationship. One branch of this growth industry has focused on older men and women, in recognition of the particular stresses that marriages are susceptible to after children have left home.

Widespread interest in marriage counseling and therapy is another facet of this new emphasis on the emotional elements of marriage. Even though the proportion of the married population that has had counseling is small and tends to be middle class, the rest of the population is reached by articles and self-administered questionnaires in mass circulation magazines, especially those aimed at a female readership. Examples from *Glamour* in the late 1980s included "Sexual

Taboos: Why Breaking Them Keeps Couples Together" and "Same Lover, Sexier Sex: 5 Ways to Make Love Better."

Although it is difficult to describe the magnitude of such attitudinal changes, the changes themselves are undeniable. The same stress on romantic love, emotional intensity, and sexual satisfaction that was long associated with premarital and extramarital relationships has spilled over into marriage itself. The decline of these qualities, the slide from emotional passion to comfortable companionship after the initial years of married life has become less acceptable. As John Gillis writes in the conclusion of his history of British marriage, people since the 1960s "expect more of the conjugal relationship. It is made to bear the full weight of needs for intimacy, companionship, and love, needs which were previously met in other ways. Couples expect more of each other." This conclusion applies far beyond Britain; it is a Western phenomenon. It must be added that the higher these emotional expectations rise, the less likely they are to be fulfilled.

Sharply rising expectations of marriage and increasing employment opportunities for women partially explain the increased marriage breakdown from the 1960s but do not directly relate to the rising divorce rate. An important factor in the greater use of divorce must have been a change in attitudes toward divorce. Public opinion polls in the United States indicate a relatively slow shift of opinion in favor of divorce between World War II and the mid-1960s, by which time divorce had already begun to increase. But from the mid-1960s, shortly before divorce rates began to rise sharply, there was a significant movement of opinion in favor of liberal divorce laws. In 1968, 33% of people thought that divorce laws should stay as they were or be liberalized. By 1974 and 1978 the figure had risen to 54%. This, it should be stressed, should be read in the context of increasingly liberal divorce legislation. The fact that more than half the population either approved of these new laws or wanted even more liberal ones suggests that American public opinion liberalized faster than divorce legislation. The main change in attitudes seems to have occurred between 1968 and 1974, the very period when laws were liberalized (beginning with the 1969 California act) and just as the divorce rate was in its phase of greatest increase. It is impossible to ascertain whether changes in attitudes fostered more divorces or whether more divorces changed attitudes, but there is no doubt that a major shift in the culture of divorce took place in the United States in the period.

A similar shift of attitudes can be detected in other parts of the Western world. Two surveys of opinion in France, one in 1969 and one in 1972, showed a significant change even in that short period. There was evidence of a decline of adherence to the Roman Catholic doctrine of marital indissolubility in that the proportion of men who believed that marriage was indissoluble fell from 30–33% in 1969 to 18% in 1972. The proportion of women with such a belief declined from 28–34% to 21%. Conversely, the proportions of men and women who believed that divorce should be available in serious circumstances or by mutual consent rose appreciably.

The familiarity with divorce that resulted from its increased incidence might well have made more people tolerant of it. This process would have been reinforced by increased positive references to divorce in the mass media and popular culture. Many more movies and television dramas focus on divorce, and American situation comedies such as "Kate and Allie" and "Golden Girls," which portray divorced women (together with widows in the latter), contribute to a wider exposure of divorce. Marriage breakdown or conflict has long been a theme of movies, but only in recent years have films such as *Kramer vs. Kramer, The Good Father,* and *The War of the Roses* focused so intensely on the social, legal, and personal aspects of divorce. Divorce has also become a minor theme in popular music. Accustomed to dealing with thwarted relationships and broken hearts, rock lyrics have taken a matrimonial turn. The theme of Elton John's "The Legal Boys" is the role of lawyers in divorce proceedings, while Billy Joel's reference to divorce in "Scenes from an Italian Restaurant" treated divorce as the routine matter it often seems to have become: a matter of course in which the spouses part the best of friends. Country music, which has a longer tradition of dealing with marriage, inevitably found inspiration in divorce, the best known example being Tammy Wynette's "D-I-V-O-R-C-E," which deals with the effects of a divorce on a small child. On television, divorce has even become entertainment. "Divorce Court" presents dramatized actions in which petitioners and defendants plead their cases before a retired judge. Finally, divorce has produced a consumer subculture of goods and services, including divorce parties, divorce cakes, divorce rings, and divorce cards (sample text: "I've just heard ... You're as free as a bird").

In short, since the 1960s, but especially since the 1970s, divorce has lost much of its scandalous reputation and is far less stigmatized as a result. This tendency has been reinforced by the adoption of no-fault rules, which means that couples no longer have to allege a specific matrimonial offense in order to divorce. Even though divorce is seldom considered desirable in its own right, though it might be desirable in particular circumstances, it is now treated more openly and less as something to be hidden from respectable society. Having been divorced did not prevent Ronald Reagan from being elected governor of California and later, in 1980, president of the United States. Canadian prime minister Pierre Trudeau separated from his wife before divorcing in 1984. In 1978 divorce even penetrated the British royal family, when the marriage of Princess Margaret (the sister of Queen Elizabeth) and Lord Snowdon was dissolved.

The dramatic shift of public attitudes toward divorce between the 1960s and the 1980s represented the collapse of one more inhibition to divorce. Like the reform of divorce laws and the changes in employment patterns, attitudes were an important part of the environment that either facilitated or discouraged divorce. If the rate of divorce is perceived as being influenced by the material, social, normative, and personal constraints on divorcing, then it should not be surprising that rates rose so markedly in this period.

Still, we should guard against thinking of divorce as having become cheap, procedurally easy, and casual, of spouses separating and divorcing without rancor and recriminations, each living happily ever after, either alone or within a new marriage or relationship. The process of marriage breakdown is an emotionally difficult one, and it is questionable how far the no-fault principles of modern divorce laws have penetrated spouses' perceptions of marriage breakdown. They are still expressed predominantly in terms of fault, and in many cases, where there is violence and exploitation, quite rightly so. Within the private sphere of marriage, the pain and bitterness of marriage breakdown persists, even if divorce is socially less stigmatized and is widely viewed as routine.

Nor have all the apparent improvements in divorce law lived up to the expectations that they aroused. During the 1960s and 1970s many jurisdictions introduced more equitable matrimonial property laws that recognized the contributions married women made to the family other than in terms of direct income. In practice, however, rules of equal division of matrimonial property have often worked to the disadvantage of women. Under the former rules, property settlements were often made on the basis of fault, and because the majority of petitioners were women, women tended to gain most of the property after divorce. In California, for instance, women received most property in most settlements up to 1970, but after the introduction of no-fault divorce and equal division of property rules in that year, their share of the property fell dramatically. It might be argued that women had been given unfairly preferential treatment under the former rules, but the fact remains that the new system worked to the relative disadvantage of women.

Property settlements are only one part of the more general economic adjustments that divorce requires. In two others, alimony and child support, women also do better on paper than they do in practice. Although court orders for these payments have increased, they are often inadequate and the rate of husbands' compliance with the orders is low. Across the United States in the early 1980s fewer than half the

248

women awarded child support payments received it in the amount and with the frequency ordered. About 30% received some payments, and a quarter received nothing at all. A 1980 survey in Canada turned up similar findings: One-third of women who were awarded support received it in full, one-third received it partially, and one-third received nothing whatsoever.

In practice, then, as distinct from legal prescription, modern divorce results in hardships on many women and their children. Women have access to the work force, it is true, and social welfare systems exist to provide assistance in particularly deserving cases (although the effectiveness of these systems varies greatly from country to country). But divorced women, especially those with children to care for, constitute a distinct, economically disadvantaged group within most societies. Even if they do have work, they are paid relatively low salaries: Women's wages have remained virtually unchanged, at between one-half and two-thirds of men's wages since the seventeenth century. Divorced women might be given an equal share of matrimonial property, but most are from the lower socioeconomic strata, such that the amount of property and money involved is very small. The courts are prepared to order former husbands to pay alimony and child support, but compliance is seen in only a minority of the orders.

The results of these factors have been detailed in a study by Lenore Weitzman, who showed that divorce has produced a new class of poor: divorced women and their dependent children. According to Weitzman, most wives "experience rapid downward social mobility after divorce, while most husbands' economic status is substantially improved." This stratum of the poor in modern society recalls the lot of the deserted wife or widow with children in traditional society. It was suggested in Chapter 5, in fact, that women in the past were deterred from leaving their husbands by the sight of impoverished women of this sort. There are vast differences between poverty and deprivation in past and modern society, however. Then it was often absolute; now it is relative. This is not to minimize the often appalling material and emotional consequences of modern divorce on women and children, but it does make them less important as deterrents to marriage breakdown and divorce. Domestic relative deprivation in modern Western society simply does not have the public character of poverty in traditional society, and fears of the economic consequences of divorce in modern times may be overridden by expectations of generous property settlements, alimony, child support payments, and social welfare assistance, even though many of these may turn out to be chimeras.

To point to some of the negative consequences of divorce is to correct an impression, sometimes given by writing on divorce, that recent reforms in laws and policies have been consistently progressive and positive. Changes in legislation and the procedures for divorce have certainly made divorce more accessible and have removed elements of adversarial procedure from the divorce process. It is far easier to exit from marriage than it has ever been in the history of Western society. Policies have been far less responsive, however, to the implications of divorce for the lives of women and children after divorce.

Conclusion

The rise of divorce during the past hundred years or so defies precise explanations in terms that can be satisfactorily applied across the Western world generally. National and state legislation, different demographic and social structures, varying economic conditions and cultural climates, all have an impact on divorce as they do on other forms of social and personal behavior. Nevertheless the rise of mass divorce during the twentieth century has been a sufficiently universal phenomenon as to lead us to seek broadly applicable explanations. The explanations that have been proposed here are of several kinds: rising expectations of marriage; economic, social, legal, and cultural changes that permit more marriages to break down; and decreasingly problematic access to divorce. All are seen as influencing one another in the manner set out earlier in Chapter 5.

Throughout this discussion, however – and this is generally true of divorce research – the feedback effect of divorce itself has been overlooked. Too often the divorce rate is seen as passive, the result of socioeconomic and historical forces that push it up in this period and down in the next. Marriages are portrayed as fragile craft, rudderless and driven by the rising seas of expectations, their crew still arguing about which sail they should raise, when the vessel of their dreams is dashed to pieces on the rocks of an economic downturn. Although it is true that social and economic conditions can favor the breakdown and dissolution of marriage, it should be clear that divorce itself has become part of the cultural environment in which marriages exist. To this extent there is a feedback effect, in which the existence of divorce as a viable alternative to marriage, together with the presence of an increasing number of divorces in Western society, contribute in turn to marriage breakdown and divorce.

A final question we might address in this chapter is the limits of growth of the divorce rate. Can it rise to the point that all marriages will be dissolved or are there limits to the extent to which divorce can penetrate the married population? In theory there seems no reason why the divorce rate should not continue to rise indefinitely, for remarriages provide a perpetually renewable stock on which divorce may draw. In practice, however, many marriages will not be dissolved by divorce. The most important reason, easily overlooked by students of divorce, is that many couples do not want to divorce; they are happily married and find their expectations fulfilled by their spouses. A recent study of marriages that had lasted fifteen or more years found that in 6% both spouses were unhappy with their marriage, in 10% one spouse was unhappy, and in 83% both spouses considered themselves happily married. It is hardly appropriate for this history of divorce to speculate about future trends. Whether the prevailing level of divorce is maintained, whether it falls, or whether it rises, only time will tell and future historians will record.

Suggestions for further reading

Albrecht, Stan L., Howard M. Bahr, and Kristen L. Goodman, *Divorce and Remarriage: Problems, Adaptations and Adjustments* (Westport, Conn., 1983).

Barnett, James Harwood, *Divorce and the American Divorce Novel, 1858–1937* (Philadelphia, 1939).

Cherlin, Andrew J., *Marriage, Divorce, Remarriage* (Cambridge, Mass., 1981).

Degler, Carl, *At Odds: Women and the Family in America* (New York, 1980).

Eekelaar, John, *Family Security and Family Breakdown* (Harmondsworth, 1971).

Gillis, John, *For Better, For Worse: British Marriages 1600 to the Present* (New York, 1985).

Golder, Hilary, *Divorce in 19th-Century New South Wales* (Kensington, N.S.W., 1985).

Griswold, Robert, *Family and Divorce in California, 1850–1890* (Albany, N.Y., 1982).

Halem, Lynn Carol, *Divorce Reform: Changing Legal and Social Perspectives* (New York, 1980).

Holcombe, Lee, *Wives and Property: Reform of the Married Women's Property Law in Nineteenth-Century England* (Toronto, 1983).

Levinger, G., and O. C. Moles (eds.), *Divorce and Separation: Contexts, Causes and Consequences* (New York, 1979).

May, Elaine Tyler, *Great Expectations: Marriage and Divorce in Post-Victorian America* (Chicago, 1980).

Phillips, Roderick, *Divorce in New Zealand: A Social History* (Auckland, 1981).

Wallerstein, Judith S., and Sandra Blakeslee, *Second Chances: Men, Women and Children a Decade after Divorce* (New York, 1989).

Weitzman, Lenore J., *The Divorce Revolution: The Unexpected Social and Economic Consequences for Women and Children in America* (New York, 1985).

Conclusion

The history of marriage breakdown and divorce is almost as long as the history of marriage itself. As Voltaire put it, "divorce probably dates from the same time as marriage. I think, though, that marriage is a few weeks older, that is to say that a man fought with his wife after a fortnight, beat her after a month, and that they separated after living together for six weeks." Whatever the broader merits of Voltaire's speculation, it does at least highlight the need to give historical depth to phenomena that are too often thought to be peculiar to modern times.

This book has focused on the most recent thousand years of marriage breakdown and divorce, and particularly on the past two centuries. It demonstrates not only that there is a history to be studied, but also that it must be carefully integrated into much broader contexts. Even the most narrow analysis of divorce must take into account marriage, sexuality, and the social relation between women and men. A more satisfying account must consider broader attitudes toward marriage and society, toward the family in general, and toward religion, morality, and the social order. Divorce, historically considered, must be placed within its social, economic, political, and cultural context, just as any historical phenomenon must.

Several broad conclusions may be drawn from the survey of divorce and marriage breakdown that this book has undertaken, although it must be admitted that no generalizations will apply satisfactorily to all parts of the Western world. As the Preface made clear, the aim of this study was to define the outline of the history of divorce and marriage breakdown in Western society, without losing sight of the diversity and divergences among states and regions, urban and rural areas, social classes, and between men and women.

One of the most evident changes traced in this book is the development of increasingly positive attitudes toward divorce. It is difficult to pin the chronology down, however. While it is clear that divorce has become far more acceptable in the course of the twentieth century, there is little reliable information on earlier attitudes. At any given period we can determine the expressed thoughts of the elites – legislators, theologians, and intellectuals – but there was rarely a consensus, and we cannot readily identify the direction of changes. We should not assume that attitudes have consistently tended toward greater tolerance of divorce. The rejection of the very principle of divorce in the 1986 referendum in the Republic of Ireland should serve as a loud reminder that there remain extensive and influential bodies of opinion that resist the dominant, more tolerant, trend of opinion.

Despite the impossibility of defining long-term attitudinal shifts very precisely, the general movement away from negative opinions is evident. Various factors have influenced this trend. Changes in secular and religious laws and policies have frequently resulted from ideological and theological consideration. The reluctant abandonment of the doctrine of marital indissolubility by the Protestant Reformers resulted from their biblical exegesis and from notions of justice, equity, and contract. There is no evidence that it was the result of social or economic changes within marriage and the family during the sixteenth century. Indeed, the same order of ideological considerations largely explains the development of divorce law and policy throughout Western society until the end of the eighteenth century. Only from this time might we give social, economic, and demographic factors some weight in the development of divorce policies.

From the nineteenth century, for example, we must take into account what might be called popular pressure. This is not to say that there was a welling up of popular sentiment in favor of divorce, although there was some evidence of this in England in the 1830s and France in the 1880s. In a more direct sense, however, petitioners for divorce were themselves influential in altering law and policy. The abandonment of legislative divorce, for example, was very often the result of the sheer number of divorce petitions that, although negligible by modern standards, cut deeply into the time allotted for legislative business. Then, too, petitioners and their lawyers pressed constantly at the bounds of divorce and progressively extended the definitions of offenses such as cruelty. A third example of the influence of divorce petitioners is their simple determination to divorce. In places as disparate as New York State, Sweden, England, New Zealand, and Italy, legal reform in the twentieth century followed on evidence that citizens were not deterred by the restrictions of prevailing divorce legislation and that widespread migration, connivance, collusion, and perjury had made a mockery of existing limitations. In such ways, even before divorce reform pressure groups lobbied legislators, and before divorce law reform figured on political agendas, there were popular influences on the shape of divorce laws and policies.

It is rather more difficult to link changes in divorce attitudes and practices to social, economic, and demographic changes. Some historians, we have seen, suggest that divorce might be seen as the modern substitute for the frequency of spousal death in earlier centuries. It is certainly tempting to ransack the various levels of social change, such as declining mortality rates, in order to locate developments that appear to have an association with divorce. We must, however, treat the findings with caution.

This study suggests – with the appropriate caution – that the broad economic, demographic, and social changes that affected most of the Western world from the eighteenth century had a distinct impact upon marriage stability. The growth of cities, the shifting balance of economies from agriculture to industry, and changes in the character of personal property, all profoundly affected relationships within the family generally and marriage particularly. The unified economic basis of what we have called traditional marriage was undermined, and separation became that much less problematic. One legal form of recognition of this social and economic transformation was the enactment of married women's property acts throughout the Western world in the second half of the nineteenth century.

Such developments need not have led to increased marriage breakdown, but this study suggests that they led in turn to changes in expectations of marriage. As expectations of marriage rose, particularly on the part of women, there is evidence – often sporadic, but pointing in the same direction – that marital conflicts and separations became more common. By this series of steps, separation became a more practicable course of action over time in urbanizing and industrializing societies.

This description and explanation of general trends in marriage breakdown over time must remain at the level of hypothesis to some extent. They comprise, however, one of the more important conclusions of this study, which is that marriages were generally stable in traditional Western society and that a significant extent of marriage breakdown is peculiar to modern times, notably the past hundred years. This conclusion is at variance with a commonly expressed notion that marriage breakdown has historically been common and that rising divorce rates in recent times simply tend more accurately to reflect an essentially constant incidence of marriage breakdown. Although at odds with this redistributive hypothesis, the conclusion of this book appears to be in accord with conservative moral assessments of the state of modern marriage, and for this reason a number of qualifying statements must be made.

The argument for marriage stability in the past rests, however, not on assessments of the quality of conjugal relationships in earlier times, but on the broad social, economic, and demographic contexts of marriage. The imperatives of marriage and the family economy produced flexible and potentially very low expectations, and a high level of tolerance, both of which have changed over time. This stress on the wider social causes of marriage breakdown and divorce is a long way from the predominantly moral assessments that explain divorce rates in terms of character weakness, lack of commitment, irresponsibility, or simply in terms of an increasingly secular society.

There are, it is clear, no simple explanations of the long-term trends in marriage breakdown and divorce in the Western world. Marriage is integral to broad social, political, economic, and cultural processes, and it is futile to expect marriage to remain constant or to have a consistent social meaning while social structures, economic relationships, demographic patterns, and cultural configurations have undergone the massive transformations of the past centuries. If this book has shown anything, it is that divorce and marriage breakdown have their place not on the margins, but in the broad sweep of the history of Western society.

Index

Protestants
  and adultery, 24–5
  and divorce, 12–27 *passim*, 157
  and marriage, 12–13, 48–50
Prussia, 50, 54, 133–34
Pufendorf, Samuel, 53
Puritans (American), and divorce, 37–9, 40–1
Puritans (English), and divorce, 33–4

Quebec, 138

Reformatio Legum Ecclesiasticarum, see divorce,
  Church of England and
Reformation, and divorce, 12–27 *passim*
remarriage, 15, 18, 25, 80, 110, 129
Reno divorces, *see* Nevada
Rhode Island, 44, 70, 141
Roman Catholic church
  on adultery, 25, 103
  councils, 9, 11–12
  on divorce, 1–2, 7–8, 10, 131, 220, 221,
    222–3
Roos, Lord, 37
Russian Revolution, *see* Soviet Union

Scotland, 15, 17, 49, 195
secularization, 47–54 *passim*, 61, 170–1
separation
  informal, 82–3
  judicial, 5–7, 54–6, 131, 132, 235–6
sexuality, 12–13, 24–5, 31, 188–9; *see also*
  adultery; double standard of sexual
  morality
Simpson, Wallis, 193–5, 197
socialism and divorce, 165–8
social purity movement, 174–5
solitary living, 41, 114–15
South Carolina, 142
South Dakota, 148, 160
Soviet Union, 182–3, 198–200
Spain, 11, 136, 201–3, 222
suicide, 90–1
Sweden, 15, 48, 49–50, 182, 187, 219
Switzerland, 153, 182, 219
Syllabus of Errors, *see* Pius IX, pope

Taylor, Harriet, 169
temperance movement, 172–3
Tennessee, 44, 142
Texas, 142
Trent, council of, 2, 11–12
Tyndale, William, 22–3

Uncumber, St., 91
United States
  divorce laws of, 139–53 *passim*, 157–9,
    196–7

divorces in, 150–3, 209, 211–12, 228,
  243
marriage in, 146, 180, 187
reputation of divorce laws in, 153–5
(*see also* entries under individual colonies
  and states)
USSR, *see* Soviet Union
Utah, 148
utopian socialists, divorce and, 165–8

Vermont, 44, 141
violence, marital, 97–102 *passim*
  attitudes toward, 6–7, 77, 98–101
  extent of, in past, 97–8, 102
  gender and, 77, 98, 100–1
  marriage breakdown and, 102
  see also correction, moderate; cruelty;
    murder, spouse
Virginia, 142, 144, 173
Voltaire, 252

Wales, *see* England (and Wales)
war, divorce and, 68, 186–91, 210–2; *see also*
  American Civil War, divorce in; English
  Civil War, divorce in; World War I,
  divorce and; World War II, divorce
  and
widows, 114, 236, 249
wife-beating, *see* correction, moderate;
  violence, marital
wife sale, 85–7
Wisconsin, 158
witch hunts, 114
women
  equal rights movement of, and divorce,
    175–8
  marriage breakdown and, 109–12
  property and, 111, 229–30, 248
  and solitary living, 114–15
  spouse murder and, 89–90, 132
  and work, 79, 111–12, 112–13, 173–4,
    226–9, 240, 244–5, 249
  see also divorce, sex ratio of petitioners for;
    divorce, women and; family economy;
    violence, marital
Women's Christian Temperance Union and
  divorce, 173, 177, 179
World War I, divorce and, 186–91 *passim*,
  238–9
World War II, divorce and, 210–2, 242
Württemberg, 15, 50–1

Zurich, 17–18, 26, 48
Zwickau, 26
Zwingli, Huldreich, 17–18

DATE DUE

HIGHSMITH 45230